THE TUDORS

The Tudors

The History of a Dynasty

David Loades

continuum

Continuum International Publishing Group

The Tower Building   80 Maiden Lane
11 York Road   Suite 704
London SE1 7NX   New York, NY 10038

www.continuumbooks.com

First published 2012

British Library Cataloguing-in-Publication Data
A catalogue record for this book is available from the British Library.

ISBN: HB: 978-1-4411-3690-9

Library of Congress Cataloging-in-Publication Data
A catalog record for this book is available from the Library of Congress.

Typeset by Fakenham Prepress Solutions, Fakenham, Norfolk NR21 8NN
Printed and bound in India

Contents

List of Illustrations

Preface

The Tudors continue to fascinate us. This is partly because of the sheer strangeness of a political world shaped by a personal monarchy whose authority was received directly from God, and partly because of the mythology which their image makers succeeded in creating. Their subjects had legal rights, and protected status, but no share in government except when called upon by the Crown. At the same time God was very real, constantly intervening in human affairs and demanding service and respect. Henry VIII and Elizabeth were also larger than life, dominating the courts with which they surrounded themselves. Elizabeth never married and 'lived and died a virgin', so her sexuality remains a subject for endless speculation. Henry, by contrast, married no fewer than six wives, and got rid of two of them by beheading, so his aggressive sexuality is taken for granted. A heady mixture of fact and fiction surrounds the representation of their lives, in which power and sex are mingled in a cocktail designed to appeal to modern tastes. For the more discriminating, Mary's marriage and her religious fanaticism have an equal attraction, as the frustrated spinster and unsatisfied wife takes it out on her heretical enemies. She, too, is larger than life.

This book is not fiction. It attempts to represent each of the Tudors as they actually were, and to assess the impact of their actions on the country which they ruled. That country was not Great Britain, it was the realm of England, which included Wales, Ireland, the Channel Islands and (until 1558) the Calais Pale. It was not a great power. For most of the sixteenth century it was a make weight in the struggle between France and the Habsburgs – not negligible but in no position to dictate terms. Only in the Elizabethan period did it begin to emerge from its European shell and to seek reputation and fortune in a wider world. However, the fact that that happened adds to the fascination. The origins of parliamentary sovereignty, the first thoughts of Empire, and the beginnings of the Church of England, all lie within this period, which the Tudors dominated with their immense personalities. So I hope that this reconstruction will bring enlightenment to those who do not know the period, and some fresh thoughts to those for whom it is familiar ground.

A lifetime of teaching and research lies behind it, and general acknowledgments are owed to students and colleagues too numerous to number. However, my immediate gratitude is due to the Oxford University History Faculty, and to its Chairman, Professor Christopher Wickham, who has given me a base in the academic world. Thanks are also due to Professor Diarmaid MacCulloch and Dr. Steven Gunn, the organisers of the two postgraduate seminars which I have been privileged to attend for many years.. I am deeply grateful to Michael Greenwood, my editor at Bloomsbury Publishing for his patience and guidance during the writing of this book.

David Loades
Burford, December 2011

1

Getting To Know the Family

The Tudors claimed descent from the ancient princely house of Deheubarth, but more realistically were a gentry family, based at Penmynydd in Anglesey. They were one of that network of families which had originally supported the Glyn Dwr revolt, and two of them, Gwilym and Rhys, were among those exempted by name from the pardon issued in March 1401. Their aunt, Elen Fychan, was the mother of Owain Glyn Dwr, and they were therefore part of his intimate kindred.[1] Nevertheless, at some point thereafter they abandoned his cause, which was dwindling towards defeat, and were included in that raft of Anglesey gentry who were pardoned in November 1406. That number also included Maredudd ap Tudor ap Goronwy of Penmynydd, the father of Owain ap Tudor, although Owain himself, who was born in about 1400, would have been too young to have needed any such pardon. Owain may well have played a part in the rehabilitation of the family by serving as a page in the household of Henry, Prince of Wales, who had been the main agent in suppressing the revolt. The evidence is unclear, but somehow or other he established a connection with the royal court because he was serving in the retinue of Sir Walter Hungerford, the Steward of the King's Household, in France in May 1421.[2] This suggests some position within the household, but whether on the king's side or the queen's is not known. After King Henry's death in September 1422 his widow, Catherine de Valois, seems to have recruited a number of his former servants, and it may well be that Owain was one of them. He is later described as being her 'sewer and servant', and that is probably accurate. At all events he was a well set-up, handsome young man, a year or so older than herself, and the Queen Dowager fancied him. At some time in 1429 or 1430 they were secretly married. Her ladies were apparently outraged, accusing him (rather unfairly) of having 'neither princely nor even gentle alliance', and of being a Welshman to boot. He summoned some of his more respectable kindred to speak for him, but unfortunately they spoke no language but Welsh.[3]

Although it was clandestine, and caused hostility among those in the know, there is no doubt about the genuineness of this wedding, and no one challenged it at the time. Catherine quickly became pregnant and withdrew from the court to one of her houses at Much Hadham in Hertfordshire, where towards the end of 1430 Owain's eldest son, Edmund, was born. Wishing to regularize her husband's position, in 1431 she arranged for his pedigree to be presented to Parliament, emphasizing his descent from one of the princely houses of Wales, and in 1432 he was granted letters of denizenship. He thus became an honorary Englishman, and not subject to the disabilities imposed on the Welsh gentry after the Glyn Dwr revolt, although it is not clear that he held any significant property in England. Over the next five years, Catherine bore Owain three further children: Jasper, who was born at Hatfield in 1432, David, and an unnamed daughter who seems to have died in infancy.[4] The young King, who was her son by her first marriage, had no difficulty in recognizing these children as his half-siblings, and when his mother's health was in terminal decline in 1436 he arranged for them to be placed in the care of the Abbess of Barking. Catherine died at Bermondsey Abbey on 3 January 1437, aged about 36, and neither her will nor the arrangements for her children make any mention of her husband. Whether she had fallen out with Owain towards the end of her life, or was a victim of that mental illness which had afflicted her father, we do not know, but her death left him dangerously exposed. In July 1437 he was summoned before the Council and consigned to Newgate, for no other reason, apparently, than having presumed to marry the Queen Dowager. He escaped from Newgate, but was recaptured and sent to the more secure prison of Windsor Castle, where he might have remained if it had not been for the intervention of the King. In 1439 he was pardoned and his goods and lands were restored to him.[5] Henry then granted him an annuity of £40 'by special grace', but did not attempt to compensate him by the award of any title. He served the Crown in various low-key ways thereafter, and was given another annuity of £100 in 1459. He remained a loyal Lancastrian, as his family ties and other obligations dictated, being eventually captured and executed after the Yorkist victory at Mortimer Cross in 1461. He did not apparently remarry, although he did beget an illegitimate son in 1459, when he was on the threshold of old age.

Meanwhile, his sons had fared rather better, being transferred from the care of the Abbess to that of the Royal Household as they reached a suitable age. Indeed Edmund, who was seven when his mother died, may never have been at Barking at all, and David, the youngest, who subsequently became a monk, may never have left. Edmund and Jasper were certainly brought up at court, where the former was knighted on 15 December 1449.[6] In recognition of their royal kinship, they were created Earls of Richmond and Pembroke respectively on 23 November 1452, and granted lands commensurate with that status. In 1453 Edmund was also granted the wardship of the ten-year-old Margaret, daughter of John Beaufort, Duke of Somerset, who had died in 1444, and two years later, as soon as she had reached the minimum canonical age, he married her.[7] By 1456 he was fighting with the Lancastrian forces in South Wales, but was defeated by Sir William Herbert and died of the plague at Carmarthen in November of that year, leaving his thirteen-year-old bride pregnant. She was immediately taken into the care of her brother-in-law Jasper and removed to Pembroke Castle where, on 28 January 1457, she gave birth to a son, who was named Henry – the future King Henry VII.

Under Henry VI, Jasper was a powerful man in South Wales. However, like his father, he was among those defeated at Mortimer's Cross, and although he escaped capture, he became a marked man to the government of the new King, Edward IV, and lost his Welsh preferments. These included Pembroke Castle, and with it control over Margaret and her infant son, who passed into the care of the Yorkist Lord Herbert of Raglan. On 4 November 1461 he was attainted and became a fugitive.[8] After several adventures, and a spell in Scotland, Jasper withdrew to France in 1462, where he was welcomed by Louis XI as a kinsman and made a member of his household. In 1468 he made a brief incursion into North Wales, but was defeated again by Lord Herbert and forced to withdraw. Meanwhile, by February 1462, Henry's marriage and wardship had been sold to Lord Herbert, and in August he was deprived of the honour of Richmond. His mother had by then been forced to go her own way, and at some time before 1464 had married Henry Stafford, the second son of the Duke of Buckingham. She can hardly have seen her son during these years, because he was being brought up in the (English-speaking) household of Lord Herbert, where he was being groomed as a future husband for one of the Herbert daughters.[9] Whatever nursery Welsh he had learned in his infancy would soon have been forgotten. He was rescued from this situation by the brief readeption of Henry VI in October 1470 and the reappearance of his uncle Jasper, who, restored to the earldom of Pembroke, was a key man in the new administration. Jasper may have taken the fourteen-year-old boy to London with him at Christmas 1470, and there is a story that he was presented to the King. However, by January 1471 they were both back in South Wales, where Jasper was commissioned to array Welsh forces. However, defeats at Barnet in April and Tewkesbury in May spelled the final end for Henry VI, and after retreating briefly to Pembroke, Jasper again took refuge in flight, sailing this time from Tenby and taking his nephew with him. Diverted by storms, they landed at Le Conquet in Brittany (then an independent Duchy) and were taken into the protection of Duke Francis II.[10]

Henry was by this time a well-educated youth according to the customs of the time. That is, he would have spoken French and understood the rudiments of Latin, known how to ride, wear armour and fly a hawk. He would have understood the Church's liturgy and calendar, learned how to dance and to pay a graceful compliment to the ladies. But of intellectual rigour and philosophical or theological argument he would have been entirely innocent, because there is no suspicion that the Herbert establishment was sympathetic to the 'new learning' – or even knew what it was. For the time being it did not matter very much. There is no sign that Jasper engaged a tutor for the young man, and his future nurture would have been that generally available at the ducal court. Indeed we know very little of how either uncle or nephew spent their time over the next twelve years or so, beyond the fact that they had periodically to dodge attempts by Edward IV and Richard III to have them returned to England. It was fortunate in that respect that they had landed in Brittany, because had they gone to France, as originally intended, there is little doubt that they would have been traded by King Louis as part of his deal with Edward IV at Picquigny in 1475. As it was, Edward kept up the diplomatic pressure on Francis II, and almost succeeded by bland expressions of good intentions. Only at the last moment was Francis convinced that these expressions were bogus, and reversed his decision to let the fugitives go.[11] Rebuffed in this manner, Edward seems to have given up; at least, no more attempts were made before his early death in April 1483.

It was the situation in England following that death which transformed Henry's prospects. Edward had left two sons, but both were under age and he had instructed that his brother Richard, Duke of Gloucester, was to act as Protector until the elder, Edward V, achieved his majority. Richard, however, became convinced that the Queen Dowager's kindred, the Woodvilles, were conspiring to oust and perhaps kill him. This fear seems to have been based on the accurate perception that the young King was much closer to the Queen's brother, Anthony, Earl Rivers, than he was to himself. As a result he seized control of the King's person from Earl Rivers, an event which caused Queen Elizabeth to take her second son, Richard, into the sanctuary at Westminster. For several weeks Gloucester maintained the face of a Protector, and even succeeded in persuading Elizabeth to surrender her son into his custody. He continued to make arrangements for Edward's coronation on 22 June, but then apparently changed his mind. Just when and why this happened remains a mystery, but suddenly postponing the coronation until November, instead he caused Ralph Shaw, a canon of St. Paul's, to preach a sermon impugning the young king's legitimacy.[12] This was on the grounds that at the time of his marriage to Elizabeth, Edward IV had been contracted to a certain Eleanor Butler. This was not news to anyone, but since Eleanor had died before Edward was born it had not been thought relevant. Richard, however, chose to take it very seriously, and on the strength of that objection caused certain of the Lords to petition him to take the Crown. He did this at the end of June, and was crowned as King Richard III on 6 July.[13] Edward and his brother Richard disappeared in the Tower of London, and it was widely believed that Richard had had them murdered. These actions, combined with the summary execution of Lord Hastings for allegedly plotting his overthrow with the Queen Dowager, split the Yorkist party in two. There were those who supported Richard on the grounds that he was an adult of proven competence, and that primogeniture was a custom of the succession, not a law. Their number also included those who, for whatever reason, were suspicious of the Woodvilles, or resented their power. The Duke's northern affinity was conspicuously loyal to him, having had a good chance to see him in action during his years at Middleham, which had been his headquarters in Yorkshire during Edward's reign. Against them stood the Grey and Woodville kindreds, and the numerous friends and dependants of Lord Hastings. Worked upon by Margaret Beaufort, Henry's mother and since 1474 the wife of Thomas, Lord Stanley, these disaffected elements began to turn their attention to the exiled Lancastrian claimant.[14]

Primogeniture was not an issue here, because if it had been – and assuming that Edward V and Richard of York were dead – the next heir was not Henry of Richmond or the Duke of Gloucester, but the young Earl of Warwick, the son of Richard's elder brother, George, Duke of Clarence. However, Warwick was only eight years old – younger than either of the sons of Edward IV – and seems not to have been considered as a candidate. While Richard III was enjoying a progress to York in the late summer of 1483, a progress which brought him the nearest thing to popular acclaim that he was ever to enjoy, the Duke of Buckingham was plotting rebellion. Buckingham had been one of Richard's staunchest allies in the actions which led up to his *coup d'etat*, and why he should have turned against him so rapidly is something of a mystery. His conscience is hardly likely to have been a factor, and the most plausible explanation is that he was dissatisfied in some way with the treatment which the new King had accorded him.[15] It appears that at first it was his intention to rescue the sons of Edward IV from the Tower, but he quickly became convinced that they were dead and transferred his allegiance to Henry of Richmond. Henry responded swiftly and, wheedling 10,000 crowns out of Duke Francis, set out with about 5,000 men and fifteen ships to try his fortunes. He went, however, to Dorset and not to Wales as his mother had advised, and by the time he arrived on 10 October he was too late. The coast was held in strength against him, and he felt that he had no option but to return to Britanny.[16] In fact, the whole rebellion was mismanaged. It spluttered to life in a series of spontaneous revolts that were neither directed nor co-ordinated. The King's response was also slow, and if his enemies had been better organized that might have cost him dear. As it was, Buckingham was caught trying to get to Wales, where he had (as he thought) assured support. He was captured near Salisbury and summarily executed there on 2 November.[17] The main consequence, however, was not to strengthen the King's position but to cause another exodus of Yorkist gentlemen to join Henry of Richmond in Britanny. In spite of this fiasco, and the consequent attainder of Margaret Beaufort, one of her ventures was successful, and the alliance between Henry and the Woodvilles was sealed at Rennes just before Christmas, when Henry undertook to marry the eldest daughter of Edward IV, Elizabeth of York. As Elizabeth was at that point still with her mother in the sanctuary at Westminster and Henry was a fugitive, that could only be described as an optimistic undertaking.

That was even more the case as Richard moved against his rival in the early part of 1484. Over one hundred persons were attainted by the parliament which met at Westminster from 23 January to 22 February, but the most important of them were already out of reach, and Margaret Beaufort was treated leniently. Her goods and lands were transferred to her husband, Lord Stanley, perhaps in a bid to secure the latter's allegiance. The King also came to terms with the Queen Dowager, inducing her and her daughters to emerge from sanctuary in return for a written safeguard under the sign manual.[18] This did not actually revoke the Rennes agreement, but it made it even more unlikely to be realized. Meanwhile the hostile relations with Brittany that had prevailed since Henry's abortive expedition were brought to an end by a truce on 8 June. Duke Francis was incapacitated by illness at that time, and although Louis XI had died in August 1483, the threat from France was felt to be growing. Richard offered military assistance and in return Pierre Landois, who was running the government of Brittany while Francis was out of action, agreed to surrender Henry and Jasper to the English King. By some unknown means, John Morton, the exiled Bishop of Ely, who was in Flanders, got wind of this intention and warned Henry in time, an action for which he earned the latter's unending gratitude. In the nick of time, and at the cost of abandoning their followers, Henry and Jasper escaped into France, where they were made welcome at the court of the young Charles VIII.[19] Fortune was now smiling on the exiles, because Duke Francis recovered at this point, and was enraged to discover what Landois had done. As some recompense he allowed the three hundred or so Englishmen still at Vannes to follow their leaders into France, and gave them money for their journey, which placed Henry under a further obligation. However, his fortunes now rested with the minority council of Charles VIII, and they were by no means certain that they wanted to entertain the risk of supporting him. They had problems of their own, and in a bid to escape the Orleanist influence which predominated in Paris, moved the centre of government temporarily to Montargis, a small town near Sens. It was at Montargis that Henry and his following joined the court, and at Montargis that he was joined by the Earl of Oxford, a stalwart Lancastrian who had broken out of Hammes Castle, where he was being held, and brought most of the garrison with him.[20] When the court returned to Paris in the late summer, Henry and his retinue went with them. Henry was now calling himself the rightful King of England, and talking of 'returning to his kingdom', but it was to be almost another twelve months before the reluctance of the minority council was finally overcome.

Henry's pretensions were justified in a sense, because the steady trickle of former Yorkists who were now joining him went on, and in the latter part of 1484 and early in 1485 the threat which he presented became more plausible. Richard, meanwhile, was suffering. His only son, Edward, the eleven-year-old Prince of Wales, died in April, and his Queen, Ann Neville, just a year later, leaving him in a dynastic wilderness.[21] There were rumours, swiftly denied, that he would marry his niece Elizabeth. Eventually, it was probably Richard's deal with Brittany that persuaded Charles's council to offer Henry just enough support to make a nuisance of himself, and to distract Richard from any attempt to aid the Duchy. He was given sufficient money to hire about two thousand mercenaries and ships to transport them to England. He landed at Milford Haven on 7 August 1485. Meanwhile, on 9 August the French and the Bretons had come to terms, removing – temporarily, at least – any call for English intervention.[22] While waiting for the Regency Council to make up its mind, Henry's own fortunes had ebbed and flowed. Following his mother's agreement with Richard, her son by her first marriage, the Marquis of Dorset, made an attempt to defect, and was only with difficulty talked back into line. Had he reached Richard's court, his knowledge of the exiles' plans could have done them untold damage. On the other hand, the Earl of Oxford's escape had left Hammes in Lancastrian hands, and the exiles were strong enough to frustrate the King's attempt to recover it, which was a good omen for their military success. At the same time, Henry was issuing 'regal' letters to his known supporters in England, warning them to be ready to support him in his 'just quarrel', and receiving encouraging messages in return. One of these, from John Morgan, told him that Rhys ap Thomas was wholly committed to his cause, and commanded extensive resources in South Wales.[23] It may well have been this message which decided him, when he left the Seine on 1 August, to head for Pembrokeshire, although it was a long way from the centres of political power. In addition to his force of mercenaries, he had with him about five hundred English exiles. Against this tiny army, Richard could in theory muster the armed might of England, so clearly a great deal was going to be determined by Henry's reception in Wales.

At first sight, he had little enough going for him. In spite of his name, he was only one-quarter Welsh by blood, his mother having been entirely English and his father half Welsh and half French. However, by means which are not entirely clear, the Welsh bards (or praise singers) had identified him as *mab darogan*, or the son of prophecy, he whom Merlin had once foretold would restore the sovereignty of the Britons to England.[24] He was not the first Anglo-Welshman to have been so honoured, but in his case his shadowy hereditary claim, and the circumstances of 1483–5, gave the designation a substance which the others had not had. It was not sufficient to rally all the faithful in Wales, but it was sufficient to induce an atmosphere of 'wait and see'. He landed at Dale, on the extreme south-western tip of Pembrokeshire, and took Dale Castle without resistance. He then proceeded by way of Haverford West to Cardigan. A few individuals joined his force, but not sufficient to make any real difference; what was much more significant, in view of the efforts which King Richard had made, was the total lack of any opposition. It was not until he reached Newtown on 12 August that his main anxiety was allayed, when Rhys ap Thomas joined him with a substantial force.[25]

Ap Thomas was a man of mixed antecedents, who had apparently been converted to Henry's cause at the time of the Buckingham rising. Richard was justifiably suspicious of his loyalty, but failed to extract his son as a hostage for his good behaviour. As we have seen, he had sent messages to Henry in exile, and now he was as good as his word. It was therefore with his army augmented to about five thousand men, and his confidence much enhanced, that Henry advanced to Shrewsbury, arriving there on 15 August. There he was joined by Gilbert Talbot, an uncle of the fourth Earl of Shrewsbury, with about five hundred men. Even thus reinforced, however, his army still appeared far too small to confront the ten thousand or so men whom Richard was assembling at Nottingham. Henry sent messages to his mother and to the Stanley brothers, William and Thomas, who responded with words of encouragement and pledges of future support, but no men and only a little money. He reached Stafford on the 17th, and there on the following day was able to make personal contact with the Stanleys. What transpired in their discussion we do not know, but it was sufficiently positive to encourage him to continue his march, and he reached Lichfield on the 19th.[26] Meanwhile, Richard was consumed with similar – only greater – doubts. He had expected the invaders to be opposed on their march through Wales, and that had not happened. The fact that Henry had managed to advance as far as Lichfield without encountering any resistance was extremely ominous. Richard knew that he was not popular, but believed that he had taken sufficient precautions to ensure to loyalty of his peers. As their retinues assembled patchily and belatedly at Nottingham, it appeared that he may not have done enough. However, he had little alternative but to respond to Henry's advance, and on 19 August set off from Nottingham, heading for Leicester. The two armies encountered on the evening of the 21st, somewhere in the region of Market Bosworth.

There is considerable dispute about the exact location of the battle which ensued on the following day, the latest speculation placing the site over two miles from the place traditionally identified.[27] Nor is there any contemporary description of exactly what transpired. Polydore Vergil, writing a number of years later, says that a marsh separated the two armies, and that Henry assembled his troops in three groups, commanded respectively by the Earl of Oxford, Gilbert Talbot and John Savage.[28] Apparently the invaders continued to advance until they were past the marsh, at which point Richard ordered an attack and the vanguards on both sides became engaged. At this indeterminate stage, the King made the fatal decision to intervene personally. He may have been worried by the failure of the Stanleys and the Earl of Northumberland to appear, and suspected treason, but he seems to have been desperate to end the battle by seizing an opportunity to take out his opponent, and led his bodyguard in an assault on Henry's standard. Henry's own guard resisted this attack with great tenacity, and that gave Sir William Stanley his cue. Launching his own horsemen into the fray, he turned the tables on the King's men, and Richard himself was killed in the ensuing melée. According to the same source, Stanley's whole force numbered about three thousand men, sufficient to establish a rough parity between the size of the armies. Not that numbers mattered very much by that time. The King's death took the heart out of his troops – who had probably had little enough in the first place – and they rapidly gave way. The Duke of Norfolk's vanguard was put to flight, and the Duke himself killed, among many others in what rapidly became a rout. Henry was proclaimed King by his soldiers on the field of battle, and the heraldic crown which would have adorned Richard's helmet was symbolically placed upon his head, Lord Thomas Stanley somewhat mysteriously emerging to perform that office.[29] Richard immediately became a usurper, and the body of the 'late Duke of Gloucester' was stripped and borne from the field in dishonour. Richard's death without heirs of his body was absolutely decisive. His designated heir was his nephew,

John de la Pole, Earl of Lincoln, but few people took that seriously, and John himself did not press his claim. The god of battles had spoken and Henry, Earl of Richmond, had become King Henry VII.

The battle of Bosworth was not the end of the Wars of the Roses, because residual pockets of Yorkist resistance remained. The first armed uprising came at Easter 1486 and was led by Viscount Lovell in Yorkshire and by the Stafford brothers in Worcestershire. This seems to have been a general expression of discontent, unconnected with any particular claimant, and perhaps for that reason was easily suppressed.[30] The message was quickly learned. In order to succeed, a Yorkist claimant must be named, and if no genuine one was available, then a pretender would have to be created. The first time this happened was early in 1487 when Lambert Simnel, the ten-year-old son of an Oxford carpenter, was passed off as the twelve-year-old Earl of Warwick. Henry had the real Warwick in his custody and wasted no time in parading him to demonstrate the imposture, but thanks to the vagaries of Irish politics Simnel was recognized there and even crowned in Dublin on 24 May as King Edward VI. He was supported by several bishops, in defiance of Innocent VIII's bull in Henry's favour, and by Gerald, the 8th Earl of Kildare, no doubt disgruntled at having been replaced as Chief Governor by the King's uncle, Jasper Tudor, now Duke of Bedford.[31] How long it had taken Richard Simons, a priest of obscure antecedents, to train Simnel for his imposture, and who was really behind his bid, are alike unknown. Rumours began to circulate in November 1486, but it was January 1487 before the boy surfaced in Ireland. The Lordship, however, was only a stepping stone, and on 4 June 'Edward VI' landed near Furness in Lancashire at the head of about two thousand eager but ill-equipped Irish soldiers and a band of German mercenaries. The similarities with his own adventure of two years earlier would not have been lost on King Henry VII, but there was one big difference. Whereas Richard had faced widespread disaffection, Henry was master of his own nobility. He raised a substantial force and, in anticipation of an attack, set up his headquarters at Kenilworth on 8 May. When news of the actual landing reached him, he moved towards Newark, and encountered the rebels near Stoke on 16 June.[32] Thanks to the presence of the Germans, the battle was hard fought, but it was also decisive. Simnel's forces were routed, and he himself and Richard Simons were captured. John, Earl of Lincoln, Viscount Lovell, Martin Schwartz, the mercenary captain, and Thomas FitzGerald, the Irish leader all died on the field. Simons was consigned to an Episcopal prison, and Simnel (as befitted his true status) was sent to work as a scullion in the royal kitchens.

Stoke is usually described as the last battle of the Wars of the Roses, but it was not the end of impostures aimed at Henry's crown. The next surfaced – again in Ireland – in the autumn of 1491 with the appearance of Perkin Warbeck, the son of a Tournai pilot, who was apparently acting as a kind of male model, showing clothes for a Low Countries merchant. Perkin, who was aged about seventeen, bore a striking physical resemblance to the late King Edward IV, and the rumour quickly spread that he was really Richard, the younger son of that king, who had somehow or other escaped from the Tower. It is very unlikely that these rumours were spontaneous; Perkin had been planted in Cork by persons unknown, but who probably included Margaret, the Dowager Duchess of Burgundy, who was Edward IV's sister and an implacable enemy of Henry VII.[33] Charles VIII, who was hoping to distract Henry from any involvement in Brittany, may also have been a party to the plot. However, the Irish had, by and large, learned their lesson over Lambert Simnel and 'Richard IV' did not get the support that he was looking for. He was backed by the more substantial citizens of Cork, and possibly by the Earl of Kildare (although the latter subsequently denied any involvement), but failed to win any general acclaim. Early in 1492 he wrote to James IV of Scotland, but a better prospect opened in France, which was at war with England from April, and where Charles VIII was looking for a catspaw. He invited Perkin to France and received him with princely honours. However, this phase was abruptly terminated in November by the treaty of Etaples between the two countries, which bound Charles (among other things) to deny any recognition to English pretenders.[34] Perkin hastily moved his base of operations to Burgundy, where he was immediately – and unsurprisingly – recognized by his 'aunt' Margaret, who was able to prime him with suitable memories of the Yorkist court. Fortunately for him, the Archduke Maximilian was also on bad terms with Henry VII at that point, and took the young man under his protection, welcoming him to Vienna in November 1493 to attend the obsequies of the late Emperor, Frederick III. Elected Emperor in his turn, Maximilian recognized 'Richard IV' as the rightful King of England, and thereby provoked a diplomatic quarrel with Henry, who forbade his merchants to trade into the Low Countries and moved the wool staple from Bruges to Calais.[35]

Maximilian, however, lacked the resources to mount any kind of a military threat, and Henry turned his attention to the ramifications of the plot nearer home. The most significant and conspicuous victim was Sir William Stanley, who had been rewarded with the office of Lord Chamberlain for his rescue of the King at Bosworth. Why Stanley became involved is a mystery. It can hardly have been through disillusionment, and may have arisen from genuine doubts about the pretender's identity, but as early as March 1493 he had begun to probe the possibilities. He entered into an agreement with Sir Robert Clifford that the

latter would travel to the court of Margaret of Burgundy and communicate with
Perkin. Clifford duly carried out his mission in June, but then at some subsequent date informed the King of what he had done. He may have been a double
agent all along, or he may have fallen out with Stanley, but it was on his evidence
that the latter was arrested towards the end of 1494. Being a commoner in spite
of his office, Stanley was tried by a commission of Oyer and Terminer on 30 and
31 January 1495 and executed on 16 February.[36] His treason – which was real
enough, although limited – is alleged to have hit the King hard, as well it might.
If he could not trust someone so close to his person, whom could he trust?
Three others were also tried and executed for their part in the plot, and a total
of twenty were attainted in the parliament which sat from October to December
1495. In spite of Stanley, it was hardly a major conspiracy, and its main consequence was to demonstrate the efficiency of the King's security arrangements.
When Warbeck attempted to land near Deal with a small force provided by
Margaret of Burgundy on 3 July 1495 he was quickly repulsed by royal forces
which had been forewarned of the attempt.[37]

Frustrated, and in desperate need of some success to bolster his flagging cause,
Warbeck turned his attentions again to Ireland. This time, rather surprisingly, he
was welcomed by the Earl of Desmond, who had presumably fallen out with the
Deputy, Sir Edward Poynings, and raised a force large enough to lay siege to the
town of Waterford. On 3 August Poynings raised the siege, and realizing that he
had no further prospects in Ireland, the pretender moved on to Scotland. There
he enjoyed what was to turn out to be his final triumph. James IV appears to have
been genuinely convinced of his assumed identity, because he not only welcomed
him with princely honours at Stirling on 27 November 1495, but he gave him his
kinswoman, Catherine Gordon, in marriage.[38] Henry VII had been at pains to
build up good relations with James III. In spite of constant friction of the border,
the two monarchs had signed a three-year truce in June 1486, and even contem-
plated a complex marriage alliance. However, this came to nothing, and in June
1488 James was defeated and killed by rebels at the battle of Sauchieburn. At that
point James IV was only fifteen, and although conscience-smitten by the part
which he had been constrained to play in his father's downfall, was unlikely to
adopt the same friendly attitude towards England. There is some evidence that
James was in touch with Margaret of Burgundy as early as November 1488, and
he might have been prepared to welcome Warbeck when the latter left Ireland
early in 1492. However, at that stage he went to Burgundy, and it was to be
another three-and-a-half years before he turned up in Scotland. Although apparently convinced that he was entertaining the rightful King of England, James did
not at first make any attempt to help him realize his ambitions. In the early part

of 1496 he was even entertaining an English embassy headed by Richard Fox, which had come to negotiate a marriage between James and Henry's daughter Margaret, then aged eight.[39] However, James came to terms with Warbeck first, and agreed to invade England on his behalf in return for the surrender of the border fortress of Berwick. The invasion duly took place on 17 September, but it was a fiasco. The Scots lords were not really behind it, and although James may have been convinced of the identity of his protégé, no one south of the border wanted to know. The banner of Richard IV provoked no response whatsoever, and after penetrating about four miles into England, and doing a great deal of damage, James retreated.

The most notable consequence of this incursion was that it enabled Henry to justify asking Parliament for a substantial grant to defend the northern marches. This grant was voted in January 1497, and in the spring the men of Cornwall revolted, unable (or unwilling) to see why they should be expected to pay any tax for an issue which did not affect them in the slightest.[40] Their action seems to have taken the government by surprise, because Henry's forces were all concentrated in the north, and this enabled the rebels to march unresisted right across the south of England. They were eventually defeated on 17 June at Blackheath by an army hastily diverted to encounter them, led by Giles, Lord Daubeney. It was their adventure, however, which tempted Warbeck to his doom. Realizing that no further help would be forthcoming from Scotland, in the middle of July 1497 he quit his refuge there and headed once again for Ireland. This time he did not get even the semblance of a welcome, and decided to try his luck in the one part of England which seemed to be seriously disaffected – Cornwall. With two small ships and about one hundred men he landed at Whitesands Bay on 7 September.[41] At first the response seemed promising and several thousand countrymen joined him, motivated, it would seem, less by any enthusiasm for Richard IV than by general discontent with the existing government. More realistically, neither Taunton nor Exeter wanted to know, and alerted by the earlier rebellion, royal forces were soon on the spot. There was no battle. Warbeck's following simply melted away, and the pretender himself fled. Captured shortly after, he made a full confession of his true identity and disappeared into the Tower. Two years later he was hanged, allegedly for attempting to escape, but really as a part of a 'tidying up' operation which also cost the life of the Earl of Warwick, and should be seen as a part of the preparations for the marriage of Henry's heir, Prince Arthur, to the Spanish princess, Catherine of Aragon.[42]

By the time he died, Warbeck was politically meaningless, but while he was active, between 1491 and 1497, he had been an uncomfortable reminder of

those struggles of York and Lancaster which had consumed so much of the
mid-fifteenth century, and had driven Henry of Richmond into a prolonged
exile in Brittany and France. Apart from the conspiracy associated with
Sir William Stanley, he had been mainly an issue of foreign policy and had
seriously disrupted relations with Charles VIII, Maximilian and James IV.
Eventually he posed no military threat, and the Wars of the Roses ended with
a whimper rather than the bang of a big battle. Of the White Rose challenge to
the Tudors, only the younger brothers of the Earl of Lincoln survived. Edmund,
Earl of Suffolk, was eventually imprisoned in 1506 and executed by Henry VIII
in 1513, and Richard, who took refuge with Louis XII of France, died fighting
at Pavia in 1525.[43] Henry rejoiced at that news, claiming that the last threat to
his family had been removed, but that was not entirely true. Margaret Pole, the
Earl of Warwick's sister, still remained, and she had borne four sons: Henry,
Lord Montague, Arthur, Geoffrey and Reginald. It was their Yorkist blood, as
much as any actual offence, which contributed to the executions of Margaret
and Lord Montague following the so-called 'Exeter Conspiracy' of 1538.
Arthur had died in 1528, Geoffrey was broken by the experiences of the trials
following the Conspiracy, and Reginald was out of reach on the Continent.[44]
The Marquis of Exeter, another nephew of Edward IV, also suffered in 1538,
and his son, Edward, Earl of Devon, died unmarried in 1556. That left only
Reginald, who was spoken of as the 'White Rose' as late as 1554. He died as
Cardinal Archbishop of Canterbury in November 1558, and the only challenge
to be posed to Elizabeth came from within the Tudor family, in the person of
Mary of Scotland, the granddaughter of Henry VIII's elder sister.[45] With the
complexities of the succession issue, we shall be concerned in due course.

Henry VII had fulfilled the prophecies of the *mab darogan* and secured the
sovereignty of England. Ironically, as an adult he neither spoke nor understood
the Welsh language, but he owed a large debt of gratitude to those Welshmen
who had rallied to him in August 1485. Without them his force would hardly
have had the 'critical mass' to have persuaded Gilbert Talbot or the Stanleys to
have joined him, let alone to have confronted Richard's army. When the victory
was won, there were numbers of his fellow countrymen to be rewarded, most
notably his uncle Jasper, who was created Duke of Bedford on 27 October 1485.
At a humbler level, men such as David Phillips and David Cecil were granted
lands and annuities, or given places at court, where a significant number were
recruited into the band of Yeomen of the Guard when that was established.[46]
Slightly later, Henry was in the habit of giving his Welsh servants a special
hand-out to mark St. David's Day (1 March) so that they could celebrate in
suitable style. The government of Wales could be described as a 'semi-feudal

mess'. The principality, north and south, was divided into counties on the English model, but the princely council which had been responsible for seeing the King's justice done seems to have lapsed with the death of Edward IV, and Richard had never tackled the problem.[47] The rest of Wales comprised something like 120 lordships where the King's writ did not run, and justice was in the hands of the territorial lord. Nearly half of these lordships were actually in the hands of the Crown, by escheat, inheritance or forfeiture, but the King's writ ran only as Lord, and did not extend beyond the bounds of the particular lordship, which made the pursuit of fugitives extremely problematic. Even if he had not been Welsh by origin, Henry would have felt bound to tackle this situation, and in the event he did so promptly. Unsurprisingly, Sir William Stanley was confirmed as Justice of North Wales and given strict instructions as to the conduct of his office. At the same time, the Duke of Bedford was made Justice of South Wales, with a similar brief, and Rhys ap Thomas became Chamberlain. As soon as Arthur was created Prince of Wales in 1489, the princely council was revived and given a supervisory role over the lordships as well as the principality, particularly in the matter of the pursuit of fugitives.[48] The fact that the Prince was an infant meant that this was in effect a royal council, and directly responsible to the King's Council in London. This was demonstrated by the fact that that the Council continued to function between Arthur's death in 1502 and the creation of Henry as his replacement in 1504. The whole patrimony of the Prince passed back to the Crown and was re-allocated for Henry's benefit. However, in practice the income continued to be paid into the Treasury of the Chamber, and the changes were more cosmetic than real.

All this could be described as Good Lordship, and was favourable to the Welsh only in a very general sense. The indentures entered into by the Lordship Stewards for their proper conduct in office have to be seen in the same way, and can be paralleled for other offices which had nothing to do with Wales. In order to find any policy which specifically favoured the Welsh, we have to look at the various charters which were issued to different communities in North Wales. Seven of these were issued altogether, the earliest dating from 28 October 1504, after the creation of Henry as Prince.[49] This exempted the inhabitants of Caernarvon and Merioneth from the operation of certain statutes passed in the fourth year of King Henry IV, which had forbidden them to hold lands or property in England or the freedom of any English borough. The charter went on to abrogate the inheritance custom of gavelkind (or partible inheritance), which was the Welsh custom, and to introduce English land law in its place. This would undoubtedly have been on the petition of the gentry of those counties, who had long sought the benefits of primogeniture in order to preserve the integrity of their holdings.[50] A further charter of March 1505 extended these benefits to the inhabitants of Anglesey, and manumitted all the bondmen of the King and the Bishop of Bangor. At a time when serfdom had almost died out in England, its continuation in Wales was seen as something of an anomaly. Two further charters of similar import in respect of the inhabitants of the Lordships of Ceri and Cedewain were issued in July 1507, and in June 1508 the Lordship of Ruthin was emancipated in the same way, the town of Ruthin being also erected into a free borough, that is under English law. Why similar privileges were not accorded to the inhabitants of the southern principality or to the lordships of South Wales remains a matter of conjecture. Perhaps they were thought of as being already substantially anglicized. The English inhabitants of the North Wales boroughs, particularly Conway, Caernarvon and Beaumaris, were not happy with these concessions to their Welsh rivals and challenged the validity of the exemptions from statute law on the ground that the King was not entitled to issue concessions which amounted to the abrogation of a statute.[51] It was indeed the received wisdom that the King could not repeal a statute without the consent of Parliament, and this dispute was really about whether such sweeping exemptions amounted to the repeal of the statute or not. The case was taken to the King's Council rather than to a court of law, and on 20 February 1509 the Council issued an instruction that no 'liberty or franchise within the Principality of North Wales' should be exercised but 'such as they of old times have used'.[52] Whether this ruling invalidated the charters was (and is) unclear, because by the time that the parties had been summoned before the King for a final resolution of the issue, Henry VII was dead, and it was 1536 before Henry VIII got round to resolving the problem with a new statute. Henry VII had in a sense favoured the inhabitants of North Wales, but he must have been aware of the equivocal status of his grants, and his purpose in issuing them remains unclear.

Henry VII, Elizabeth of York, Henry VIII, Jane Seymour

Henry VII, Henry VIII, Edward VI

Henry VIII and Cranmer

Thomas Cromwell

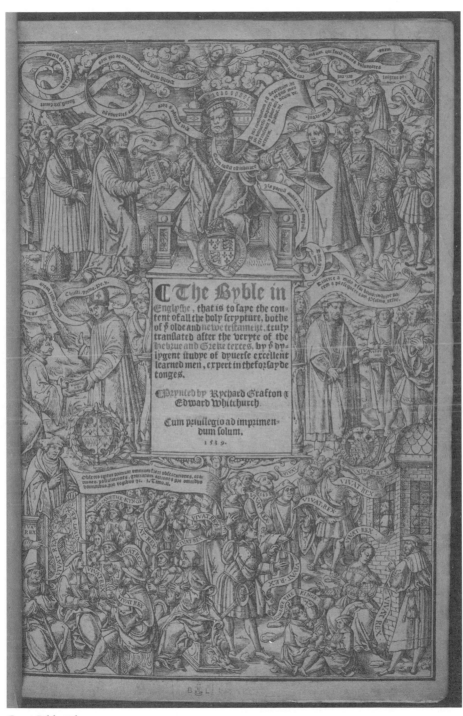

Great Bible title page

THOMAS CARD „ WóLCEVS
creat anº 1515 mort 1530

Thomas Wolsey

Design for Field of Cloth of Gold pavilion

The Kings and Their Marriages: Henry VIII's 'Great Matter'

Henry of Richmond's pledge to marry Elizabeth of York in December 1483 was a calculated dynastic move. Her two brother being presumed dead, Elizabeth bore the bloodline of her father Edward IV, and, because there was no Salic Law in England, her claim to the throne was actually stronger than that of her cousin Edward of Warwick, let alone that of her prospective bridegroom. When the Queen Dowager came to terms with Richard III in 1484 and tacitly withdrew the pledge, it was a blow to Henry, because if Elizabeth had been married elsewhere in the early part of 1485, his dynastic prospects would have been diminished. The union of York and Lancaster which she promised to bring would not have happened, and the future of the Tudor family would have become a serious problem. However, that did not come about, and in the event the defeat and death of Richard at Bosworth nullified his agreement with Elizabeth Woodville, restoring the Rennes pledge to the agenda. Consequently, when his first parliament petitioned the King to marry in December 1485, it was Elizabeth of York that they had in mind.[1] The parties were not, in fact, very closely related, because one has to go back to Edward III to find a common ancestor, but they were technically within the prohibited degrees, 'the fourth and fifth degrees of kindred', and perhaps also the fourth degree of affinity, so a dispensation was needed. Moreover, Elizabeth was illegitimate by a statute of Richard III's parliament, which needed to be repealed before a dispensation could even be applied for. That proved to be tricky, but was successfully accomplished.[2] The procedures of the papal bureaucracy were cumbersome and slow, requiring the testimony of eight witnesses, so it was 16 January before a faculty could be issued in the proper form. Time was also needed for the couple to become acquainted, because Henry's exile meant that he had never set eyes on his nineteen-year-old bride. Fortunately their personal chemistry worked exceedingly well, and it is possible that they were sleeping together as early as Christmas 1485. If that was so, it added a degree of urgency to the situation, and the couple were actually married at Westminster on 18 January. In spite of its great significance, and the fact that it was celebrated in panegyrics both contemporary and later, little is known of the actual ceremony beyond the fact that it was conducted by Archbishop Bourchier – one of his last services to the Crown, since he died on 30 March.[3]

It was a conspicuously successful union, both in personal and in dynastic terms. Prince Arthur was born with exemplary promptness on 19 September 1486, setting the seal of Divine approval not only on the marriage but also upon the Tudor regime. We do not know how many pregnancies Elizabeth endured thereafter, because there seem to have been a number of miscarriages and still births, but four other children are known by name, three of whom grew up to marry and have children of their own: Margaret, born in November 1489, who went on to marry first King James IV of Scotland and then Archibald, Earl of Angus; Henry, born June 1491, of whom more anon; Mary, born in March 1496, who later married Louis XII of France and Charles Brandon, Duke of Suffolk; and Edmund, born in 1500, who died in the same year. Elizabeth was crowned with great splendour on 25 November 1487, in what must have been an interval between pregnancies, but her political influence appears to have been slight. Indeed, she was later described as being much loved precisely because she was powerless.[4] There is some reason to suppose that she was deemed to have inherited the Earldom of March, but the main financial provision was made for her in a series of grants which followed her coronation. Other grants were made from time to time, particularly following the death of her mother in 1492, and her endowment seems eventually to be been similar to that awarded to other Queen Consorts previously, with a total income of about £4,000 a year. No accounts survive, other than Privy Purse expenses, so it is hard to be sure.[5] She used her resources mainly for charitable works of a pious nature, and never attempted to establish an independent clientage. She had, of course, her own Privy Chamber, apart from that of the King, staffed by ladies of her choice, but as she spent little time away from the court, her household staff must have been largely notional.

Briefly, in 1500, she was the mother of three sons and the dynastic future must have seemed secure. However Edmund died after about two weeks, and on 2 April 1502 Arthur succumbed to what appears to have been pneumonia. This was less than six months after his marriage to Catherine of Aragon, a union which was supposed to secure the family's future. The ceremonies surrounding their wedding in November 1501 had been replete with fertility symbols, but it is by no means certain that the marriage was ever consummated.[6] It was immediately proposed to transfer the seventeen-year-old widow to Arthur's brother Henry, but Henry was only eleven years old at that point, so any dynastic ambitions had to be put on hold for the time being. Both Henry and Elizabeth were devastated by the loss of their heir, and took the fatal decision to try and repair the damage with a further child. Elizabeth was thirty-six and still fertile, so she conceived without great difficulty, and on 2 February 1503 was delivered of a daughter in the royal lodgings at the Tower. Then disaster struck. The child, named Catherine, lived only a few days and then, on 11 February – her thirty-seventh birthday – Elizabeth died of puerperal fever, that scourge of the medieval marriage bed. Henry was deeply affected, and in spite of the fact that the dynasty's future now depended wholly upon the twelve-year-old Henry, he did not marry again. He considered various possibilities, including Joanna of Naples, another Juana who was Catherine of Aragon's widowed sister, and even Catherine herself, but these were mainly diplomatic ploys and it is difficult to know how seriously they were intended.[7] During the last two or three years of his life his health was in any case poor, and he may well have felt that the effort was not worthwhile. So he concentrated on training the young Henry for the succession, a training which consisted of a rigorous humanist education and physical exercise of the most strenuous nature. By the beginning of 1509 he had reared a splendid specimen of youth, both physical and intellectual, but one absolutely lacking in any kind of political experience.[8] It was enough – just – because when he died on 21 April his son was still a few weeks short of his majority. However, no one suggested a minority council, and Henry VIII took over the Crown with full powers.

The new King must have been aware what a narrow escape he had had, and seems to have been determined to fix his own succession as quickly as possible, or perhaps he just fancied his sister-in- law. At any rate he married Catherine in the Franciscan church at Greenwich on 11 June, alleging his father's dying wish. In doing so, he swept away a whole cobweb of doubts; doubts about the dispensation from consanguinity which had been originally obtained from Julius II in 1503; doubts about Catherine's dowry, which had been the subject of long and anxious negotiations with Spain; and doubts about his own repudiation of the original agreement, which had been registered in 1505.[9] He also (and this was to be important later) fulfilled Catherine's long-standing ambition, which had been the subject of many hours of careful prayer since the idea had first been mooted. They were crowned together on midsummer's day, and the whole world seemed to rejoice. They were, by all accounts, a magnificent-looking couple – he fair of colour and immense of stature; she auburn, petite and pretty; both in the full flush of youth. The court festivities, maskings and other entertainments went on for weeks, although the King did not joust until the following January – warned, perhaps by his council, of what a dangerous undertaking that could be. Within a few weeks of their marriage, Catherine was pregnant, and January 1510 was prematurely delivered of a stillborn girl.[10] In the light of subsequent events this looks ominous, but it did not appear that way at the time. It was sad, but a routine hazard, and neither of them brooded about it too much. Meanwhile Catherine, who had a lively political intelligence and some diplomatic experience, was busy furthering an alliance between her husband and her father. It was Henry's express wish to wage war on France, and for that he needed allies. Ferdinand was the obvious choice, having quarrels enough of his own with Louis XII. In choosing this policy, the King was partly motivated by a romantic dream of errantry (inspired by his admiration for King Henry V) and partly by the desire to emancipate himself from the control of the Council which his father had bequeathed him.[11] That Council, which was dominated by clergy, did not approve of his bellicosity and he was determined to have his own way, so he not only permitted but encouraged Catherine's efforts. Meanwhile, not neglecting her primary function, she had fallen pregnant again, and on 1 January 1511 was delivered of an apparently healthy boy. The child was named Henry, and the rejoicings were thunderous – the succession was once again secured. So it seemed, but a few weeks later, almost before the sound of celebration had died away, the child was dead. This time both parents were seriously distressed, and Catherine particularly so, since conventional wisdom blamed any constitutional weakness in a child on its mother. The King had gone on pilgrimage to Walsingham to celebrate Henry's birth and was beginning to wonder whether he had done anything to upset God, who was clearly displeased over something.[12]

Meanwhile, he had his war to think about, and the entertainments of the court to divert him. The latter included the game of courtly love, which Henry played with more enthusiasm than discretion, causing rumours about the chamber that he was taking mistresses, which were almost certainly unfounded at this time. Nevertheless, the rumours caused distress to the Queen, and by 1513 the honeymoon between them was definitely over. Like most strong physical relationships, theirs was subject to stormy outbursts, but too much should not be made of them, and by 1514 Catherine was pregnant again. This time it ended in a miscarriage, and a strained relationship can again be detected. This was not aided by the fact that Ferdinand had double-crossed Henry and made a separate peace with France, an action which virtually forced the King to follow suit in 1514.[13] Moreover, Henry had by this time found in Thomas Wolsey a councillor after his own heart, and the rise of Wolsey measured the decline of the Queen's political influence, so that by 1515 she was somewhat in the wilderness. Nevertheless, her marriage was by no means over and late in the year she was pregnant again, this time going to full term and being delivered of a healthy girl in February 1516. Coupled with the death of her father at about the same time, this offered redemption – up to a point. The child was female, and that reduced the rejoicings. Henry was upbeat, talking about a 'token of hope', but Catherine was getting seriously worried about her body. She was now thirty-one and four pregnancies had taken their toll. Time was no longer on her side if she were to discharge her prime responsibility to deliver a male heir. Also – although it is not certain that the Queen knew about it – Henry was beginning to show a serious interest in a young lady of her chamber called Elizabeth Blount.[14] At what stage Bessy Blount actually became the King's mistress is not known, and it may not have been until 1518, but by the latter part of that year they were certainly sleeping together because in the summer of 1519 she delivered him the token of her affection in the form of an illegitimate son, who was promptly acknowledged and named Henry Fitzroy. This was a bitter blow to Catherine, whose last pregnancy had ended in a still birth the previous year. It also demonstrated that Henry was perfectly capable of begetting a male child which could survive, and thereby increased the perception that her own failure to do the same was due to some constitutional weakness in herself.[15] Bessy did not return to the royal bed after her reproductive feat, and the King went on sleeping with his wife, but more in hope that expectation. After 1518 she did not conceive again, and it is possible (although nothing was said) that at the age of thirty-three she had undergone her 'climacteric' – that is, passed the menopause.

By 1520, when she played a full part in the ceremonies of the Field of Cloth of Gold, Catherine was on the defensive. She probably knew that, barring a miracle, she would bear no more children, but went on hoping, redoubling her pious exercises. Rumours of Henry's exploits continued to circulate, but it was probably 1522 before he took another mistress. It is likely that Mary Boleyn was already married to William Carey before she began to share the royal bed, but since she did not conceive it is hard to be sure. Perhaps she had some contraceptive knowledge, or (more likely) Henry's potency was becoming fitful. When their relationship came to an end and she began to sleep with her husband in 1525, she conceived promptly enough – so promptly indeed that some people believed Henry Carey to be the King's son, but since he was never acknowledged as such that is extremely unlikely.[16] Meanwhile Catherine continued to be the Queen, to keep her court, and to accompany her husband on all formal occasions. It was probably some time during 1526 that the King began to find this situation intolerable. He had to do something about the succession. As things stood, his daughter Mary was his heir, but female succession was unprecedented in England, and raised all sorts of uncomfortable questions about the man she would marry and the prospect of a foreign king. The previous year he had sent her off with a royal entourage to the Marches of Wales, as Prince Arthur had been sent in the past, only without the acknowledgement of any formal creation as Princess of Wales. At the same time he had created Henry Fitzroy as Duke of Richmond and sent him with a similar team to the north of England. Richmond was a royal title, and the King seems to have been keeping his options open.[17] Catherine obviously thought so, and resented Fitzroy's elevation bitterly. There is no evidence that the King ever seriously considered legitimating his bastard, but he had to do something. At the same time, fretting about the reasons for his dilemma, he recalled the worries which had been expressed at the time of his marriage about the adequacy of the dispensation which had permitted it. He had paid no attention at the time, but suppose the impediment arose not from the canon law, but from the law of God, which no earthly power could dispense? The more he brooded upon this problem, the stronger his conviction became that he had broken the precept laid down in the Book of Leviticus, and that marriage between such kindred was contrary to the Law of God.[18] So he had never been truly married to Catherine at all! Consequently he was a free man who could marry and beget children on any woman whom he might choose. In May 1527 he arranged for Wolsey, as Cardinal Legate, to summon him to answer to the charge of having cohabited with his brother's widow.

However, this was no straightforward business, because Wolsey's authority did not extend to abrogating a papal dispensation; only the Pope could do that, and it would be necessary to take the issue to Rome. Whatever he might think, Henry's case was problematic, and in June 1527 it suffered two crucial blows. In the first place, an Imperial army (although not under the Emperor's control) took and sacked the city of Rome, leaving the Pope as a helpless prisoner; and in the second place, the King confronted the Queen with the news that they had never been married, which understandably produced a furious denial.[19] Catherine was the Emperor's aunt, and she immediately appealed to him for help – help which he was in a unique position to give, thanks to the Pope's imprisonment. Pope Clement was released in due course, but was understandably averse to causing any offence to Charles V. So, in addition to his own reluctance to undo a dispensation issued by one of his predecessors, he was locked into an Imperial embrace which made it virtually impossible for him to give Henry what he wanted. The King tried all manner of diplomatic pressure to no avail, eventually securing in 1528 a commission to Wolsey and the Cardinal Protector of England, Lorenzo Campeggio, to hear the case in England.[20] This commission, on which great hope were pinned, turned out to be a fraud, because it was not a decretal commission and Clement had no intention of confirming its findings should they be in the King's favour. The result was the court which convened at Blackfriars in London in June 1529 and was adjourned at the end of the following month with nothing accomplished – an outcome which drove Henry apoplectic with fury and spelt the end for Cardinal Wolsey.[21]

The King's anger was twofold: in the first place, the sheer frustration of dealing with a Curia which had no intention of giving him what he wanted; and in the second place, desire for the woman whom he intended to marry, but who was holding out on him for that very reason. The woman in question was Anne Boleyn, the daughter of his servant Sir Thomas Boleyn and the sister of his recent mistress, Mary Boleyn. Their relationship seems to have grown out of another courtly love dalliance at some time in 1526. Anne, who had spent several years at the court of Francis I of France, was an accomplished flirt, and expert in all the graces required of a lady of the court. She seems to have been surprised – and not a little alarmed – at the size of the fish she had hooked, but, having an astute mind, rapidly began to turn her advantage to political ends, with the result that her family became important in council and high in royal favour.[22] They played a key role in the disgrace of Cardinal Wolsey following the Blackfriars fiasco and did much to shape royal policy over the next few years. What she could not do, however, was to solve the problem of Catherine, who clung to her position with great tenacity and rejected any suggestion that she might take the veil. Queen she was, and Queen she had every intention of remaining. Henry, however, neither could not would do without Anne, and the result was a curious *ménage a trois* which lasted from 1529 until the King finally brought it to an end in 1531 by dismissing Catherine from the court. Anne did the honours at the Christmas celebrations that year, while Catherine was in exile, but she was not the Queen and many courtiers did not accept her pretensions.[23] The impasse was finally broken in 1532. Henry had been considering for at least two years the possibility of 'going it alone' – that is, finding his own solution within England, irrespective of what the Pope might say. Catherine's defences had proved impregnable, but they could perhaps be outflanked. This would require two things: a collaborative Archbishop of Canterbury, and some means of making his decision final. A way was opened to the former when the aged and extremely conservative Archbishop Warham died in August. Henry could now appoint his own man to that crucial position, and that seems to have finally decided him to take the risk of defying the Curia. On 1 September he created Anne Marquis of Pembroke in her own right, and the following month he took her off with him to Calais for his long-planned meeting with Francis I. He had already taken the precaution of browbeating the English clergy into submission with threats of praemunire and had suspended the payment of annates to Rome. In other words, he had spelt out his intentions clearly enough, in the hope that the pontiff would read the warning signs and grant him his wishes even at this late date.[24] Clement was unmoved, because he could not afford to be anything else, and so Henry's Great Matter moved towards its dramatic climax.

Francis was embarrassed at being expected to treat Anne Boleyn as though she were the Queen, but confined his protest to keeping his own consort well out of the way. Then, at some time during their stay in Calais in October 1532, Henry and Anne eventually slept together. Whatever impotence the King may have suffered in the past was not evident on this occasion, and in January 1533 the Marquis was discovered to be pregnant. This news had the effect of concentrating minds. Whatever timetable Henry may have had in mind for his declaration of independence, it now had to be shortened if the expected child was to be born legitimate. Thomas Cranmer was immediately summoned home from his diplomatic mission in Germany to take up the Archbishopric, and on the 25th of the month Henry and Anne were secretly married. Although he knew Cranmer's track record, Clement made no difficulty in issuing his pallium, and he was duly consecrated on 30 March. On 5 April the southern convocation gave its verdict that the marriage between Catherine and Henry was invalid by the Law of God, and on 23 May Cranmer, in a specially convened court, endorsed that decision and proclaimed the King's second marriage good and lawful.[25] On 1 June a visibly pregnant Anne was solemnly and splendidly crowned at Westminster in a ceremony noticeably boycotted by the Imperial ambassador. By that time also, Parliament had given its verdict on the proceedings. When the session closed on 7 April, the Act in Restraint of Appeals passed into law. This statute, which was largely the work of Thomas Cromwell, forbade all appeals whatsoever to the Court of Rome, and effectively severed jurisdictional links between England and the Curia.[26] Then, on 7 September, Anne Boleyn was delivered of a daughter, and the courts of Europe were shaken with merriment. The King of England had moved heaven and earth to secure the legitimacy of his new child only to be confronted with another girl! Henry and Anne were bitterly disappointed, but at least the omens for future success were good. The Queen had had a trouble-free pregnancy and an easy delivery. Next time, it would surely be a boy.

Only it wasn't. An outraged Pope had ordered Henry to take Catherine back under pain of excommunication, but he ignored the threat, and an equally offended Catherine had refused the title of Dowager Princess of Wales which she was offered. She did not, however, refuse the settlement which the King made for her, at around £3,000 a year, and diplomatic relations with the emperor were not broken off.[27] Then, in July 1534, the Queen miscarried, and the King's old demons began to revive. Surely he could not have offended God a second time? There was no breakdown of relations at this time, but Anne had many enemies, and they began to talk. The King was enamoured of another wench, and the Queen was taking it badly. Sometimes they were not speaking to each other for days at a time – and so on. Much of this was mere malicious gossip, but Henry was occasionally finding his wife tiresome. She had a political agenda of her own, and that was not proper; also she had not learned to curb her old feisty self. She threw tantrums and upbraided him for real or imagined faults – behaviour which he had found fascinating during their prolonged courtship, but which was not becoming in a married woman.[28] She also found herself being blamed for actions which the King was taking in defence of her position. She was blamed for the house arrest under which a recalcitrant Mary was placed after November 1533, and – more unrealistically – for the executions of Thomas More and John Fisher in the summer of 1535 for refusing to accept the Royal Supremacy over the Church, which was the condition under which they were married. In other words, by 1535 she was becoming a liability, and unless (or until) she could bear the King a son, that situation was likely to get worse. Like most physical relationships, this one blew hot and cold, and there were no doubt days when they could not stand the sight of each other. However, they were still in love, and toward the end of 1535 Anne was pregnant again. Then, in January 1536, Catherine died and the political landscape shifted. Gone now was the threat that, by abandoning Anne, he would be forced to return to her, and half the pretext for his excommunication had disappeared as well. Gone also was the main obstacle to a diplomatic rapprochement with the Emperor, whose honour would not allow him to abandon her cause, and this meant that a way was opening for the foreign policy which Thomas Cromwell favoured.[29] So, although Henry may have expressed relief at Catherine's departing, Anne had every reason to be anxious. The Queen was, after all, the main upholder of that pro-French policy which was now bound to come under attack.

Shortly after Catherine's death, Henry had a heavy fall in the lists. He was no longer as agile and skilful as he had been in his youth and he was left unconscious for over two hours. He recovered, but about a week later Anne miscarried again, allegedly from the worry that his accident had caused her. The foetus was male, and it was later claimed that it was deformed, which convinced Henry that he could not be the begetter and that Anne had been guilty of adultery. This story is plausible insofar as it was a common belief at the time that deformity in an infant was the result of sinful conception, but there is no contemporary evidence to that effect.[30] However, Henry was distressed at the loss of 'his boy', and his nagging worries about his second marriage were rekindled. Just what turned these doubts into convictions we do not know, but on 24 April the King established a commission to investigate his wife's conduct. The commission returned a few days later with numerous charges of adultery, which, in a Queen consort, constituted treason because of the threat posed to the succession. Anne, who was in complete ignorance of these proceedings, was suddenly arrested on 2 May and consigned to the Tower.[31] It appears that her natural flirtatiousness had betrayed her into a number of indiscreet words and gestures which could be construed against her. Mark Smeaton, a musician of her chamber, had also been arrested and induced to confess intercourse with her, which was almost certainly false and probably induced by the threat of torture. Her alleged accomplices were tried on 12 May and convicted on the flimsiest grounds, largely because the King would have it so. Three days later Anne and her brother George, Viscount Rochford were arraigned on the same charges, to which were added incest. Of course, the conviction of Henry Norris and Mark Smeaton meant that the result was a foregone conclusion, and both Anne and her brother were rushed to their executions on 19 May.[32] The true reason for their dramatic fall lies, almost certainly, not in any misconduct on the Queen's part, but in the desire of Thomas Cromwell to destroy the Boleyn family as a rival political influence. As long as the Royal Supremacy had been the leading issue, they had been natural allies, but since the death of Catherine they increasingly stood in his way, and it was a tribute to Anne's political gifts that he decided that she could not simply be shunted aside. Her death was an indication of her power.

On the same day that Anne was executed, Henry betrothed Jane Seymour, and they wedded on 30 May. Given that he still had no male heir, he was bound to marry again, but his haste in doing so provoked much comment. Infatuation with Jane was alleged to be one of his prime reasons for wishing to remove her predecessor, but that is unlikely to have been the case.[33] He had known Jane for several years as a lady around the court, and his motives are likely to have been more prosaic. He had taken the trouble to cause Archbishop Cranmer to annul his second marriage before Anne's death, thus bastardizing his second daughter, a step which the former Queen's execution made strictly unnecessary.[34] Moreover Pope Paul III was convinced, now that Catherine and Anne were both dead, that Henry would return to his allegiance. The King, however, had no intention of renegotiating his relations with the papacy, or of marrying any of the ladies whom Charles V dangled under his nose. He wanted a clean start on his own terms, and that is what Jane represented.

Unlike Anne, Jane had no political talents, or baggage. Her brother, Sir Edward, was already an established courtier with a career of his own, and her main quality seems to have been imperturbable good humour – a quality which Anne had conspicuously lacked.[35] Once Mary had made peace with her father by surrendering to his imperatives at the end of June, the two became close friends. Jane was twenty-seven and Mary twenty, so they were more like sisters than step-mother and step-daughter. The burden on the new Queen to bear a son must have been immense, but she showed no visible sign of it. The Duke of Richmond had died on 22 July, greatly to his father's distress, and the second succession Act which became law on 18 July had taken the precaution of authorizing the King to bequeath the Crown by his last will and testament, in case there should be no male heir.[36] Henry now had no son and two illegitimate daughters, so if he should die the chances of a disputed succession were very real. By the beginning of 1537, Jane was pregnant, and as her condition developed the country held its breath.

The King cancelled his summer progress in order to be on hand if complications should develop, but everything appeared to be going smoothly. The astrologers were predicting the arrival of a prince. They had done that before, but this time Henry was sufficiently convinced to order a stall to be prepared in the Garter Chapel at Windsor for the new Prince of Wales. Jane 'took to her chamber' at Hampton Court at the end of September, not, apparently, being certain when her time was due. She was no doubt confused by the many experts, mostly female, by whom she was surrounded, because less than a fortnight later, on 9 October, she went into labour. After an easy pregnancy, the birth was bitter and protracted. Anxiety mounted and intercessions were ordered in the city churches.[37] Then, on 12 October, after two days and three nights of struggle, the baby finally arrived. It was a boy and apparently normal and healthy. The whole court exploded with relief and the news travelled like wildfire, provoking bonfires and street parties throughout the land. The child was named Edward and was christened a few days later with sumptuous splendour, Archbishop Cranmer standing as godfather and the Lady Mary, his sister, as godmother. Jane was sufficiently recovered from her ordeal to sit in the antechapel and receive the congratulations which flooded in. However, appearances were deceptive, and while the new Duke of Cornwall flourished, his mother became progressively sicker. By the 18th she had developed puerperal fever and her life was in danger. Her attendants were later accused of having allowed her to catch cold, but the true reason for her condition was almost certainly defective hygiene. By the afternoon of the 23rd, septicaemia had developed and she became delirious. The following morning, extreme unction was administered and, after lingering through the day, she died late that night.[38] Henry's search for a male heir had claimed yet another victim, but at least the heir himself survived. Whether he had been with his wife at the end we do not know; what we do know is that her death hit him hard:

> And of none in the realme was it more heavilier taken than of the Kynges Majesty himselfe, whose death caused the kyng immediately to remove into Westminster wher he mourned and kept him selfe close and secret a great while…[39]

He had waited almost thirty years for this moment, only to have its joy snatched from him by the loss of the woman whom he later described as his first true wife.

This time there was no rush to find a replacement. The king was forty-six and his fires were burning low, quite apart from his grief. Nevertheless, life was uncertain, particularly for a small child growing up in the sixteenth century and subjected to the vagaries of Tudor medicine. Well nigh half of those who survived birth did not make it to their fifth birthdays, so there could be no complacency. A second son was urgently needed, and that meant a fourth wife. This time Henry was prepared to look abroad and toyed with several ideas, including Christina of Denmark and a range of French princesses, before being persuaded by Thomas Cromwell of the merits of an alliance with the Duchy of Cleves.[40] The King had been given a big scare in the early part of 1539 by the sudden coming together of Francis I and Charles V in the treaty of Nice. This appeared to threaten a joint Franco-Imperial campaign against the schismatic realm of England, and Henry hastily ordered the erection of fortifications all along the south coast. The threat quickly disappeared, but it left the King feeling diplomatically isolated, and the merits of a German alliance grew on him. He negotiated with the Protestant Schmalkaldic League, but was not prepared to meet their terms, and in the autumn of 1539 reached an understanding with Duke William of Cleves. One of the features of this agreement was a marriage between Henry and the Duke's sister, Anne. Such a decision was unprecedented, because he had never set eyes on her and knew of her only by the flattering reports of envoys anxious to please.[41] Each of his three earlier wives had been well known to him before he had ventured to marry them, but Anne was an unknown quantity. Had he been better informed, he might well have hesitated, because Anne, although passably good-looking, was a bumpkin. She had been educated only in the domestic virtues, as became the prospective bride of a minor German prince, knew no Latin and was innocent of intellectual interests. She spoke no language other than German and had no known musical talents or other courtly graces. In other words, she was a most unsuitable bride for an ageing but highly educated monarch who was also a connoisseur of the arts of the chamber, both male and female.

The result was fiasco. Anne was held up by bad weather at Calais until 27 December, forcing Henry to spend a lonely Christmas. Impatient to meet her, he then decided upon an ill-advised act of gallantry and, intercepting her at Rochester, invaded her room in disguise on 1 January. The poor girl was naturally terrified, never thinking that such a breach of security must have been connived at. She believed that she was going to be abducted, and her lack of English contributed to the confusion. At length the King was forced to reveal his true identity and a measure of order was restored, but he was bitterly disappointed by her lack of wit and sangfroid.[42] After that, it was downhill all the way. The public formalities were all observed, but the wedding night was a disaster. He had no desire, and she was so ignorant of the facts of life that she did not even know what was supposed to happen. 'At this rate', one of her ladies observed the next day, 'it will be a long time before we see a Duke of York.' After persevering with courteous correctness for several nights, Henry gave up and decided that this so-called marriage would have to be dissolved. For the time being he was distracted by the events surrounding the fall of Thomas Cromwell, and Anne continued to appear as Queen with her full entourage. However, on 24 June, she was sent to Richmond ostensibly to avoid an outbreak of plague, and the following day was visited by the King's commissioners and informed (through an interpreter) that her marriage was invalid.[43] The ground alleged was non-consummation, although it is not clear that the commissioners explained that. To their enormous relief, Anne made no fuss; indeed their news was probably a great relief to her. She accepted the settlement which he proposed and showed no desire to return to her homeland. Instead she became the King's 'good sister' and stayed on the fringes of the court until she died, still unmarried, in 1557. The court gossips were subdued, non-consummation not being the stuff of scandal, and a depressing omen for those still hoping for a second son.

To their rescue came Catherine, the eighteen-year-old niece of the Duke of Norfolk. Norfolk had been chief councillor since Cromwell's fall and undoubtedly used her as a means of consolidating his ascendancy, so she had a lot of political baggage, but that did not at first matter. Henry had been increasingly smitten with her since April 1540, when the stream of gifts began, and on 28 July they were married. The King, the gossips were delighted to notice, could scarcely keep his hands off her, even in public, and their hopes of further procreation were understandably high.[44] It did not happen. Far from being the innocent girl Henry thought he was marrying, Catherine was young lady with past, because that sexuality which had attracted the King had also attracted others. While growing up in the rambling, disorganized household of the Dowager Duchess of Norfolk, she had been bedded by at least two men, one of whom, Thomas Culpepper, was now a member of the King's Privy Chamber.[45] Her education had in other respects been neglected, and excellent though she may have been in bed, she was no fitter as a companion for Henry than Anne of Cleves had been. She was given a very generous endowment and her household, which rapidly filled up with Howard kindred and clients, cost the King about £4,500 a year. Within a few months, however, things started to go wrong. The patronage of her family was bitterly resented, and men began to regret the passing of Thomas Cromwell. Even the King sensed this mood about the court.[46] Moreover, her splendid new husband turned out to be a most unsatisfactory lover, and Catherine became bored and frustrated. When the King was ill in the spring of 1541, he even withdrew from conjugal relations entirely, and that added to her woes. The last thing that Catherine needed was to be a nurse to a sick husband. Henry, however, recovered and took his nubile young wife off with him on progress to the north of England. This was a business trip, including a failed attempt to meet his nephew James V of Scotland at York, and the King may well have had little enough time for dalliance, but others were only too willing to fill the gap.

Catherine's chief gentlewoman, Jane Rochford, should have known better. Her late husband George, Viscount Rochford, had been brought to his death by sexual scandal, and she knew the perils attached to such intrigues. Nevertheless, she facilitated – and even encouraged – Catherine's adventures.[47] Thomas Culpepper reappeared, and another old flame, Francis Dereham, now the Queen's private secretary. We do not know exactly what happened, because Catherine denied intercourse, but both men admitted that they had intended it, and Jane believed that it had taken place. Given the ubiquitous presence of servants at court, these goings-on would have been likely to come out sooner or later anyway, but what actually happened was that they were revealed indirectly. The Howards had many enemies and one of these, Mary Hall, knew all about Catherine's earlier life. She told her brother. John Lascelles, and on 1 November John told the Archbishop of Canterbury.[48] Of course, what they knew did not include the events of the summer, and so only related to pre-nuptial intercourse and not to adultery, but Cranmer realized that the information was serious enough and told the King. Henry at first was incredulous. Someone was trying to blacken the name of his beloved wife. Nevertheless he established a commission to investigate, in order, as he put it, to clear her name. Unfortunately the result was the opposite. Not only did the commissioners establish the essential truth of Mary Hall's charges, but because two of the same men were involved, the story of the summer's adventures came out as well.[49] Culpepper, Dereham, Jane Rochford and several other ladies were placed under arrest and the Privy Council went into emergency session. On 7 November, Catherine was interrogated and the whole story came out, interspersed with fits of hysterics.[50] Henry was devastated and vowed that he would torture the ungrateful girl to death, but in the event he confined himself to the due processes of the law. On 1 December Dereham and Culpepper were arraigned for the treason of violating the Queen and both were found guilty. They were executed at Tyburn on the 10th. Catherine and Jane Rochford were not tried, but an Act of Attainder was passed against them on 8 February 1542 and they were executed on the 12th, Catherine being almost too weak to walk to the block. She was just twenty years old. The King was an old man, and his failure to satisfy his young wife was a prime cause of this tragedy, but no such thought could be uttered at that time. In fact, in spite of his initial ardour, there is no evidence that this union was ever consummated, and Catherine's fertility remains unknown. Henry married three times after Jane Seymour's death, but he never created another pregnancy. By the time he married Catherine Parr, Lady Latimer, on 12 July 1543 it was generally recognized that his fires were spent. There was not going to be a Duke of York.

Henry's last marriage does not really belong to the story of the succession, because Catherine was mainly nurse and companion to an ailing man. That was virtually acknowledged by the King's last Succession Act, passed in the spring of 1544, ostensibly designed to cover the situation arising from Henry's decision to campaign personally in France.[51] This was a hazardous occupation and the King was a lumbering hulk of a man. He had left Catherine in charge as regent during his absence, which was an outstanding mark of trust, but there is no sign that he expected to leave her pregnant.

'...[R]ecognising and knowledging also that it is the only pleasure and will of Almighty God how long his highness or his said entirely beloved Prince Edward shall live, and whether the said Prince shall have heirs of his body lawfully begotten, or whether his Highness shall have heirs begotten and procreated between his Majesty and his said most dear and entirely beloved wife Queen Catherine that now is...'[52], he set out to deal with the situation which actually existed. Edward was, of course, his heir, and his children after him. But failing any such, and failing the birth of any son to his present or subsequent marriages, the crown was to pass to his natural daughter Mary, on condition that she married with the consent of the council. Failing her and her heirs, the next in line was to be her half-sister Elizabeth, with the same condition, and in default of her and her children, Frances Grey, the daughter of his sister Mary who had died in 1533. It was a comprehensive document, which concluded with a clause (similar to that in the Second Succession Act of 1536) that the King might either confirm or alter this order by his last will and testament. The Scottish line, represented by Mary, the infant daughter of James V, was completely bypassed. [53] In the event, these arrangements were confirmed by his will, drawn up in December 1546, which controlled the English succession down to 1558. The most remarkable thing about this act was the fact that it included two illegitimate women, without legitimating either of them. It was, in other words, an entirely constitutional settlement, drawing deeply upon the new-found powers of Parliament. Had such a facility been available in 1460, the Wars of the Roses might never have happened!

One of the reasons why the Scottish line was omitted from this act was that Henry had other plans for Mary. Following his victory over the Scots at Solway Moss in November 1542, the King had conceived a scheme to exploit his ascendancy by marrying her to Prince Edward, thus merging the two lines which had the strongest hereditary claim.[54] Any child of that union would be the undisputed sovereign of Great Britain. The Scots had reluctantly consented to this arrangement by the Treaty of Greenwich in the summer of 1543, and although the Scottish Parliament had refused to ratify the agreement, Henry was still determined to bring it to fruition. It would not have been convenient to acknowledge a claim to England in one who was primarily intended to bring about a union of the Crowns. Edward stayed, in a sense, engaged to Mary until 1548, when renewed Anglo-Scottish warfare caused her to be betrothed instead to the Dauphin of France, and physically removed to France to enable this to come about. They married eventually in 1558, and meanwhile Mary had been brought up as a French princess.[55] Edward died, without achieving his majority, in July 1553. He was unmarried and the Tudor male line died with him. He was, in fact, betrothed to Elizabeth, the daughter of Henry II of France, in the summer of 1551, but she was only six years old and he died long before she had attained the minimum age for cohabitation. Child marriages were common at that social level and there was no reason why they should not have been wed, but it did not happen. Ironically, Elizabeth eventually became the third wife of Philip II of Spain.

Unable to transmit his crown to the heirs of his body, Edward nevertheless made his impact upon the succession issue. Early in 1553, before he became fatally ill, he had written a kind of school exercise about what would happen if he should die without direct heirs. In this essay, he had ruled out both his half-sisters on the grounds of their illegitimacy and declared that the throne should pass to any boy who might hypothetically be born to one of the women of the Grey/Brandon line.[56] This envisaged a longish time scale, because Frances Grey was too old and none of her daughters was yet married. It was not real politics, but when the situation became urgent in June 1553 it was brought out because it was the only scheme which existed. Overcoming his aversion to female succession, the King allowed his 'device' to be altered to permit the eldest Grey girl, Jane, to be placed first in the order.[57] This overturned both Henry's will and the statute which had authorized it, and its legal standing was highly questionable. Members of the council and the law officers of the Crown objected, but were overruled by the King and compelled to sign an instrument embodying his wishes. When Edward died, it looked for a few days as though those wishes would prevail. The foreign ambassadors in London at the time certainly thought so, but they reckoned without Mary. Rallying her affinity in East Anglia, she claimed her rights under her father's will, and her party rapidly grew.[58] Even the Protestants, who had been expected to rally to Jane because of Mary's well-known religious conservatism, failed to do so. The Duke of Northumberland, who had taken it upon himself to see the King's last wishes respected, was left isolated as first the council and then the nobility declared for Mary. This has been described as the only successful rebellion against a Tudor government, but in fact it was a Tudor rebellion against a Grey/Dudley government, and a rebellion in favour of the enhanced power of statute. By 19 July Mary was accepted as Queen, and in spite of the desperate efforts which Henry and Edward had made to avoid such a consummation, England had its first female ruler.

Two Queens in Search of an Heir

Having secured her throne, at the beginning of August 1553, one of Mary's first thoughts was of the need for a husband. She had been betrothed several times in her youth – to the Emperor Charles V, to the Dauphin, and even to Francis I – but these had all been political moves and nothing had come of them. Since 1536 there had been various other negotiations, but always her father's suspicions and her own illegitimate status had stood in the way. In 1544 she had been given a wedding portion of £10,000 and a place in the succession, on condition that she married with the consent of the council, but no firm offers had resulted.[1] Edward's council had been nervous of her and had no desire to see her position strengthened, so she had come to the throne at the age of thirty-seven unwed. It is difficult to know what Mary's personal attitude to marriage may have been. Towards the end of her father's reign she had lamented her single state, declaring that as long as her father lived she would be 'only the Lady Mary, and the most unhappy lady in Christendom', but when the opportunity finally presented itself, she professed herself unwilling to marry, recognizing it merely as a public duty. Because of the care which had been taken over her upbringing, she had enjoyed none of those sexual adventures which normally accompany adolescence and which her sister Elizabeth had certainly experienced, so she may well have dreaded the whole prospect of sexual intercourse as some kind of diabolical mystery which she would have to grit her teeth to endure. Nevertheless duty was duty, and the succession had to be secured, if at all possible. In spite of her advanced education, Mary was also a very conventional woman and regarded marriage as a kind of natural destiny for anyone of her sex. Also, although she was very conscious of her royal status, there were aspects of government with which it was not proper for a woman to meddle – such as leading an army into battle.[2] A husband was therefore a necessary helpmate, especially since the political world was exclusively male and all the imagery of monarchy was masculine. As England's first ruling Queen, she was going to find the way difficult enough in any case, so the need for someone to share the burden and father her children was absolutely irrefutable, whatever her personal inclinations may have been.

Her council took it for granted that one of her first concerns would be marriage. Her age alone made it an imperative, if indeed it was not already too late. However, she was also aware that there was a strong party within that council who wanted her to find a husband within the realm, and who favoured Edward Courtenay, the twenty-six year-old son of the late Marquis of Exeter, as a candidate.[3] Although she freed him from prison and created him Earl of Devon, Mary was aware that Courtenay would make a most unsuitable consort. Well-educated and Catholic in his religion, he was nevertheless a feckless youth, with no idea how to conduct himself in the real world of courtly politics. The Queen therefore did not consult her council, but instead sought the advice of the Emperor's ambassador, the clever and self-serving Simon Renard. Knowing how xenophobic the English were, Charles V had at first been inclined to advise an English husband, but quickly realized the advantage which Mary's approach to Renard had given him.[4] Nearly twenty years earlier, when she had been particularly grateful for his support, she had vowed that he was her true father and that she would never marry without his consent. Now that the possibility was a real one, she had remembered her promise, and intended to keep it. Although he was a widower, Charles modestly disclaimed any such ambition for himself; his age and precarious health precluded it. That left two possibilities: Dom Luis, the brother of the King of Portugal, who had sued for her hand in the past, and his own son Philip, recently widowed and the father of one son. Philip was deep in negotiations with the Portuguese for the hand of the Infanta, so it was by no means certain that he was available. However, Charles instructed Renard to suggest Philip as a hypothetical possibility and see what happened.[5] The ambassador proceeded cautiously, expecting a head-on conflict with the Queen's ladies, who were thought to favour Courtenay, but he need not have worried. Mary immediately became enthusiastic and the opposition melted away. Philip, it turned out, was available, and on 10 October Renard formally proposed the marriage. On the 28th the Queen accepted with many tears, and the following day swore on the sacrament that she would wed the Prince of Spain.[6]

Although a number of members of her council had, by this time, a fair idea of what was going on, she had not consulted them, and this left them with a dilemma. Towards the end of November the Parliament petitioned the Queen to marry within the realm, and several councillors, particularly Stephen Gardiner, the Lord Chancellor, were suspected of aiding and abetting them. Such suspicions were almost certainly unfounded, but they had to decide what line to adopt. In the event they accepted her decision with a good grace and concentrated their attention on negotiating a suitable treaty to accompany the marriage. In this they were remarkably successful, largely because they were dealing with the Emperor and not with his son. Charles was concerned to secure a power base for Philip in northern Europe from which he could maintain his claim to the Low Countries when the Emperor carried out his intention of abdicating. This was a complex story, but Charles had settled the succession to The Netherlands on Philip in preference to his brother Ferdinand, who would take over the Empire, and this had caused tension within the family.[7] Philip as King of England would be in a much better position to defend his right, so Charles was prepared to be generous in other ways in order to bring that about. Consequently the treaty which was signed in early January and proclaimed in London on the 14th gave the new King very little in the way of regal power. He was not to take any executive action on his own, to appoint his own servants to English offices, or to involve England in the on-going war with France. When Philip realized what had been done, he was indignant and registered a secret protest, but he did not withdraw from his undertaking, and preparations for the marriage were put in hand.[8] However, it was not only Philip who was annoyed by the prospect of what might await him in England. English opinion in general was bitterly averse to the match, treaty or no treaty, and towards the end of January a widespread conspiracy resulted in rebellion in Kent. This rising, which is known by the name of its leader, Sir Thomas Wyatt, was briefly dangerous and cost the lives of over a hundred rebels, including Wyatt himself, Jane Grey and Jane's father, the Duke of Suffolk, who was unwise enough to be implicated.[9] Unwilling to admit that the Queen's marriage was so unpopular, the council blamed the rising on the Protestants, who were opposed to the government for their own reasons, and that provided the pretext for the execution of Jane Grey. English opinion was not reconciled to the prospect of a Spanish King, and as the time of his coming drew nearer, Renard underwent paroxysms of anxiety, seeing heretics and other enemies behind every bush.

Nor did the Spanish side of the preparations go altogether smoothly. Philip had to find a Regent to take over his duties, and enough men and money to satisfy his father's needs for his war against the French. Both of these arrangements took time.[10] For several months the Prince did not communicate with his bride, and doubts about the seriousness of his intentions arose. In England, a household was prepared for him and a commission established to adjudicate disputes between the nations, each being accustomed to a different code of law. Ships hovered in the western approaches, ready to provide an escort, and the Queen moved to Bishop's Waltham in order to receive him. At length, on 11 June his harbinger, the Marquis de las Navas, arrived, bearing the expected gift, but still there was no sign of Philip himself. By 9 July his household was becoming restive and some of them went home.[11] But eventually, on 20 July, he arrived and was received by the nobility of England in pouring rain at Southampton. He was accompanied by an honourable escort of Spanish nobles, but his ships and the troops which he had brought with him proceeded straight to The Netherlands. He had been warned by his father not to make his coming seem like a military occupation. Proceeding immediately to Winchester, he took up the residence which had been prepared for him in the Deanery, while the Queen moved to the Bishop's Palace in preparation for their wedding, which was due to take place on the 25th – St. James's day. As soon as he arrived, Philip changed out of his wet clothes and went in search of his bride who 'very lovingly, yea and most joyfully received him'. It was the first time that the pair had met, and the court watchers were on the lookout for every blink and gesture, but what they saw reassured them. The couple 'chatted pleasantly' for half an hour before he returned to his lodgings, although what language they used is not recorded.[12] Her Spanish was not up to a sustained conversation, and nor was his French, so presumably they used Latin, in which both were fluent. Philip spoke no word of English, and this problem of communication was to dog his stay in England, although there is no suggestion that it affected his relationship with his wife. Two days later they were married with great splendour in the cathedral, Bishop Gardiner performing the ceremony in what was still, theoretically, a schismatic church.

Philip did not appear to mind, although the couple refrained from communicating during the mass. In fact, he carried off the whole occasion with great good humour, and his display of affection for the Queen was very well received. His Spanish entourage, however, were less pleased. They noted that the symbolism of the occasion was reversed, with the King taking the left-hand, or consort's, side. Nor was any sword (the symbol of authority) borne before him until after the wedding was completed, emphasizing that his position depended entirely upon his wife. Even at the wedding feast, they complained, he was served off silver while the Queen was served off gold.[13] Nevertheless the prevailing atmosphere was one of hope. When the couple retired for the night, the bed was publicly blessed, and the servants then withdrew. Nobody knows, one commentator observed, what happened thereafter, 'but if they give us a son, our joy will be full'. As was customary for a new wife, Mary remained in seclusion for several days after the wedding, while Philip went sight-seeing. Then they set off in a leisurely fashion towards London. Given that the Queen was completely inexperienced, her husband probably found his sexual function difficult, and he confided later to one of his intimate servants that she was not much good in bed (*para la sensualidad de la carne*).[14] Nevertheless, relations seem to have been more or less normal, and in November Mary announced rather coyly that she believed herself to be pregnant. Philip busied himself with the reconciliation of the English Church to Rome, a task which had been expressly reserved for his attention, and did not attempt to intervene in the regular government of the country. He was well aware how touchy the English could be about such matters, because his household had caused endless problems in the weeks following his marriage. He had originally undertaken to use English servants while in England, but had nevertheless brought a full Spanish establishment with him. Disputes were inevitable, and the King had sought to resolve these by decreeing that his public service would be conducted by the English and his private service by the Spaniards, because he needed to understand what they were saying to him![15] This sensible arrangement provoked immediate complaints from both sides; the Spaniards felt dishonoured, and the English had no access to the privy apartments. Both side got used to their allotted roles in due course, but the moaning went on throughout the time of his residency.

When he was not negotiating with the papacy, Philip kept himself busy with the affairs of his father's continental war (for which he had his own separate council) and in playing war games with the English aristocracy. He was well aware that he had a party among the latter, some of whom found the notion of a woman sovereign preposterous, and who looked to him for real, masculine leadership. He did not know how to present himself as a King of England, but there was nothing like a few tournaments to bolster his image as a warrior.[16] Meanwhile Mary's condition was apparently progressing normally and commentators assiduously noted her changing body shape. The Parliament duly gave him the protection of the treason laws and confirmed his right to a Regency if the Queen should die in childbirth.[17] On 20 April she withdrew into the customary female seclusion at Hampton Court; rockers were appointed and a nursery established. Nobody knew just when the happy event was due, but it was expected to be sometime in May. Letters making the announcement were prepared and the court settled down to wait. They waited … and waited. On 22 May Ruy Gomez, Philip's confidential secretary, confided that he could see no sign of an incipient birth, and scandalous tales began to multiply; the Queen was sick, or bewitched, or even dead.[18] By early July it was clear that Mary's pregnancy was a delusion, and by the end of the month the trappings were removed and an exhausted and bitterly disappointed Queen re-emerged into the public sphere. No announcement was made, and it is not clear now what caused the illusion, whether it was psychological or a symptom of some physical illness. Philip, who had been persuaded to remain in England for his wife's lying-in, was anxious to depart, and convinced that Mary, now thirty-eight, would never bear a healthy child.

Mary's false pregnancy was in many ways the turning-point of the reign, because whatever she might think herself, it was no longer possible to believe that there would be an heir of her body to continue her work when she died. Philip's interest in the realm would end with her life, and there was no longer any prospect of a union between England and The Netherlands as provided in the marriage treaty for an heir of the union.[19] There was no reason to suppose that Mary would die in the near future, but the succession was now firmly back on the agenda. The King began to agitate for a coronation, perhaps thinking that it would give him the additional status needed to enable him to claim the crown for himself. English opponents, suspecting some such intention, resisted the idea furiously, and Mary was eventually constrained to refuse his request, a refusal which strained relations between them.[20] Meanwhile, she declined to face the main issue. The heir in law was her sister Elizabeth, but the Queen had made it clear very early in her reign that she would not recognize her – she was, it was alleged, too much like her mother. The princess had been imprisoned following the Wyatt rebellion and had narrowly escaped execution, so she kept a low profile while Mary's pregnancy resolved itself, but that event undoubtedly strengthened her hand. The Queen herself seems unofficially to have favoured Margaret Clifford, the daughter of Eleanor Brandon and grand-daughter of Henry VIII's sister Mary, but no pronouncement was ever made, and Margaret had virtually no support in the country. The English wanted Elizabeth, and by 1556 Philip had also come around to that point of view. The King, however, wished to exercise some control over his sister-in-law, and that meant a suitable marriage, so for over two years he tried by every kind of threat and blandishment to induce her to consent to a union with the Duke of Savoy.[21] Emmanuel Philibert had been dispossessed of his Duchy by the French, and was serving as a commander in the army which Philip had inherited from his father when the latter had abdicated in 1555-6. He was not a Spaniard but he was the next best thing, a reliable ally and subordinate. However Elizabeth, knowing perfectly well what the King was about, would have none of him, and by the summer of 1558 Philip had acknowledged that if his wife were to die, he would have to take her successor on her own terms.

Mary's health fluctuated. When Philip returned to England briefly in the summer of 1557, she bloomed, but after his departure in July she became subject to fits of lethargy and depression. She also had menstrual problems, which had afflicted her since adolescence and may well have accounted for her phantom pregnancy. In January 1558 she declared again that she was pregnant, but at the age of nearly forty-three no one took that seriously and no prepara-tions were made for a confinement. Philip sent his congratulations, but there is no reason to suppose that he believed it either.[22] In March she was forced to confess her error, and once again became depressed. Meanwhile, she had written a will which declared the succession to the heirs of her body, with no suggestion that there were not likely to be any. In August she was ill of a fever, but appeared to throw it off. Then in October she became sick of what was described as a 'dropsy', which may well have been an ovarian cancer, and by the end of the month was obviously in serious danger. In June Philip's special envoy, the Count of Feria, had visited Elizabeth and negotiated with her in a light-hearted sort of way. Now, at the beginning of November, he came again with an altogether more serious purpose in mind.[23] Although he must have suspected the worst, Philip did not come himself because he did not want to be caught in England by Mary's death. Had he been in England at that time, he would have felt bound in honour to bid for the succession himself, and that he had no desire to do. Feria's instructions were to facilitate the accession of Elizabeth in whatever ways might be most appropriate. Having paid his respects to the dying Queen, he therefore made his way to Hatfield, and reported to the best of his ability on what was likely to happen under the new regime.[24] Meanwhile, Mary had added a codicil to her will, admitting the uncertainty of heirs of her body and decreeing the succession to the 'next heir by the laws of England'. She did not name Elizabeth, but everyone who knew of her will knew what she meant. About a week before she died, she sent a message to her sister, acknowledging her right to succeed and asking only that her debts be paid and her church settlement upheld. Elizabeth appears to have made no response and the women did not meet. Relations were too bad for such a meeting to have served any useful purpose, and the new Queen ignored most of the provisions of her predecessor's will. Mary received extreme unction and quietly slipped away early on the morning of 17 November. By midday her successor had been proclaimed in London, to the sound of great rejoicing. After all the uncertainty, Elizabeth had come to the throne peacefully and unopposed. Cardinal Reginald Pole, the Archbishop of Canterbury and the man most likely to have resisted her claim, lay mortally sick at Lambeth and died later the same day. Circumstances had conspired to give the new Queen a remarkably clean start.[25]

Elizabeth was twenty-five, and neither marriage nor the succession pressed upon her in the same way that they had pressed on Mary. Matrimony might have been on other people's agenda, but it was not, for the time being at least, on the Queen's. Remarkably, the first suitor in the field was her brother-in-law, Philip of Spain. How serious Philip was we do not know, but he felt that it was a gesture which he was bound to make. In practical terms it was quite unrealistic, because he would have had very little time to spend in England, and Elizabeth had no intention of going abroad. She turned him down, politely but firmly, in January 1559 – no doubt to his great relief.[26] Like her sister, Elizabeth as an infant had played her part in her father's diplomatic games and, again like Mary, these games had been brought to an abrupt end by her bastardization in 1536, when she was barely three years old. There, however, the similarity had ended, because whereas Mary had passed her adolescence under the strictest security and had been allowed no dubious company, Elizabeth had been barely fourteen when Sir Thomas Seymour made a pass at her. This had involved a good deal of horseplay of a sexual nature, and although the council quickly put a stop to it, it made a lasting impression upon the young princess.[27] She had enjoyed herself a good deal, and knew that she was attractive to men. That gave her a sense of power. It also brought out that natural flirtatiousness which she had inherited from her mother, and taught her how dangerous such games could be. In spite of her denials, her encouragement of Seymour had helped to bring him to the block, and the same fate might well await any other man who attempted the same tactics with one so close to the throne. Thereafter she had kept a close guard upon her behaviour and did nothing to encourage the Duke of Savoy (whom she never met), nor Eric of Sweden, who sent envoys to pursue her in the dying days of her sister's reign. Consequently, when she became a free agent in November 1558, she had a limited but real fund of experience to draw upon, knew the power of sexuality, and set a very high price upon her own head. When Parliament petitioned her to marry in January 1559, she used the same rhetoric which Mary had used about being wedded to the realm, only in her case time was to show that she meant it.[28]

However, at first that was not anticipated. Eric of Sweden kept up his suit, Sir William Pickering was mentioned by the mischievously minded, and tentative feelers were put out for a negotiation with the Archduke Charles, a younger son of the Emperor Ferdinand. Her council were of one mind that she should wed, and her trusted secretary, Sir William Cecil, was particularly insistent. However, these careful plans, and her own agenda, were thrown into disarray in 1559 when the Queen fell in love.[29] She had known Robert Dudley for a number of years and may well have been attracted to him before. He was the younger son of the Duke of Northumberland and they had been thrown together as children. They had even shared a spell in the Tower of London after the Wyatt rebellion, and after their release he is alleged to have loaned her money. Nobody had thought much of it when she had appointed him Master of the Horse at the outset of her reign, but that was a position which involved a lot of access to the monarch and their intimacy seems to have grown rapidly. By the summer of 1559 there was scandalous gossip; she was visiting him in his chambers, day and night; it was clear that she intended to marry him.[30] There was just one snag in this speculation – Dudley was already married, to Amy, the daughter of a neighbouring Norfolk squire, Sir John Robsart. The speculation therefore took a sinister turn; Dudley was intending to do away with his wife in order to marry the Queen. The court became divided, the older nobility particularly resenting him as a parvenu, the son and grandson of traitors. Rumours inevitably spread abroad through the diplomatic network, and did the Queen's reputation no good at all. 'A young princess cannot be too wary what countenance or familiar demonstration she maketh more to one than to another...' wrote Sir Thomas Challoner to Cecil, expressing a general sentiment.[31] Kate Ashley, her mentor and old friend, was of the opinion that she should settle her marriage swiftly in order to scotch these rumours, but Elizabeth did not respond. In the early part of 1560 the rumours did indeed die down, because she was preoccupied with other business, but in August they started up again with renewed vigour. It was even reported in some quarters that she was pregnant by Dudley. Then, on 8 September, Amy Dudley was found dead in the house which they shared at Cumnor in Oxfordshire.

She had apparently fallen downstairs and broken her neck. There were various suspicious circumstances; her injuries were not entirely consistent with a fall, and the servants had been given the day off. Inevitably, suspicion focused on Dudley, and the Queen was forced to suspend his access to the court. An inquest was immediately ordered, which returned a verdict of death by misadventure.[32] This was reasonable enough on the evidence available. Amy had been afflicted with an 'ailment' in one of her breasts, which was almost certainly breast cancer and which would have made her bones brittle, and Dudley had been miles away at the time. Nevertheless there were accusations of a cover-up, and Elizabeth was left with a terrible dilemma. Now that her favourite was free to marry her, the circumstances made it impossible to contemplate. At some point before Christmas, Elizabeth recognized this fact, and although when he returned to the court the rumours inevitably started up again, Lord Robert's matrimonial ambitions were effectively laid to rest at that point. They remained close friends, and he was admitted to something like his earlier intimacy, but when the Queen believed herself to be close to death from smallpox in 1562, she swore that she had never had intercourse with him, and that was almost certainly the truth.[33] To the scandal of her council, she named him as Protector of the Realm in the event of her own demise, but that was the nearest he ever came to the Crown Matrimonial. He became a member of the Privy Council and was created Earl of Leicester in September 1564, but the rest of their relationship does not really belong to a history of the succession. There was not going to be another Dudley on the throne of England.

For a number of years Sir William Cecil was not quite sure, and from 1563 to 1567 he promoted, to the best of his ability, the negotiation with the Archduke Charles. This was a controversial matter, because Charles was a Catholic, although of no very strenuous kind, and Cecil's more ardent Protestant colleagues were opposed to the move. There were those in Germany, notably the Duke of Wurtemburg, who were looking for an alliance between the Lutherans and England as a means of shoring up the religious peace of Augsburg, which had been negotiated in 1555. Charles was apparently thought to be convertible.[34] At the same time, Elizabeth made a few calculated gestures intended to demonstrate the conservatism of the English Prayer Book, and apparently embraced the doctrine of the real presence.[35] Cecil's main motivation, however, remained in domestic politics rather than foreign affairs. He continued to be morbidly anxious about the influence and ambitions of Robert Dudley. He need not have worried. By 1565, when the negotiations moved up a gear, Elizabeth had clearly decided against a domestic marriage; the real choice lay between Charles and the young King of France. The problem with the latter lay in the fact that he was barely thirteen years old, not even old enough for cohabitation, while the Queen was thirty-one. Unsurprisingly, the French offer remained mainly a paper option. Cecil was not alone in his enthusiasm for the Austrian choice; the Earl of Sussex and the Duke of Norfolk also backed him keenly. The principal opposition came from the Earl of Leicester and his friends, motivated less by his own ambitions than by anxiety about a Catholic marriage and what that might entail. Meanwhile the Queen's body clock was ticking on, and she does at least seem to have decided to marry someone, because as she pointed out, 'she had formerly purposed by all means to remain single, but in consequence of the insistent pressure that was brought to bear upon her by the Estates of her realm, she was now resolved to marry...'.[36]

However, when it came to the point, religion proved the sticking point. The English had hoped that Charles, having no great continental responsibilities, would come to live in England and would conform (outwardly at least) to the Protestant settlement. The Austrians, on the other hand, were insistent that he must have access to the Mass, at least in private. This seems to have been the desire of the new Emperor, Maximilian, Charles's brother, rather than of the Archduke himself, but it was an impossible condition. The Mass was illegal in England, and any such indulgence would have set the worst possible example. The Queen was pressing Archbishop Parker to discipline those who, for conscientious reasons, were rejecting the ceremonies of the established Church, and it would be out of the question to be punishing Protestants and indulging Catholics at the same time.[37] Negotiations continued, with the advantage going now one way, now the other. At one point, late in 1567, it seemed that a compromise formula had been identified, with which the Emperor was alleged to be satisfied, but on 10 December the Queen rejected it, and that brought the negotiations to an effective end. Protestant opinion in general was greatly relieved, but the Queen was now thirty-four and no nearer getting married than she had been at the time of her accession.

The next possibility arose from developments in Anglo-French relations. Since the treaty of Cateau Cambrecis in March 1559, France had become increasingly immersed in civil strife. This had originally been caused by the unexpected death of King Henry II in a jousting accident in the summer of that year, and had been aggravated by the death without heirs of his young successor, Francis II in December 1560. This had brought his brother, the nine-year-old Charles IX to the throne, and with him the Queen Mother, Catherine de Medici, as Regent. Since then Catherine had been struggling to uphold the King's authority and to stabilize the realm. In spite of England's ill-fated intervention on the Huguenot side in 1563, she had increasingly looked to an English alliance to achieve this. The idea of a marriage had originated with the Montmorency interest, which was in alliance with the Crown, rather than with the Queen Mother herself, and involved the sixteen-year-old Duke of Anjou, the King's younger brother.[38] The English council responded, less out of any enthusiasm for the Duke than because of deteriorating relations with Spain. The Regent of the Low Countries, Margaret of Parma, had suspended commercial relation with England in 1566 over alleged interference in the discontent which had produced the Compromise, in defence of religious freedom and noble privileges. This action had harmed Antwerp more than London, but Margaret had subsequently been recalled and replaced with the Duke of Alba. Alba had brought an army with him which had crushed all dissent and sent the refugees flying in all directions, many of them to England. Both the Queen and her council viewed Alba's activities with the gravest suspicion, and a French alliance seemed the obvious answer.[39] Such an alliance would diminish the influence of the ultra-Catholic Guise party and provide at least some security against the Duke of Alba. From the French point of view, marriage to the Queen of England would also detach Henry of Anjou from the Guises, upon whom he was currently heavily dependent. Anjou at length consented to the opening of negotiations in mid-February 1571, but insisted that the integrity of his religion must be respected. Secret discussion then ensued, because Elizabeth did not want to raise another storm in England, and Catherine was worried about the reaction of the Guises if they found out what was going on. Missions went backwards and forwards, and various compromise formulae were considered, but the sticking-point was the same as that with the Archduke Charles – Anjou's freedom to hear the Mass.[40] However, Mass or no Mass, opinion at the French court was increasingly in favour of an understanding with England. Huguenot influence was temporarily in the ascendant, and Charles was serious considering intervening against Alba in The Netherlands. As a result, the marriage proposal was shelved, and the two parties instead signed a mutual defence alliance at Blois on 19 April 1572. In spite of the massacre of St Bartholomew's Day a few months later, which resulted in the overthrow of Protestant influence at the French court and in which Catherine and the King were at least implicated, that treaty survived and formed the basis of Anglo-French relations until the death of Henry III in 1589.[41]

This was largely due to the determination of Catherine de Medici, who regarded the treaty of Blois as a fragile protection on its own. Almost as soon as it was clear that the Anjou marriage would not work, she substituted her youngest son, François, Duke of Alençon. The fact that he was barely eighteen and the Queen was thirty-nine was not allowed to obtrude. The negotiations which followed went on for nine years, and fall into two quite distinct phases. The first phase, which lasted from 1572 until 1578, has been described as a 'masterpiece of protracted dalliance' on Elizabeth's part.[42] She was, almost certainly, not seriously interested in marrying the Duke, but he was thought to be more flexible in religious matters than his brother, and that gave some plausibility to the discussions.

'Then he is not so obstinate and forward, so papisticall and (if I may say so) so foolish and restive like a mule as his brother is...' wrote Sir Thomas Smith, Elizabeth's special envoy in France, who favoured the match.[43] Although a Catholic, Alençon was a sworn enemy of the Guises and had attracted a number of Huguenots into his service. Elizabeth, meanwhile, was under renewed pressure from her Parliament to find a husband – any husband – and that gave her sufficient incentive to prolong the pretence. The Duke was supposed to come to Dover in person in September 1573 to be inspected, although it was not put in those terms, but this time it was he who backed off, claiming illness. He sent the Comte de Retz in his place, but the resulting negotiations made no perceptible progress. In April 1578 the whole moribund process was started up again, on this occasion because the Queen was desperate to distract the Duke of Anjou (as he had by then become) from a projected venture into The Netherlands.[44] Charles IX had died in 1574 and his brother, the erstwhile Duke of Anjou, had become King as Henry III (which was why Alençon had become Duke of Anjou), but it is clear that in seeking to intervene in The Netherlands the Duke was acting on his own initiative and not as an agent of the King. In fact, Henry was finding his brother a bit of a nuisance, and would have been glad to see him married in England. On the other hand (the King being childless), he was now the heir to the throne of France. Towards the end of 1578, with the Queen still expressing interest but professing reluctance to marry any man she had not met, the Duke sent a trusted household servant, Jean de Simier, as his harbinger to arrange a visit.

Simier's arrival in January 1579 elevated the whole protracted business to a new level, partly because Anjou's adventure in The Netherlands had run into the sand, and partly because Elizabeth took an instant liking to his agent, who was a most accomplished courtier.[45] The Duke obtained leave of his brother and arrived secretly at Greenwich on 17 August. He stayed for less than a fortnight, but his visit was by any standards an outstanding success. There were no public protests, and he was lavishly entertained. In spite of his unprepossessing appearance, Elizabeth seems to have been genuine impressed. She began to act like a woman in love, carrying his portrait in her prayer book and writing him affectionate little poems. How far this was a genuine menopausal flurry, and how far a calculated act, no one can now be sure.[46] She may have been influenced by the Duke of Parma's successes against the Dutch rebels, or by the Earl of Leicester's clandestine marriage to Lettice Knollys, or simply by her own emotional state. As soon as word of her apparent infatuation got out, trouble arose. Lord Burghley was loyally supportive, but most of her council were horrified, having calculated that, at forty-six, the Queen's childbearing years were over and that a marriage would compromise her independence for no good reason. The succession would merely be complicated by having a husband when there was no prospect of an heir. At a more popular level, John Stubbs gave vent to the general feeling when he published *The Gaping Gulf*, castigating his sovereign for falling into a subtle French trap. Stubbs lost his right hand, and but for the secret support of the Earl of Leicester might well have lost his life.[47] Nevertheless his point was well made, and the negotiations returned to limbo – to the Duke's great frustration – during 1580 and most of 1581. Then, on 31 October 1581, in what was apparently a make-or-break attempt to salvage his marriage prospects, Anjou returned to England. On 22 November, Elizabeth suddenly announced that she would, after all, marry him, kissed him publicly and gave him her ring as a token. What possessed her to behave in this manner is not known. It must have been a desperate emotional outburst by a woman who saw her last chance of matrimony slipping away; no more political explanation will fit the evidence. The Duke was as mystified as any, but understandably elated. Then it all ended in tears. The Queen's ladies were as horrified as her council by this sudden rush of blood to the head and worked through the succeeding night to dissuade her. In the cold light of dawn, Elizabeth surrendered. She withdrew her pledge, leaving Anjou fuming about the inconstancy of women, and of Englishwomen in particular.[48] He departed soon after, and the longest-running of all the Queen's matrimonial negotiations collapsed in disarray. Elizabeth was now forty-eight and there was no point in further pretence; there would be no heir of her body to claim the succession. A virgin she had come to the throne, and a virgin she would remain. It remained for her image-makers to exploit that fact to the best advantage, but her council would have to look elsewhere for an heir to England.

The question of Elizabeth's marriage had dominated the succession issue for more than twenty years, but it had never been the only consideration. When she came to the throne, her accession had been in accordance with Henry VIII's last Succession Act, and with his will which that Act had authorized. By the same statute, the heir in default of issue by Elizabeth should have been Catherine Grey, Jane Grey's younger sister, and there were many councillors and courtiers who thought that her right should be recognized.[49] At the same time, if the statute was set aside as having been *ultra vires*, which was Edward VI's position, then the true heir was Mary of Scotland, the granddaughter of Henry's elder sister, Margaret. However, if that were done, Mary had a better claim to the throne than Elizabeth, who was illegitimate, and that no one in England was prepared to countenance. Mary was not only an alien born, but was also in France, married to the Dauphin Francis and likely in due course to become Queen of France by marriage, as she was already Queen of Scotland by birth. As a rival to Elizabeth, Mary was therefore a non-starter, but as a possible heir in the event of Elizabeth dying childless, her position was good deal stronger. The Queen herself was understandably reluctant to make any decision between these two possibilities and did her best to suppress any discussion of the issue.[50] Paradoxically, Mary's misfortune then strengthened her position considerably, because, having come to the throne somewhat unexpectedly by the death of her father-in-law in the summer of 1559, she was left a widow at the age of nineteen in December 1560. Finding herself surplus to requirements in France, she had then returned to Scotland in August 1561 and had begun the difficult task of picking up the threads of Scottish politics. She was a Catholic ruling a Protestant kingdom, but by keeping her religion as a private matter she at first had some success, and encouraged her English supporters to believe that she would be able to do the same thing in England.[51] Meanwhile, a little before Mary returned to Scotland, Catherine Grey was discovered to be pregnant. Her marriage had been discussed in the same terms as that of Elizabeth by Imperial diplomats, anxious to secure the maximum advantage, but in the event she had gone through a secret ceremony with Edward Seymour, Earl of Hertford at some time earlier in 1561. Since she was so close to the throne, any such marriage required the Queen's consent, which this one obviously had not received. The Queen was angry, suspecting a conspiracy for which there is no evidence, refused to recognize the marriage, and imprisoned the luckless Catherine in the Tower. A commission subsequently headed by Archbishop Mathew Parker found their marriage unlawful, and although modern research questions that verdict, it stood at the time.[52] Catherine was subsequently released, and died in 1568, but Elizabeth never recognized the legitimacy of her daughter. In spite of her disgrace, Catherine continued to enjoy support for her claim as heir, particularly in Parliament, but it is not surprising that the Queen would not countenance it.

Meanwhile, the Scottish Queen's circumstances had changed dramatically. For several years she had maintained good relations with her 'sister', hoping no doubt to secure the coveted recognition as heir to the throne of England. Marriage was as high, or higher, on her agenda, and Elizabeth tried to influence her choice. However, the Queen could not expect to command the right of consent in an equal, and confined herself to making helpful suggestions. It was not in her interest that the Queen of Scots should marry powerfully, and she put forward the claims of her own favourite, Robert Dudley. Mary was not impressed and eventually, in 1565, married Henry, Lord Darnley, the son of the Earl of Lennox and of that Margaret Clifford whom Mary I had once considered for the succession.[53] This displeased Elizabeth, who saw in her choice another step in her bid for England, and relations between the two women cooled. Mary promptly fell pregnant and in June 1566 was delivered of 'a fair son' who was given the traditional Scottish name of James. In other respects, however, Darnley turned out to be a very unsatisfactory consort. The couple quarrelled furiously, and she refused him the Crown Matrimonial. Then in January 1567 he was murdered, and the Queen was suspected of complicity. Suspicion was confirmed when she was 'abducted' by, and subsequently married, the chief suspect, James Hepburn, Earl of Bothwell. Combining against her, the Scottish nobles forced her abdication in July 1567 and imprisoned her in Loch Leven Castle.[54] The following year she escaped and made an unsuccessful bid to recover her crown. Defeated again, she fled across the border into England, in search of recognition and support.

Mary's arrival was an acute embarrassment for Elizabeth. She could not ignore the charges against her, but continued to recognize her as a sovereign. She did not want her in England, but could not afford to allow her to travel on to France. In the event, Mary remained in more or less honourable confinement for nearly twenty years, and became the focus for progressively more serious plots against the Queen's life and estate. Since the disgrace and death of Catherine Grey, she was the only possible heir, unless one counted the remote claim of Henry Hastings, Earl of Huntingdon, descended from the Staffords through the female line.[55] For that reason, Elizabeth refused to condemn her, or allow her to be condemned, in spite of the danger which she presented. To English Catholics, of course, she was the true Queen, but they recognized that Elizabeth would have to be made away in order to realize her claim. The rebels in 1569 planned to rescue her; the Ridolfi and Throgmorton plotters aimed to assassinate the Queen in her interest. In 1570 there was a plan to neutralize her by marrying her to the Duke of Norfolk, but Elizabeth regarded that as treasonable and it cost the Duke his head.[56] How far Mary herself was implicated in these plots is uncertain, but the Parliament was convinced of her guilt and kept up a steady clamour for her execution. Many of the council shared their view, but the Queen was not to be moved. Then in 1586 she was trapped into an express consent to the Babington Plot, and even Elizabeth could not resist the pressure to put her on trial. It was very doubtful whether any court in England had jurisdiction over her, but that was not allowed to stand in the way of her condemnation. England was by then at war with Spain, and Mary had expressly commended herself to Philip's protection several years before. After much hesitation on the Queen's part, she went to the block in February 1587, parading herself at the last as a Catholic martyr.[57]

The death of the Queen of Scots meant the end of the direct Catholic claim, which devolved on her remote kinswoman the Infanta of Spain, a pretension which hardly anyone apart from Robert Parsons was prepared to take seriously.[58] It did not, however, put an end to the Scottish line, which was now represented by her twenty-one year-old son, James. Elizabeth made it clear that she did not regard his claim as being debarred by his mother's attainder, which was reasonable enough since they had not seen each other for nearly twenty years, and he had been brought up as a Protestant. Although the Queen made no specific pronouncement in his favour, and indeed forbade all discussion of the issue, James now emerged as the favourite for the succession. Elizabeth had given up all pretence of marriage, and there would clearly be no heir of her body, so apart from Arabella Stuart, a niece of Lord Darnley, there was not a rival in sight. Only those who were doggedly opposed to the thought of a Scot on the throne favoured Arabella, and James went out of his way to make himself agreeable.[59] For several years he was in secret communication with Robert Devereux, Earl of Essex, the Queen's latter-day favourite, promising him many favours, until that correspondence was cut short by Essex's disgrace and execution in 1601. Although at first deterred by this misfortune, James soon learned that the key man in England was now Robert Cecil, and he began to cultivate his goodwill with similar offers. Whether or not the Queen made a deathbed declaration in favour of 'her brother of Scotland', we do not know, but it was Robert Cecil who managed the succession, smoothly and peacefully, when Elizabeth died on 24 March 1603.[60]

The Tudors had survived for one hundred and eighteen years, and the succession had been an issue throughout, but at no time more than during the forty-five-year reign of she who has gone down in history as 'the Virgin Queen'. Although she may have been warned by her sister's misfortune, it is by no means certain that Elizabeth ever made a conscious decision not to marry. It was just that every time a negotiation seemed to be on the brink of success, the price became too high and she backed off. The one genuine love of her life was Robert Dudley, and the circumstances which made marriage to him impossible were a personal disaster for the Queen. Her duty had to prevail over her personal inclinations – not a problem which had ever afflicted her father.

The Monarch and the Realm: The Uses of Parliament

The Tudors would not have understood the meaning of the word 'constitution'. They operated within a framework of law and custom which determined the relationship of one authority to another. The nobleman had duties, rights and privileges according to his status and the tenure by which he held his lands; the urban corporations had similar responsibilities, as laid down by their charters of foundation; and of course the Church exercised autonomous jurisdiction in respect of its spiritual functions.[1] The monarch was similarly constrained, and the distinction between law and custom was not clearly made. It was, for instance, the custom that the Crown descended to the eldest heir male, but it was not law, and other considerations such as competence to govern could be taken into account. It had been this factor which had made the accession of Henry IV in 1399, or Edward IV in 1461, possible. The succession of a female was untested since the twelfth century, when Henry I's daughter Matilda had made her unsuccessful bid, and no one knew what would happen if the daughter of the last incumbent was challenged by a man with a more remote claim. It was, on the other hand, accepted as law that the King could only raise direct taxes with the consent of Parliament, and that only Parliament could make new law, as distinct from interpreting that which already existed.[2] However, both these laws existed more by virtue of unchallenged prescription over a number of years than by any exercise of legislative will. Royal edicts on their own were not laws and could not be enforced in the King's courts. They were implemented by the council, and could be judicially challenged. Since the days of Henry II the country had enjoyed a common code of law, and the King's courts enforced that common law wherever his writ ran – that is, throughout the country except in those franchises which were specifically exempted, such as the Welsh Marcher lordships. These franchises had been created by the King's progenitors and would escheat to the Crown if the heirs of the holders should fail, but there was no recognized method of terminating them in any other way. Even when such liberties did fall to the King, as happened with the Duchy of Lancaster in 1399 or the Earldom of March in 1461, their jurisdictional structures were left intact, and the King's writ ran as the franchise-holder and not as the monarch.[3] The common law itself was customary in origin, and for centuries the only method of extending or adapting it was by judicial interpretation. It was only comparatively recently that the concept of statute law had been accepted, and it was still a matter of dispute whether statute could abolish or amend existing laws, as distinct from legislating on new matters.

The Parliament had come into existence originally as a means of communication between the King and his subjects, either when he felt the need to justify executive decisions which he had made, or wished to consult them on some specific subject. At first, only the magnates and prelates had been summoned to a meeting which would later be known as the Great Council, but from the middle of the thirteenth century knights of the shire were summoned occasionally, and from the early fourteenth century knights and burgesses appeared regularly.[4] By the middle of the fourteenth century a meeting was only recognized as a Parliament if all four constituencies were present. The main reason for this was the King's increasing need for money to fight his wars, and because it was recognized that the Commons provided by far the greatest share of this taxation revenue. It became customary for these demands to be initiated by government requests to the Lower House, and by the early fifteenth century this custom had become a rule. For similar reasons, the House of Commons also became a principal channel for the presentation of petitions to the Crown, on both public and private matters. A petition presented by this route had both more weight and more authenticity than a similar request offered through less prestigious channels.[5] The Parliament was also a High Court, and by the middle of the fifteenth century the House of Commons had adopted the practice of casting petitions of grievance against named individuals as indictments by a process known as impeachment, whereby the Commons acted as accusers and the Lords as judges. The decision of the Lords in such cases was final and could not be challenged in any other court of law.[6] By a similar process, the Parliament also assumed the right to declare an accused person guilty of any offence – particularly treason – without recourse to any other court. In other words, the Lords constituted themselves both judge and jury in that particular case, thus bypassing the defendant's normal right to trial by due process, in a form known as attainder. In all these developments it must be remembered that the King was a constituent element of the Parliament, which could pass no measure without his consent, so he was a party to all these changes. Even during the years of weak royal government under Henry VI, the Parliament existed primarily to do the King's business, and for that reason could only be summoned and dismissed by him. A Parliament, in other words, was an occasional event rather than a regular part of the government, and there was no legal or customary requirement upon the monarch to convene it – provided that he could do without direct taxation.[7] By 1485 the House of Lords consisted of all adult peers, about fifty in number, twenty-six Bishops and a similar number of mitred Abbots (at the discretion of the Crown); just over one hundred members in all. The House of Commons was made up of seventy-four knights, representing thirty-seven counties, and two hundred and twenty-two burgesses from one hundred and ten towns (two from each constituency except London, which sent four) – a total of about three hundred, making it the largest such representative assembly in Europe. Unusually, there was no House of Clergy, the Church being represented by the Bishops and Abbots in the Lords.[8]

The regular executive body at the centre of government was not, therefore, the Parliament but the King's Council. The council was omnicompetent, but it existed to carry out decisions, not to make them. The King might delegate that process to his councillors, or to some of them, or to his officers of state, but that was at his discretion – the responsibility remained with him. In theory the composition of the council was also at the King's discretion, but during the period of weak royal government under Henry VI that discretion had been challenged by those advocating the idea that some persons were 'councillors born' – in other words, men whose status made them too powerful to be ignored, such as the Duke of York. This idea was never accepted while Henry was at liberty to make his own judgements, but was forced on him from time to time, and remained part of the agenda for those who continued to believe that the council should represent the power structure of the realm.[9] Once they had taken the council oath, its members had three rather different functions. In the first place, they advised the King on whatever matters he chose to lay before them. This advice might be proffered formally by the whole council, or informally by groups and individuals – it depended upon how the King had chosen to consult them. This was perceived to be the most important function of a councillor, and contemporary theorists reserved their most severe strictures for princes who governed without 'good council'.[10] Its second function was executive – to carry out the King's policy. This also might be done collectively or by select groups acting as standing committees. In addition, individual councillors served on Royal Commissions, where the King's authority was delegated for specific purposes to groups of named individuals. The presence of a councillor on a commission was intended to guarantee both the direction and the effectiveness of its work. Finally, the council had a judicial function: to adjudicate disputes (particularly those between magnates) where the effectiveness of the normal courts was questionable; and to exercise the King's prerogative of equity. This latter function dealt with cases where the common law provided no remedy, or where the jurisdiction of the courts was questionable.[11]

The council underwent one major transformation during the sixteenth century. In 1540 it was reduced in size and consolidated. Thereafter it consisted of the Privy Council proper, about twenty men, mainly office-holders, who took the council oath and were expected to attend meetings regularly, and the Councillors at Large. These latter were more in the nature of occasional advisers, usually specialists in some recognized field such as warfare or taxation. They did not take the council oath and attended only when specifically summoned. This corresponded roughly to the distinction between the Inner Ring and the council as a whole, but was now formalized. The Privy Council was expected to meet regularly, to follow an approved agenda, and to keep minutes of its meetings, but its communication with the King continued to be on an informal basis, as before. Unfortunately, when sensitive political issues were under discussion the clerk who kept the minutes was excluded, so we have no record of those parts of the meetings.[12] The Council at Large became an amorphous body and disappears during the mid-century period. During the minority of Edward VI the Privy Council became the governing body of the realm, and appointments to it became the subject of factional strife, whereas Henry VIII, Mary and Elizabeth all kept recruitment strictly in their own hands. For a variety of reasons, Mary enlarged her Privy Council to more than forty members and revived the practice of using standing committees, with the result that her council was more effective administratively than it was politically.[13] Elizabeth reduced it in size again and kept its membership under very tight control, so that by the end of her reign it numbered no more than a dozen, but it enjoyed enhanced executive authority as the Queen increasingly delegated routine matters for decision. The conciliar courts of equity – that is, Star Chamber and Requests – flourished exceedingly from the 1520s onward, as confidence increased and their business grew, but they were more in the nature of modern tribunals, and their decisions did not have the status and enforceability of the common law. Requests in particular became increasingly detached from the Privy Council, special Masters of Requests being appointed who were not councillors.[14]

The council operated within the court, because it depended upon regular contact with the King, but other aspects of government had long since moved out. The central courts of common law, the King's Bench and the Common Pleas, sat during the law terms in the Great Hall at Westminster, and although the King could in theory preside at either of these courts in person, in practice he did not do so, and they were controlled by their Chief Justices.[15] The Chancery, originally the King's writing office, which controlled the Great Seal and issued the royal writs, also had institutional independence by the fifteenth century, and the King did not interfere personally in its functions. The same was true of the Exchequer, which handled and audited the formal accounts of the King's revenue under the (somewhat notional) control of the Lord Treasurer. By the reign of Edward IV, most of the actual money received by the Crown had been diverted to the Household department – the Treasury of the Chamber – but the Exchequer held on to certain traditional revenues, such as the sheriffs' farms, and continued to audit all accounts, in addition to adjudicating fiscal disputes in its own court.[16]

Finally, there was the court itself, the theatre of royalty and of the King's magnificence. It was divided into two sections, the Household and the Chamber. The former constituted the service departments, such as the kitchen and the cellar, which catered for the King's personal requirements and those of his servants; the latter provided the King's ceremonial and business environment. It was through the Chamber that contact was made with the monarch or his consort, patronage solicited, foreign ambassadors received, and scholars and musicians entertained. It was particularly important that the court should be seen to be lavish, and should be open to all comers with the right credentials.[17] Although the central administration had long since gone 'out of court', it remained the political focus because it was the monarch's environment; it moved with him, and was immediately affected by his mood changes, illnesses or other incapacity. It had been Henry VI's failure to maintain any balance in access to his person that had created that factional dominance of patronage which had been one of the main causes of his downfall. Edward IV, in spite of his Yorkist origins, did not make the same mistake. Nor did Henry VII, for whom a willing acceptance of his position was a sufficient passport to favour. Henry is alleged to have been mean, and his fiscal policies were indeed harsh, particularly in his later years, but he always knew better than to stint on the expenditure of his court. Large-scale building projects, lavish hospitality and generous entertainments were features of his reign, as well as heavy expenditure on jewellery. It was essential that he compete in the European League if he wished to be taken seriously in international diplomacy, and both his own coronation and the marriage of his son Prince Arthur have to be seen in that context.[18] In the latter part of his reign, Henry tended increasingly to withdraw from the Chamber, with its public face, and took refuge in a Privy Chamber, which was staffed largely by menial servants and where the pressures of a public existence were eased. His son continued this practice, less with a view to withdrawing than of gathering round himself a group of congenial young men, and these Gentlemen of the Privy Chamber became the new hub of the court. The gentlemen were used on all sorts of confidential missions, both at home and abroad, but their principal task was to entertain the King and to share in his amusements. Because of their unique opportunities for access to the King, they also became patronage brokers on a large scale, and their services could work out very expensive for petitioners.[19] Female monarchs, of course, needed female attendants about their persons, and after 1553 the Privy Chamber became a sort of boudoir – a place where Mary or Elizabeth could withdraw from the male-dominated world of politics and indulge in a little gossip or needlework. Its political importance, therefore, disappeared, but it remained – indirectly, at least – a major centre for patronage.[20]

Apart from appointing his own men to the Chancellorship and to the Privy Seal, Henry VII did not interfere with the working of the 'out of court' departments. He continued Edward's practice of diverting most of his income to the Treasury of the Chamber, and in other respects the officials concerned would hardly have noticed the change of regime – at least in the performance of their regular duties. The council, on the other hand, saw some significant changes. Like his predecessors, Henry operated with an 'inner ring' of particularly trusted advisers, but unlike them he did not rely primarily upon his peers. With the exception of his uncle, the Duke of Bedford, most of these intimate councillors were either commoners, such as Sir Reginald Bray, or prelates, such as John Morton, the Archbishop of Canterbury and Richard Fox, Bishop (eventually) of Winchester. Henry was very much concerned to repudiate the notion that anyone had a 'right' to sit on the council, and this select group was chosen very largely because of their complete dependence upon the King. The humanist notion of 'good council' in the service of the Commonwealth was gaining ground among the political writers of the period, and the King embraced it, wishing above all to be seen as well advised.[21] Another way in which the King built upon his predecessors' practice was in his use of committees – groups of councillors to whom specific tasks were allocated. Some of these were essentially ad hoc and were discontinued when the task was completed, but others could be described as 'standing committees'. Of these, the most notorious was the King's Council Learned in the Law, which was charged, among other things, with the taking and enforcement of bonds and recognisances – those pledges of good conduct which became the hallmark of the latter part of the reign. Another was the Council in the Star Chamber, which dealt particularly with those magnate disputes where abuse of the normal legal processes might reasonably be suspected. Although all councillors were eligible to sit in the Star Chamber, some made it their regular responsibility and others do not appear to have served as councillors in any other capacity.[22] All councillors took the council oath, but some attended meetings only when their other duties permitted and other seem to have appeared when summoned. There was a large penumbra of these occasional councillors, some forty or fifty at any given time, as opposed to about twenty regulars. Altogether two hundred and twenty-seven men were described as councillors over the twenty-four years of the reign, but of those only about thirty would have belonged to the inner ring. There was no regular presidency of the council, but it seems to have met under the chairmanship of the most senior officer of state, normally the Lord Chancellor. The monarch did not attend, but received the results of its deliberations either from his secretary or from a delegation of councillors summoned to his presence for that purpose.

There was also a council in the Marches of Wales, which was equally a royal council, but was quite distinct from the main body. This had originally been set up for Prince Edward, the son of Edward IV, and was responsible for overseeing the government of the Principality and of those Marcher lordships which were in the King's hands. It had survived his accession and death, and had been reactivated for Henry VII's son Arthur when he was created Prince in 1489. After Arthur's death it was created again for Prince Henry in 1504, but never seems to have been very effective, and was moribund by the time of the King's own death in 1509.[23] A similar council had existed in the north of England under Edward IV and Richard III, but its existence became shadowy after 1485, and it seems that Henry VII relied upon the Warden General of the Marches to keep an eye on the government of the region and to oversee the working of the county commissions of the peace. Both these regional councils were reactivated by Cardinal Wolsey in the mid-1520s and continued to function for the remainder of the period. At first they were nominally headed by Princess Mary in Wales and by the Duke of Richmond in the north, but after the withdrawal of the one and the death of the other, the councils continued independently as agencies of the central government.[24]

The Commissions of the Peace formed the backbone of local government under the first Tudor. They had originated in the fourteenth century and consisted basically of the elite of each county, mobilized to do the King's business. The context of these commissions was highly complex, but they were devised as means of keeping local law enforcement in the hands of the Crown, rather than allowing it to devolve to the clientage systems of the nobility. By the end of the fifteenth century the Commissions of the Peace had taken over most of the duties originally discharged by the sheriffs, with the exception of such formal responsibilities as the return of writs.[25] They had also taken over most of the judicial duties originally performed by the private courts of the feudal honours and manors, which were left with little beyond the regulation of land use. The Commissioners were also beginning to discharge the purely administrative function of implementing statutory regulations of an economic or social nature. This had begun before 1485, but became increasingly important after the Parliament of 1495, which introduced a whole raft of such measures. There were other commissions – of Sewers, Gaol Delivery and Oyer and Terminer – but the Commission of the Peace remained the principal one, and the one by which the gentry came to measure their status within their counties. The purpose of all these commissions was the same: to intrude the royal authority into county systems of government which would otherwise have been too independent. In other words, to centralize control.[26]

The Parliament served a similar purpose. Although only summoned once in the last twelve years of the reign, it consolidated its position as the main representative assembly of the realm, and as its prestige increased, elections became matters of local political interest. A seat at Westminster signified the arrival of a gentleman among the counties' elite, and increasingly led the gentry to seek borough places. A borough was supposed to be represented by resident burgesses, who were to be paid their expenses, which might be significant, so the temptation to give one or both places to local gentlemen who would serve without claiming was particularly great in the case of small or poor boroughs. By 1504 the majority of borough members were of this kind, and only the major cities such as Bristol, Norwich and London continued to be represented by resident citizens in the traditional manner.[27] Henry's use of Parliament also increased its political muscle. It confirmed his title to the throne, defined the functions of Justices of the Peace, and withdrew the privileges of a number of sanctuaries. This last impinged upon the privileges of the Church, but was accepted by a complacent Archbishop and by a Pope who was anxious to strengthen the position of the English Crown. Parliament voted taxes, not without protest, but without serious opposition, notably in 1497 – a levy which caused revolt in Cornwall because the pretext was war in Scotland. In doing so, it used the traditional method of collective assessment, and made it clear that this taxation was intended as an extraordinary measure. For normal purposes the King was expected to 'live of his own', that is, on the traditional revenues of the Crown, which Henry was at pains to augment.[28] In no respect did Henry VII's parliaments transcend their traditional limitations, which has led to the observation that 'nothing very much happened' during the reign. However, the King did make more use of Parliament for legislative purposes than any of his predecessors had done, particularly in 1495, and this strengthened it both politically and institutionally. The fact that no assembly was called during the last five years of his reign does not mean that he was contemplating the possibility of doing without it. He just did not need its support to the same extent that he had done earlier. Although we do not know too much about what went on in the Parliament chambers between 1485 and 1504, it would appear that debate was lively and engaged, and that the members of both houses were concerned to uphold the King's position by every means in their power.[29]

For the first twenty years or so of Henry VIII's reign, that situation did not fundamentally change. Henry convened parliaments in 1510, 1512, 1515, 1523 and 1529, more evenly spaced than his father's, but not much greater in frequency. The beginning of individual assessments for subsidies can be traced to 1512, and Cardinal Wolsey hit the buffers when he tried to get £800,000 out of the House of Commons in 1523. But on the whole, Parliament continued to build up its legislative competence and did not exceed its traditional functions until the anti-clerical Commons received petitions against clerical abuse of mortuary and probate fees in 1529.[30] These produced statutes which were an undoubted infringement of ecclesiastical jurisdiction, and should be seen as early steps in the King's campaign to put pressure on the Church over the annulment of his marriage. Meanwhile, there were those among his advisers who were advocating a domestic solution to his problem, and to that end he began to argue that the Pope's jurisdiction over his kingdom was limited to specifically spiritual issues and did not include, for example, matrimony. However, that left him with the problem of how to reach a domestic solution, of who had the right to declare his marriage invalid.[31] The archbishop of Canterbury, William Warham, was unco-operative, and such an issue clearly could not be referred to the courts of Common Law. Parliament was the only institution with the right sort of credentials. It had trespassed on spiritual jurisdiction before, not only over sanctuaries and benefit of clergy, but also in the great Praemunire Act of 1393, which had declared it to be an offence to exercise such jurisdiction without the King's licence. That had come close to denying the papal prerogative altogether, and successive Popes had tried in vain to have it removed from the statute book. It pointed an appropriate way ahead.[32]

Still hoping to avoid a confrontation with Rome, in 1530 Henry had brought charges under the Praemunire Act against the whole clerical estate of the realm. They had bought him off, but in pardoning them the King had insisted that they surrender their legislative autonomy, a condition also included in the Act of Parliament which confirmed their submission in 1531. By this time, Henry was convinced that a domestic solution was possible and was looking to Parliament to bring it about. The question was, how to achieve that? While he awaited an answer to that question, the king went ahead and married Anne Boleyn, a move which he knew would be condemned by the Pope. Thus forced to an issue, Thomas Cranmer, his newly appointed Archbishop of Canterbury, declared his first marriage invalid and Cromwell, his leading adviser since 1532, devised a succession of statutes, commencing with the Act in Restraint of Appeals in 1533, which culminated in the Act of Supremacy the following year.[33] These measures, which he forced through by a mixture of management and persuasion, effectively terminated the papal authority in England, replacing it with that of the King. It is probable that most of the members who voted for these new laws believed that they were coping with an emergency situation, created by the King's urgent need for a son and heir, and that once that had been achieved, negotiations with Rome would follow and the status quo would be restored. If they were thinking in that manner, however, they were deceiving themselves, because once Henry had grasped the enormous extension of royal power which was now available to him, there was no way in which he was going to give it up. Parliament had been very careful not to make it appear that they were conferring this power on the King – they were merely recognizing an authority which was already deemed to exist – but in practice the Royal Supremacy was a new creation, and one which the King, Lords and Commons had conspired to create.[34] Once it had thus swallowed the great autonomous franchise of the Church, there was no limit to Parliament's ambitions – or rather, the ambitions of the King with their collaboration. The succession was arranged, secular franchises were abolished and the monasteries were dissolved, all matters which would have been considered *ultra vires* before the Act of Appeals. In a few short years after 1533, the medieval estates, with their limited functions and defined competence, had become in effect a sovereign legislature, competent to address all issues, both public and private.

This situation was not to be clearly defined for many years, and in the meantime there was one theoretical snag to such a comprehensive development – all positive law was supposed to be consistent with the law of God.[35] This presented a challenge to the framers of statutes, and a cause to their opponents, because the Royal Supremacy was manifestly not consistent with the Canon Law of the Church, which had always been accepted as the positive expression of that Divine Law. The case was made by arguing that it was indeed consistent with the law of the early Church, before the advent of papal corruptions and distortions, an argument which you could believe if you wanted to, and for which the coercive power of the King offered a compelling incentive. God's law – in the sense of natural law – hardly presented an obstacle, because although there was a broad consensus about what it meant, it did not address issues such as the distribution of power between a monarch and the Church.[36] However, the Canon Law had to be constructively ignored. It was also possible to argue that the statutes of the 1530s had effectively preserved the traditional faith of the Church, and to that extent constituted God's law. This was particularly true of the Act of Six Articles of 1539, which demonstrated the king as Supreme Head defending the Mass. However, such a defence became more difficult when statute turned to the implementation of Protestantism after 1547. It was still possible to argue that this legislation represented true doctrine, but that jettisoned the support of conservative upholders of the Supremacy such as Stephen Gardiner, the Bishop of Winchester, or Cuthbert Tunstall of Durham. Princess Mary, indeed, went so far as to argue that such legislation did not create true law, because it was contrary to the received faith.[37] This was a point of view which the minority council could not possibly accept, and led to a long stand-off with the Princess. The official line continued to be that all that law which had been created between 1533 and 1553 was consistent with the law of God, and represented a growing understanding of what that law might be.

This, however, created a fundamental problem when it came to the question of repeal. It was well accepted by the 1530s that only Parliament could repeal a statute which it had created, and that caused a problem over the second and third Succession Acts of 1536 and 1544, each of which effectively repealed its predecessor. It could be argued that these were purely secular adjustments to fit changing circumstances, and did not touch the Divine Law. A similar argument could be addressed to the repeal of the Act of Six Articles in 1547, as representing an improved understanding of the will of God, but when Mary decided in 1553 to sweep away the whole Edwardian establishment, the problem arose in an acute form. Mary regarded the Acts of Uniformity of 1549 and 1552 as being 'no true laws' – so should she simply ignore them as *ultra vires*? Cardinal Reginald Pole advised her to do no less, pointing out that she had a solemn duty to restore the true faith.[38] Mary, however, was cautious and listened to her legal councillors, who argued the necessity of repeal. Consequently, all the reformation statutes going back to 1533 were repealed in two Acts: the first of November 1553 dealing with the Edwardian enactments, and the second of January 1555 with the Henrician ones. A further Act of the latter date also restored to the statute book those early fifteenth-century heresy laws which had been repealed in 1547.[39] Consequently, whatever the theory of the Catholic restoration, the Church in England between 1553 and 1558 was the Church by Law Established, no less than its predecessors had been. This meant that the need for a valid religious statute to be consistent with the law of God was surreptitiously jettisoned, because there was no way in which the Edwardian and Marian establishments could be equally in accordance with the will of God. This in turn meant that Parliament was accepted by all parties as the proper forum to decide what the constitution of the Church should be, who should run it, and what its worship should consist of. There was a strong party in the House of Lords which opposed the Elizabethan Bill of Uniformity in 1559, but no one did so on the grounds that Parliament was not competent to decide such matters.[40]

By 1565, when Sir Thomas Smith wrote his famous account of the constitution of England, the omnicompetence of Parliament was an established fact.

> The Parliament abrogateth old laws, maketh new, giveth orders for things past, and for things hereafter to be followed, changeth rights and possessions of private men, legitimateth bastards, establisheth forms of religion, altereth weights and measures, giveth forms of succession to the Crown, defineth of doubtful rights whereof no law is already made, appointeth subsidies, tallies, taxes and impositions, giveth most free pardons and absolutions, restoreth in blood and name as the highest court, condemneth or absolveth them whom the prince will put to that trial. And, to be short, all that ever the people of Rome might do either in *Centuriatis comitiis* or *tributis*, the same may be done by the Parliament of England. [41]

The reason for this authority was perceived to be the manner in which Parliament had come to express, and indeed monopolize, the consent of the realm. The Privy Council had long since ceased to be a representative body, and the system of government by commissions, although it constituted a partnership between the Crown and the gentry, was represented at the centre only through the House of Commons. As Smith went on to point out, the peers and prelates were present in person, and every man in England 'by his procurators and attornies'. There was more than a touch of fiction about this, because the franchise was restricted, in the counties to the forty shilling freeholders and in the boroughs to heads of households, which meant that the vast majority of men (and all women) did not have a vote. Nevertheless, comparison with the republican constitution of Rome was not altogether inappropriate.[42] On the whole, and as a result of varying degrees of manipulation and management, Parliament had been supportive of the Crown, even running ahead of Henry VIII in some aspects of anti-clericalism. It had accepted the religious changes, in both directions, largely because these were manifestly in accordance with the monarchs' will, and had dutifully legislated changes to the succession when called upon to do so. Opposition there had been, and much grumbling over the Royal Supremacy, but real resistance was largely confined to issues of taxation. One of the reasons why the House of Commons had accepted the dissolution of the monasteries with such equanimity was because it was felt that such an accession of wealth to the Crown would reduce its demands for financial support – and so it transpired, in the short term at any rate. Thomas Cromwell had placed a number of men in the House, both to vote and to argue his causes, but on the whole the Crown was not very successful at dominating the Commons by this method. The Marian council's attempts to secure the election of men of the 'wise, grave, and Catholic sort' in 1554, for example, did not much affect the composition of the House, and Giovanni Michieli's attribution of the stroppiness of the 1555 Commons to the fact that it was full of gentlemen rather than citizens is now generally considered to be misinformation.[43] Mary's parliaments caused annoyance to the Queen by rejecting a number of measures which she was supporting, but none of first-rate importance, and when the Parliament of November 1554 was required to petition the King and Queen for reconciliation with the Pope, it duly did so, with very few dissenting voices.

Paradoxically, it was largely those same men who, just over four years later, voted for the end of the Catholic restoration. It used to be argued that the Commons in 1559 was influenced by the religious exiles returning from abroad, indeed that some of them actually sat in the House, but several years ago this was demonstrated to be untrue.[44] The continuity between 1554/5 and 1559 was about normal, which means that something between sixty and seventy per cent of the attendance was the same. It was the will of the Queen which had changed, and that is sufficient to account for the difference. The absence of any strong Catholic party in the House of Commons, to match that in the House of Lords, is one of the most remarkable features of this Parliament, and casts doubt upon the whole commitment of the gentry to the Marian restoration. We know that some magistrates were keen persecutors, but many even of these turned their coats with the new regime, and Elizabeth on the whole was content to have it so, without enquiring too closely into antecedents.[45] Within a few years, those radical Protestants who believed that the Queen had stopped the reformation half-way were making their presence felt in the House of Commons. They never constituted a majority, and talk of the 'the Commons' demanding this or that additional reform is misleading. What they did was to constitute a vocal and troublesome lobby within the House, continually trying to introduce radical measures.

When Anthony Cope brought in his alternative Prayer Book in 1587, he accompanied it with a bill 'containing a petition that all the laws now in force touching the ecclesiastical government should be void, and that it might be enacted that the Book of Common Prayer now offered might be received into the Church of England...'.[46] He was informed by the Speaker that the Queen had 'commanded the House not to meddle with this matter'. Opinion was clearly divided, because the House first decided to hear the book, irrespective of the Queen's prohibition, until one Dalton reminded them of the consequences of

Elizabeth's indignation, when the majority had second thoughts, '[a]nd so the time being passed the House brake up, and the petition nor book read'.[47] This passage of arms was fairly typical of the puritan tactics used from about 1570 onwards, the assumption being that the Queen was insufficiently careful of her own security and well-being, tolerating not only Papists, but also priestly authority in a manner most unbecoming a Protestant Supreme Governor. What this lobby in the Commons wanted by the 1580s was a Presbyterian system of government, whereby the real authority would be vested in a hierarchy of synods rather than in the Crown. This was partly doctrinal in its inspiration, and partly based on mistrust of a woman in supreme ecclesiastical power. Elizabeth knew this perfectly well, and would have nothing to do with it. She had set up an Ecclesiastical Commission to run the Church on a regular basis, anticipating precisely this objection, but she never made any secret of the fact that she regarded the Bishops as her servants – a fact which Archbishop Grindal of Canterbury ignored at his peril in 1577.[48]

It was during the long reign of Elizabeth, from 1558 to 1603, that Parliament came of age as an institution of government. Peers continued to place members in the House of Commons; indeed it was clients of the Earl of Leicester and the Earl of Bedford who made such a nuisance of themselves over the puritan issues. The even more numerous clientage of Lord Burghley was equally prominent on the conformist side, but these men constituted only a small minority, some seventy or eighty members in a House which by 1603 numbered four hundred and sixty. [49] The great majority were duly elected, either by the gentlemen of their counties or by the borough franchises of the towns. It was the nomination of these latter members which was not free, rather than the elections. As we have seen, small boroughs were often willing to put up gentlemen from the neighbouring countryside, and contested elections were rare. The numerous boroughs in Cornwall, which was not typical, regularly returned Duchy officials. The House so constituted was not particularly biddable, unlike the Lords, where the effect of royal indignation was liable to be immediate and personal. Opposition would probably be too strong a word to use for their attitude to the Queen and her council. Except over issues like the Anjou marriage, outright resistance to Elizabeth's wishes was not common, especially on the part of the House as a whole, but a vociferous minority kept up a running fire of criticism, and not only on religious matters.[50] One of their most persistent concerns was over the treatment of Mary, Queen of Scots. Mary had sought refuge in England in 1568 and had been a source of embarrassment to the council ever since. After she had been a focus for the Catholic rising in the north of England in 1569, they had decided to keep her in more or less honourable confinement, and Mary got her own back by lending credence to a sequence of Catholic plots against Elizabeth, most of which envisaged her assassination. After her suspected involvement in the Ridolfi plot of 1572 and the campaign to marry her to the Duke of Norfolk, which cost that nobleman his head, an agitation began in the House of Commons to put her on trial.[51] It was by no means clear which court in England would have jurisdiction over such a person, who was not only a Scot, but also (in the eyes of Elizabeth) still a sovereign princess. However, that did not stop the agitation against her, particularly as it was countenanced by several members of the Privy Council, including Lord Burghley. Eventually, unable either to persuade or to coerce the Queen, these councillors adopted what had originally been a private device and recognized the Bond of Association in 1584. This was an agreement, eventually signed by thousands of gentlemen, never to accept anyone on the throne in whose name an attempt had been made on Elizabeth's life. Should such an attempt be successful, the person concerned, far from securing the Crown, should be executed as a common criminal.[52]

The substance of this Bond was included in an Act of Parliament passed in the following year 'for the surety of the Queen's most royal person', which included provision for the interim government of the realm in the event of such an assassination, and the pursuit of the criminal or criminals concerned. What the Bond included, but the Act did not, was a further provision that the Lords of the Council, in consultation with the Parliament, should have the right to determine the next successor to the throne. Elizabeth would have no truck with so revolutionary a constitutional suggestion and withheld her consent to its inclusion.[53] Lord Burghley, on the other hand, had been prepared to promote it, probably on the grounds that the right of Parliament to determine the succession had already been established under Henry VIII. Elizabeth was deliberately vague about her own right to the throne, preferring to base her claim on the fact that she was Henry's daughter rather than on anything so 'republican' as an Act of Succession, which was why she was so reluctant to exclude Mary. It was, however, under the provisions of this Act that the Scots Queen was eventually trapped, having been deceived into giving an explicit endorsement to Anthony Babington's plot in 1586. She was tried by a special commission (the validity of which she did not recognize), found guilty and, after a long hesitation on the Queen's part, executed in February 1587. [54] On this issue the House of Commons eventually had its way and registered, in a sense, its claim to be consulted on issues of state. At the same time, Elizabeth was reluctant to concede any such right. Freedom of speech – that is, the privilege to speak freely to an issue that was before the House – had long been established, but the freedom to raise any issue which a member might determine was a different matter altogether. It was this claim that Peter Wentworth put forward in 1587, arguing to a ten-point agenda that the Parliament was a council of the realm, and could not properly discharge its function unless it were free to air its public concerns. The House of Commons, however, was not ready for so revolutionary a suggestion, and the Speaker had no difficulty in preventing Wentworth's questions from being put.[55] It was his own traditional function to determine the timetable and agenda for the House and, in insisting on that, he was supported not only by the councillors in the Commons, but also by the majority of members. The Queen was not amused by Wentworth's presumption, and he spent some time in the Tower.

Nevertheless, by the end of the reign Wentworth's ideas were gaining currency. Part of the problem with his earlier intervention was that he spoke only for a minority, as had been the case with the puritan agitations of the 1570s and 80s. When the House was of one mind, it was much harder to resist its pressure, as was revealed by the monopolies debates of 1597 and 1601. Monopolies were grants of trading privileges with which the Queen rewarded favoured courtiers. They did not mean that the courtier concerned intended to trade in that commodity, but that he had the right to sell licences to those who did, a cost which the trader then passed on to his customers. It was a method of giving rewards at no cost to the Treasury, and was bitterly resented.[56] Faced with the almost unanimous wishes of the House, the Speaker had no option but to allow a debate. This was cast in suitably deferential terms, but the outcome was a clear criticism of the Queen:

> [...] So it was put to the Question and concluded, that thanks should be returned by the Speaker, and some twelve were named to go with him as a convenient number, and entreaty made to the Privy Council to obtain liberty to be admitted.[57]

No issue of constitutional principal was directly involved in this case, and Elizabeth chose to give way graciously, but the writing was on the wall. It was not long before the House of Commons was claiming (quite wrongly) to be a Court of Record, and to determine issues relating to its own composition which traditionally belonged to Chancery. By taking advantage of its ancient fiscal and legislative prerogatives, and by exploiting the ambiguities in the Queen's position on many issues, by the early seventeenth century the Parliament (and particularly the House of Commons) had made itself an aggressive and effective partner in the government.[58] By that time, too, the collective political and economic clout of the Commons outweighed that of the House of Lords. It is important not to ignore the latter, which still enjoyed the prestige of its social superiority, but it was not proactive in the same sense as the Commons. The clientage networks of individual Lords no longer had the importance which they had enjoyed, even in the middle of Elizabeth's reign. The peers, as one member reminded them, represented only themselves, whereas the Commons represented the whole realm. There was more than a hint of republicanism about these pretensions.

Noble Ambitions

The medieval nobleman derived his wealth from his lands, but his status from his affinity – that is, from those men who wore his livery and followed his fortunes, especially in war. At any time after the Norman Conquest, his estates would have been granted on a military tenure by the King, who was deemed to possess the whole realm. That favour might have been given to an ancestor and his position been one of inheritance, but equally his own services might have been similarly rewarded, and his estate created or augmented within his own lifetime. Originally, his affinity would have been directly related to his land-holdings, consisting of his tenants or vassals and their sub-vassals, with the infantry being provided by those villains who worked the soil, and who would have had little option if called upon for military service.[1] It was upon this basis of feudal tenure that a royal host was created. However, the military obligations of such tenure were limited, and if the King needed his host for more than a few weeks then he was expected to pay for the additional service. By the end of the thirteenth century, he might very well hire mercenaries in the first place.[2] Nevertheless, the culture of the nobility was military, and their retinues formed natural constituencies, so they served in peace as well as in war, using their own men to enforce the King's laws, and their own courts of honour and manor to maintain discipline in the countryside. Although no King from Henry II onwards was prepared to admit it, the lands of a powerful nobleman might therefore constitute a state within a state, owing allegiance to the King but channelling that obedience exclusively through their lord. Even the sheriff, who protected the King's rights within each shire, might be nominated by the Earl of Essex or the Earl of Northumberland, and although his obedience was in theory directed exclusively to the Crown, in practice he looked to his lord for guidance.[3] In principle, medieval England was a unified state, but in fact it contained many noble satrapies, which fluctuated in importance according to the personalities of the men involved.

Consequently, a nobleman's status depended upon three things: his honour, his lineage and his wealth, of which the third was the least prestigious. His honour, similarly, was divided into two sorts: that which was derived from the size of his following, and that which arose from his own reputation as a soldier. These two factors were sometimes connected, sometimes not, but both were up to a point under his own control. His ancestry, however, was something that was given to him by the will of God, and therefore was uniquely important. This was based on the assumption that virtues were hereditary, and that every nobleman possessed the qualities which had glorified his progenitors – however well they might be concealed.[4] This did not inhibit successive monarchs from ennobling whom they chose, but it did lead to some creative genealogy! In fact, the royal authority was to some extent at odds with this culture of lineage, because it had long been accepted that only the King could create an Earl, and that was extended to the other ranks of Viscount, Marquis and Duke as these were introduced during the fourteenth century. The same principle was extended in the early fifteenth century to the ancient estate of Baron, so that by about 1450 it was accepted that the King made noblemen, not God.[5] This was not an issue before 1485, because, on the whole, Kings were respectful of the claims of ancestry, and Edward IV in particular shared the aristocratic culture of chivalry of which it was a part. However, a nobleman with lineage and a large retinue (to say nothing of extensive wealth) could well come to believe that he had both a right and a duty to participate in the government of the realm, irrespective of the will of the monarch for the time being – hence the idea of the 'councillor born'. During the minority of Henry VI, which lasted from 1422 to 1437, the country was effectively run by its nobility, some of them members of the minority council, some not, but all equally insistent about having their own way within their respective 'countries'.[6] When he assumed personal responsibility for the government, Henry VI proceeded to make this centrifugal situation worse by governing through a narrow circle of favourites, whose retinues more or less did what they pleased in the country. This not only alienated those nobles not within the magic circle, but also led to conflicts between favoured and unfavoured clients, and to their mobilization and military deployment. The warlike culture of the aristocracy, which had previously been exploited for the wars in France, now took the form of private battles in the shires, and led to the conviction among the excluded party that only a regime change could cure the ills from which England was suffering. Hence the mobilization of the rival forces of York and Lancaster, and the so-called 'Wars of the Roses'.[7]

Henry VI had been largely responsible for allowing this noble feuding to get out of hand. The central government was weak, and its officers and agencies diverted to factional ends. 'The law', as Jack Cade's rebels protested in 1450, 'serveth for naught else but to do wrong'. He was thus to blame for his own downfall in 1461, and his successor, Edward IV, did not make the same mistake. He participated personally in the processes of government, reconciled as many Lancastrians as possible, and was reasonably impartial in his distri- bution of patronage. However, he was very respectful of the code of chivalry and effectively re-founded the Order of the Garter, refurbishing the chapel at Windsor Castle for the knights' use. He was also respectful of his nobles and governed as far as possible through them, the best example of that being the extensive powers which he conferred on his brother Richard as Lieutenant of the North, a confidence which was ill-rewarded by the latter's behaviour in 1483.[8] Henry VII was brought up alongside this noble world, a part of it by birth, yet excluded from it by circumstances, and he had plenty of opportunity to view its effects with a jaundiced eye. He was glad enough of the support of his uncle, the Earl of Pembroke, and of the Earl of Oxford and the Marquis of Dorset who joined him in exile, but was not overwhelmed by noble adherents when he landed at Milford Haven in August 1485. His victory at Bosworth owed more to Sir William Stanley than it did to any nobleman, and he therefore came to London as King with singularly few obligations of gratitude to honour. He was also understandably suspicious of the culture of lineage and military prowess. He might well need soldiers to protect his newly acquired status, but he preferred to have them under his own control. He was not – and did not wish to be – dependent on noble retinues, and although he ennobled several of his more prominent supporters, he did not on the whole admit them to his inner council.[9]

The exception to this rule was his uncle Jasper, newly promoted to the Dukedom of Bedford, and to a lesser extent John de Vere, the Earl of Oxford, who was restored to his dignities and properties and created Lord Admiral. Lord Thomas Stanley was created Earl of Derby and Sir Peter Courtenay Earl of Devon, but none of them, with the exception of Jasper, was given any substantial role in government. Altogether forty-three peers served as councillors in the course of the reign, as against forty-nine officials and sixty-one churchmen, so it is not true, as Polydore Vergil alleged, that Henry cold-shouldered the nobility.[10] However, he preferred churchmen in high office, and relied more on the advice of his officials than he did on his peers. His policy was rather to create a royal affinity of gentlemen within each county by giving them offices of profit and by linking them, or their kindred, to the royal court by service. He then depended on this affinity to run the Commission of the Peace, and to govern the county in his name. Sheriffs were henceforth the King's men, and the proviso that neither sheriffs nor Justices of the Peace might wear any livery other than the King's was strictly enforced.[11] He did at first rely on the Earl of Northumberland as Warden General of the Scottish Marches, but when the Earl was killed in 1489 he was succeeded in office by the three-year-old Prince Arthur, which meant that the work was discharged by royal officials as deputies acting in his name, but in fact responsible to the King. The first test of this policy came in 1487 with the invasion of Lambert Simnel, which could have spelt serious danger. However the only peers to join the rebels were the Earl of Lincoln and Viscount Lovell, and the former was killed at the battle of Stoke. The King's own forces were sufficient to win that battle and secure his throne.

The dangers inherent in private armies had long been recognized, and statutes against retaining had been passed as far back as 1399. The most recent had been in 1468, just before the affinities of George, Duke of Clarence and the Earl of Warwick had risen in revolt against Edward IV.[12] They had not been effective, as the events of the Wars of the Roses had demonstrated, and in 1504 Henry repeated the device. His Statute of Liveries recalled these earlier enactments, and went on:

> And over that our said sovereign lord the King, ordaineth, establisheth and enacteth by the said authority that no person of what estate or degree or condition he be [...] privily or openly give any livery or sign, or retain any person other than such as he giveth household wages unto ...[13]

This struck the nail firmly on the head, because not even the grandest peer kept in 'household wages' more than two hundred individuals, whereas his affinity had traditionally been many times that size. As we have seen, a retinue had originally consisted of a lord's vassals and tenants as well as his servants. By the fifteenth century, this following had been augmented by those known more generally as his 'well willers' – men who were attached to him for their own protection or through some other kind of dependency. During the uncertain years of the mid-century, when trust in the royal justice was at a low ebb, a great lord like the Duke of York might have many thousands who had 'commended' themselves to him in this way, and thus potentially a private army which could be deployed for his own purposes.[14] However, with the return of effective royal government in the latter part of Edward's reign, the military need for these affinities had faded away, and had not really returned during the brief and troubled reign of Richard III. When Henry needed an army, as for the invasion of France in 1492 or on the Scottish border in 1497, he issued commissions of array. These might still be directed to peers, but they were peers acting in the King's name and for his purposes. The soldiers they raised might still be, in a sense, their dependents, but that no longer constituted a threat. Consequently the King was able to insist on the enforcement of this act in a way which had not been possible with its predecessors. The penalty on the lord for every infringement was a fine of 100 shillings, and the same from the recipient, and the records of the last five years of the reign are full of bonds taken for obedience to this statute.[15] Actual prosecutions were not numerous, but George Neville, Lord Abergavenny, was fined the enormous sum of £10,000 in 1507 for persistent infringement. Most of this fine was eventually pardoned, but it served as notice of intent. On this issue, as on many others, the King was intent to be obeyed.[16]

Henry VII had made war seldom and reluctantly, and used his peers very sparingly. This created discontent among the nobility, most of whom still saw their service to the Crown primarily in military terms. Henry used war games as court entertainments, but never pretended to share the culture of chivalry which they represented. So when he died in April 1509, his nobles were looking for a new world in the hands of his magnificent and warlike son. Henry VIII was concerned not to disappoint them. In spite of continuing most of his father's officers and councillors, the new King did not share his predecessor's suspicion of the ancient nobility, nor did he share his parsimonious attitude to fines and recognisances. Many of the latter were cancelled, and the old King's two chief enforcers, Edmund Dudley and Sir Richard Empson, were speedily arrested and consigned to the Tower.[17] At the same time, he recalled to favour and restored to their titles Thomas Grey, Marquis of Dorset and William Courtenay, Earl of Devon, both of whom had been attainted in 1504 on suspicions arising from their proximity to the Plantagenet royal family. With the exception of the former Earl of Suffolk, who was the 'White Rose' claimant to the throne and who remained in the Tower, Henry did not share his father's suspicions, and went on to restore Margaret Pole, the sister of the Earl of Warwick, to her title as Countess of Salisbury in 1513. He also created peers for their service in war, the most notable being Thomas Howard, raised from the Earldom of Surrey to the Dukedom of Norfolk, and Charles Brandon, created first Viscount Lisle and then Duke of Suffolk in 1514.[18] Admittedly he had Edmund de la Pole executed in 1513 for no better reason than being who he was, but no rash of attainders greeted the new regime, for the simple reason that it had been unopposed.

However, the influence of Thomas Wolsey after 1515, and Catherine's continued failure to bear him a son, wrought a change in that attitude, signalled by the fall of Edward Stafford, Duke of Buckingham in 1521. Edward was descended through the female line from Thomas of Woodstock, the youngest son of Edward III, and he had been mentioned in some well-known discussions at Calais some time between 1502 and 1506 as a possible successor to the throne.[19] At first, Henry had shrugged off any possible challenge, but Edward's pride in his ancestry, and his ill-disguised contempt for the parvenue Tudors, began to become irritating. He also made several rather foolish mistakes. He persisted in pressing his claim to be High Constable of England in perpetuity; he fell out with the powerful Cardinal; and he flaunted his retinue by proposing to tour his Welsh estates at the head of five hundred men. At the same time, he fell out with some of his own servants, who were easily induced to testify to his pretentions. He was summoned to London, arrested and tried for high treason. It is fairly clear that his offences were those of an abrasive personality rather than a conspirator. Nevertheless, he was executed, and the King drew back from ennobling or promoting any more of his remote kindred.[20] He went on creating peers at the rate of about one a year, but they were all either members of his immediate family or servants either in administration or in arms. For example, he created his bastard son, Henry Fitzroy as Duke of Richmond and Somerset in 1525, his potential father-in-law Sir Thomas Boleyn as Earl of Wiltshire in 1529, and his brother-in-law Sir Edward Seymour as Earl of Hertford in 1537. Sir William FitzWilliam became Earl of Southampton ahead of his promotion as Lord Privy Seal in 1537, Sir William Paulet became Lord St John in 1539 and Sir John Dudley became Viscount Lisle in March 1542.[21] At the same time, he turned against his earlier associates: Henry Courtenay, Marquis of Exeter, was executed for treason in 1538; Lord Montague, the eldest son of the Countess of Salisbury, died for the same cause in the same year, and the Countess herself in 1541. Even the Howards, who had seemed to bear a charmed life, fell foul of Henry in the last months of his life. The Duke of Norfolk and his son, the Earl of Surrey were attainted for flaunting their blood royal in a dubious claim to control the minority which was clearly impending, and Surrey lost his head just a few days before the King's death.[22]

Altogether Henry created forty-three new peers, but because of attainders and natural wastage, at the time of his death there were only fifty-six lay nobles, as against forty-three at his accession. He is alleged to have lamented on his deathbed that he had allowed the nobility to fall into decline, and proposed several new creations to make good the deficiency. That lamentation looks spurious, but what he had undoubtedly done was to transform the nature of the peerage. Of the thirty-four barons who were alive at that time he had created sixteen, and of the seventeen greater peerages eleven were of his making. He had thus transformed the nobility from a 'lineage base' to a 'service base'.[23] The House of Lords now consisted primarily of men who were there for services to King Henry VIII rather than his ancestors, and that signalled a major change of emphasis. Unlike his father, Henry had been perfectly willing to promote his trusted servants to the peerage, but he changed the significance of their promotion in the process. He also transformed the balance of power within the House of Lords. By dissolving the monasteries, he eliminated the constituency of the mitred Abbots, thereby removing about twenty ecclesiastical peers and leaving the laity with a permanent majority. After 1540 the Church was represented in Parliament only by two Archbishops and twenty-one Bishops; since there were normally a few vacancies, and some who were excused attendance, the clerical voice was much diminished, which became a matter of great significance once Parliament was established as the forum for ecclesiastical legislation after 1547.[24] Apart from their function in Parliament, it would be no exaggeration to say that the main appearance of these men as peers was decorative. They were regularly summoned to adorn the court for special occasions, whether it was the celebration of Christmas, the christening of a royal child, or the ratification of a new treaty. The King's honour required that he be nobly accompanied on such occasions, and his peers were expected to provide that presence. Their ladies provided the Queen Consort's Privy Chamber, and their children (or some them) accompanied the royal offspring to their lessons.[25] In short, they were part of the necessary trappings of monarchy, but their political significance had been much diminished. The number of servants which they might bring with them to court was strictly limited by the Eltham Ordinances, and the possibility of their pursuing private quarrels in the country by using their servants to coerce opponents had been reduced to nil. Because of the circumstances of their elevation, all were committed to the enforcement of the King's laws. In this context it was highly significant that when Henry Percy, the sixth Earl of Northumberland, died childless in 1537, he was coerced into making the King his heir, rather than his brother Sir Thomas.[26] It had been said that the north east of England 'knew no prince but a Percy'. Not any longer!

When death removed Henry's awesome personality in January 1547, the nobility ostensibly took over. Sir William Paget's testimony resulted in a spate of promotions and new creations. The Earl of Hertford (Edward VI's maternal uncle) became Duke of Somerset and Lord Protector, Viscount Lisle became Earl of Warwick, the Earl of Essex became Marquis of Northampton and Lord Thomas Wriothesley became Earl of Southampton. Each of these creations was accompanied by a suitable grant of lands, and the minority council was dominated by these newly promoted peers.[27] Superficially it looked as though the circumstances of Henry VI's minority nearly a hundred and thirty years before had been recreated. However, there was one major difference. Whereas the peers of the 1420s had been deeply rooted in their countries, and commanders of considerable *manred* (that is, personal service – usually of a military nature), their successors in 1547 had no such base. John Dudley, Earl of Warwick, was typical in this respect. His power base was the court, and his office Lord Admiral with its accompanying membership of the Privy Council. Although he had great estates, he treated them as commercial assets rather than a source of manpower, buying and selling land regularly, so that he had no consolidated constituency of tenants, and his servants and dependents relied upon his influence at the centre rather than in the country.[28] The importance of this difference was well demonstrated by the fall of the Duke of Somerset in October 1549. Somerset had pursued a number of controversial policies over the previous two years. He had converted the Church of England to Protestantism, and given undue priority to the subjection of Scotland. Above all, he had countenanced movements of social protest aimed at the gentry (and noble) proclivity to enclose arable land for sheepruns. These protests had got out of control in the summer of 1549 and shown a strong anti-aristocratic bias, which had eventually needed forceful suppression. Somerset, who had shown an arrogant tendency to reject advice and to rule without the agreement of his council, had been forced to act, but had apparently done so reluctantly. As a result, a majority of the council decided that he would have to be removed from office, and early in October gathered in London for that purpose.[29] Somerset became alarmed and whisked the King off to Windsor, where he presumably intended to defend himself. However he had no retinue to come to his aid, and his appeal for support produced only a few unarmed peasants. Faced with the forces which the Earl of Warwick had recently led to defeat the rebels in Norfolk, and with the army which Lord Russell was leading back from the South West, he had no option but to surrender. Whereas a fifteenth-century Duke of York, similarly placed, would have been able to call upon a private army several thousand strong, the Duke of Somerset had only a handful of personal servants. He was deposed and imprisoned without the slightest resistance.[30]

Having ostensibly settled his dispute with the council, Somerset was released and a few months later restored to its ranks. His daughter married Warwick's eldest son and the quarrel between them was apparently appeased. However, appearances were deceptive. Disliking Warwick's domestic policy, and still more his rapprochement with France, the Duke became a leader of opposition. He allied with conservative leaders such as the Earl of Arundel and began to pose a threat to the unity of the council – a unity which was of particular importance in the circumstances of a minority, and when the country was still seething with social unrest. Warwick, who was to be created Duke of Northumberland a few days later, decided in October 1551 that he was a threat which would have to be confronted. Somerset was arrested at a council meeting on the 16th, and charged with a fanciful array of offences, including a plot to assassinate several councillors and raise the City of London.[31] Several other peers were arrested with him in order to maintain the plausibility of the accusations. He was eventually charged and convicted for the lesser offence of felony, and executed in February 1552. In this context, the important thing about this second and final fall is that nobody came to his assistance. He was the wealthiest man in England, yet he was unable to raise a retinue to defend him, and in the aftermath of his fall his estates were simply split up and redistributed. One or two of his dependants, including Sir Michael Stanhope, were executed with him, but others, including Sir William Cecil, made their peace with the winner and continued to serve in public office.[32] What none of them did was resort to arms. The days when a peer would able to protect himself against political enemies by calling upon his clientage were gone as a consequence of the policies of the first two Tudor Kings.

The same point was made during the situation following Edward VI's death in July 1553. The King had been determined that his sister Mary should not follow him upon the throne and had settled the succession on his cousin, Jane Grey. Jane's cause was upheld by the Duke of Northumberland, and ostensibly by the rest of the council. However, Mary challenged this decision, and gathered a force at Framlingham in Norfolk. This force consisted largely of her own affinity, drawn from her Norfolk estates, and was made up of the followings of several loyal gentlemen, collectively significant although not individually of great size.[33] When Northumberland set out to oppose her, his force consisted largely of household troops such as the guard and the followings of the gentlemen pensioners. Very few of them were his own men, or committed to him personally, and when his cause collapsed on 19 July because of the defection of most of the council his force simply disintegrated, leaving him to face arrest, trial and execution for High Treason. Again, the wealthiest man in England, and one who had apparently held all the strings of power in his own hands, was undone by a lack of *manred*.[34] Once Mary had established the validity of her claim, he had neither a cause to fight for nor yet the means to continue the struggle. A hundred years earlier he could have retreated to his power base in the north and defied the King to come after him, but his northern estates were of recent acquisition and it was over a decade since he had last visited the area. The apparent revival of the 'overmighty subject' in the reign of Edward VI was almost entirely illusory. Northumberland's power was at the centre, and when he had lost that, he had nothing to fall back on.

Up to a point, Mary's policy in respect of the nobility was the opposite of her father's. Having seen off Jane Grey, she was not suspicious of rival claimants, and in any case the nearest to her in blood was Cardinal Reginald Pole, her confidant and Archbishop of Canterbury.[35] Whereas Henry had taken the chivalric culture seriously, at least as a basis for sport and display, Mary showed not the slightest interest in war games. This was not entirely the result of her gender, because although she would have been barred from taking part, she could have appeared, as Elizabeth was to do, as the 'Queene of Faerie', presiding over the noble feats of her gallants. She did not do so, and the possibility never seems to have crossed her mind. She also set out to right some of the wrongs which she perceived to have been inflicted on the nobility during her father's reign. One of the first things she did after arriving in London was to restore the aged Duke of Norfolk to his titles and estates. She could not bring the Earl of Surrey back to life, but she could make sure that his title was recognized in respect of his fifteen-year-old son, who would succeed to the Dukedom in the following year.[36] Similarly, she released from the Tower the twenty-six year-old Edward Courtenay, who had been kept in confinement since his father's execution in 1538. He was created Earl of Devon and the bulk of his father's property was restored to him. There was even a rumour current that the Queen would marry him, but she never showed the slightest inclination to do so. The Duchess of Somerset was released at the same time and suitable provision made for her maintenance, but her son was not recognized as Earl of Hertford, and there were clearly limits to the Queen's policy of restitution.[37] Some time later, in 1557, she recreated the Earldom of Northumberland for Sir Thomas Percy in an extremely conservative provision for the defence of the border against Scotland.[38] This may be an indication that, had she lived longer, the traditional nobility would have acquired again something of the local power which they had lost during the reign of Henry VIII, but there are few other indications of that happening. Of those nobles who had been members of Edward VI's council, a surprising number continued to serve Mary; a few, such as the Marquis of Northampton, were attainted and lost their titles, but only two, the Duke of Northumberland himself and his colleague the Duke of Suffolk, were actually executed. On the whole, local jurisdiction continued to lie where it had come to rest during the reigns of Henry VII and Henry VIII, with the various commissions which governed the counties. Mary did follow a policy of including one or more Privy Councillors on each Commission of the Peace, and these were often noblemen, but there is little indication that they actually functioned as justices.[39]

When the rebellion of Sir Thomas Wyatt threatened London in February 1554, Mary tried at first to rely on the 'White Coats' – the trained bands of the City of London – to defeat him, but that turned out to be a mistake when most of them deserted. The court was briefly exposed to attack, and it was the noble retinues of the Earl of Pembroke and the Marquis of Winchester which came to the rescue.

However, these had been raised through hastily issued commissions of array, and no one could have been less military in normal times than Lord Treasurer Winchester.[40] The same method was used to assemble the expeditionary force which Pembroke led to St Quentin in 1557 in support of Philip's campaign. It was a familiar device, used by both Henry VIII and Edward VI. Such commissions were addressed to experienced military men, who might or might not be nobles, instructing them to raise so many men for the King's (or Queen's) service. The men so mustered did not necessarily have any previous connection with their commander and were certainly not expected to be his retainers. They were also taken onto the royal payroll from the moment of their assembling and their commanders were not expected to foot the bill, even in the first instance. By the end of Henry's reign, they were normally raised from the county militias and the link with aristocratic retinues had been effectively broken.[41] It did not return during Mary's short reign, although the provisions in the Earl of Northumberland's commission raise the possibility that it might have done. As with her Church, Mary's policy with respect to the nobility was conservative, but it does not feature prominently in her regime. Apart from the restorations, she created only a few Barons, and they did not feature prominently in her government.

In this respect, as in many others, Elizabeth was her own woman. Like her father and grandfather, she avoided using peers in the normal processes of government and retained the ban on retinues, but like her sister she made very few creations. With the notable exception of Francis Russell, Earl of Bedford, most of the peers which she inherited were conservative in their religious views, and whereas this did not at first prompt them to resist the regime, it was good reason for not using them in high office.[42] On the whole, the Queen was content to allow them to go on exercising their traditional influence in their home countries, but did not pretend to govern through them, nor was she any more willing than her father had been to allow Justices of the Peace to be 'commended' to any peer. Her court was secular and highly educated, dominated by men like William Cecil and Nicholas Bacon, while the Privy Chamber was in the capable hands of Katherine Ashley. All Mary's intimates had either withdrawn or been retired and replaced by gentlemen and women led by the families of Boleyn, Carey and Seymour.[43] The Earl of Oxford retained his place as Lord Great Chamberlain and the Earl of Arundel as Lord Steward, but they remained in the background, as did the other established peers, who were expected to put in an appearance and serve on ceremonial occasions but were not allowed to dominate. Indeed, it was made clear to them that they were servants of a demanding mistress. Apart from restoring the Marquis of Northampton and the Earl of Hertford early in 1559, Elizabeth's first peerage creation was that of her personal favourite, Robert Dudley in September 1564. Lord Robert was ennobled for services of an intimate nature, and he was no friend to Sir William Cecil, but the rivalry between them had nothing to do with Lord Robert's new status. When he joined the Privy Council soon after, their counterpoint kept that body divided for many years, which was how the Queen preferred it, because it increased her own freedom of action.[44]

Sometimes, however, the tensions were between court and country parties, and in 1569 these flared into open rebellion. This quarrel began with the arrival of Mary, Queen of Scots in 1568. Her marriage to James Hepburn, Earl of Bothwell not being recognized on either side of the border, the idea arose of neutralizing her as a political influence by marrying her to the Duke of Norfolk, England's premier peer and only Duke. Norfolk liked the idea, but the Queen, influenced by Sir William Cecil, did not. In fact, she forbade it in forceful terms, which caused Norfolk and his conservative allies to view Cecil's power with increasingly hostility. They allied with the Earl of Leicester to form a formidable conspiracy against the secretary, but Leicester, correctly reading Elizabeth's mind in the matter, made a clean breast of the whole affair, which prompted the Queen into an unequivocal endorsement of Cecil's position.[45] This, and the general chill which had come over their relations with the court as the religious establishment began to settle down, prompted the Earls of Northumberland and Westmorland to reassess their position. They were not militant Catholics, but they disliked the whole drift of royal policy and thought that Elizabeth should acknowledge Mary as her heir. Northumberland had also lost the favoured position in the borders which he had enjoyed under Mary and felt that his access to the court was blocked. Now, with Norfolk and Leicester both in full retreat, he felt his position to be uniquely exposed. Rumours began to circulate about the intentions of the two Earls and they were interviewed by the Earl of Sussex, the Queen's Lieutenant in the north. Sussex professed himself satisfied, but Elizabeth was not, and on 24 October they were summoned to court to explain themselves.[46] This put them on the spot and, fearing arrest, they began to mobilize. At first, they did this on the pretext that the Queen had ordered it, and confusion reigned. The Earl of Northumberland had what was probably the largest affinity in England among the traditionally minded northern gentry, and they were accustomed to obeying his orders, so they came, unaware at first that they were committing themselves to rebellion. By the time Sussex had proclaimed them traitors on 13 November, they were too far committed to retreat. Northumberland himself seems to have been forced into action by a radical element among his own supporters led by Richard Norton, who appealed at once to the Pope for recognition and to the Duke of Alba in The Netherlands for support.[47] This was probably well beyond the Earls' intentions, which seem to have extended no further than freeing Mary of Scotland and making a demonstration against the religious settlement. The rebels marched from Brancepeth, where they had assembled, to Durham, where they staged a Solemn High Mass in the cathedral and then set off south. They got as far as Bramham Moor, near Leeds, on the 24th, when their momentum petered out. Their men began to desert and royal forces were gathering against them. They called off the rescue of Mary and began to retreat.[48]

The reason for this failure was that Northumberland's grip on his affinity was nothing like as strong as it appeared to be. The Percy and Neville followers in County Durham and North Yorkshire responded reasonably well, but their colleagues in Northumberland itself, the rest of Yorkshire and the north west hardly at all. Their force was therefore less than half of what might have been expected, and when Lord Hunsdon advanced from the south in command of a royal army, these absent gentlemen were among the first to declare their loyalty to the Queen.[49] It became obvious that Charles Neville no longer commanded much allegiance in Cumberland and Westmorland, and that the Percy affinity had been only imperfectly restored with the re-erection of the Earldom in 1557. On 15 December the Earls disbanded what was left of their force and fled, first to Hexham, then to Naworth, and then over the border into Scotland. Both were attainted, and the Earldom of Westmorland extinguished for the time being. Henry Percy, Thomas's brother, was allowed to succeed to his brother's title in spite of his attainder, but was given only a greatly reduced patrimony.[50] The third northern Earl, Henry Clifford of Cumberland, was a sick man, and died during the crisis. He was not involved at all, and his heir, who succeeded as a minor, was brought up in the south as a good Protestant. His estates were not touched, but his affinity caused no trouble and gradually withered away. The effective destruction of the traditional Earldoms of Northumberland and Westmorland wrought a major change in the politics of the north of England. Their lands were split up and, apart from the rump estates of the Percys, distributed among those gentlemen who had been most conspicuous for their loyalty during the crisis.[51] Quite fortuitously, the remaining border affinity, that of Dacre, was extinguished at the same time, because Leonard Dacre, a disappointed claimant to the inheritance, raised a force in January 1570 which threatened to collaborate with the disaffected clans across the border. He was too late to join the northern rising proper, but could have been a nuisance if he had not been caught by Lord Hunsdon, who was still in the vicinity with the army raised against the Earls. In a skirmish near Naworth, the rebels left three hundred dead, and a number were taken prisoner. It was the only bloodshed during the campaign, and Dacre joined the Earls in Scotland. He had little in the way of lands to forfeit, but his name had been sufficient to raise the affinity, which was largely destroyed in the battle.[52] The Earl of Westmorland kept on running and ended up in the Low Countries as a pensioner of King Philip of Spain, but Thomas Percy was handed over by the regency government of Scotland and executed at York on 22 September 1572.[53]

The northern rebellion was a warning. It did not constitute a serious threat to the stability of Elizabeth's government, but it did serve to alert the council not only to the residual perils of Catholicism, but also to the dangers which could still lurk in the noble affinity.[54] A close watch was kept on such nobles as the Earls of Derby, Shrewsbury and Pembroke, who were expected to show themselves at court from time to time and were discouraged from riding 'well accompanied'. Their military pretentions were accommodated by service as Lords Lieutenant, which satisfied their dignities, while the actual functions were mainly discharged by their Deputies, who would be loyal gentlemen with court connections. The Earl of Leicester fancied himself as a soldier, but only overseas and in command of men raised in the usual way through the county levies. In the 1570s these militias had been reorganized to make them more amenable to this kind of deployment, being divided into 'trained bands' and the rest. The former consisted of the more substantial citizens, those who had property and other interests to protect, who were to be armed at the expense of their counties and used only for home defence. The remainder were to be available for service wherever required, and were to be armed at the expense of the Crown once they had been mustered.[55] In spite of the dubious quality of the men raised in this way, they were to acquit themselves well in battle, both in the Low Countries and in Brittany. Leicester went in command of such forces to the Low Countries in 1585, but became ensnared in the politics of The Netherlands and was eventually recalled in disgrace because he had allowed his own ambition to exceed that of his mistress. The only nobleman who allowed his military ambitions to outrun both discretion and common sense was Robert Devereux, second Earl of Essex. Devereux succeeded Robert Dudley, who was his stepfather, as Elizabeth's personal favourite, and used this especial status to get himself appointed to commands in France in 1592, against Cadiz in 1596 and on the Islands voyage of 1597.[56] Of these, only the second could be rated a success, but they inflated Essex's self-conceit to the point where he literally talked himself into being appointed Lord Deputy of Ireland in 1599. However, he more than met his match in the Earl of Tyrone, and after wasting his resources in failing to bring the Earl to battle, signed an ill-considered truce. Elizabeth was furious. He returned in disgrace and comprehensively forfeited the royal favour, a fact which drove him into a state of paranoid depression.[57] Convinced that he was the object of malicious plots, he staged a rebellion early in 1601, which demonstrated conclusively how far the nobility had declined from their earlier power. Although he was a second-generation peer with extensive estates in North Wales and Cheshire, he made not the slightest attempt to raise an affinity in that region, but relied instead on the swordsmen and disappointed place-seekers who had gathered round him at court. This motley crew of about three hundred was supposed to raise London and seize control of the court, with the object of forcing Robert Cecil and his cronies from power and compelling the Queen to receive Essex into favour again. It was a forlorn hope. London did not stir, and Cecil was prepared for him, with the result that he was driven into a forlorn retreat to Essex House and eventual surrender.[58] A few weeks later, this misplaced ambition cost him his head.

With the exception of Leicester and Essex, both of whom were failures, Elizabeth had not entrusted either an army or a navy to any major nobleman since the Earl of Warwick had commanded at Le Havre in 1563. Her favoured soldiers were either minor peers such as Lord Mountjoy, or gentlemen professionals such as Sir John Norris and Sir Francis Vere – men without political pretensions. The same was even more true at sea. Although the Lord Admiral was a peer by definition, Lord Howard of Effingham was a comparatively minor member of that distinguished family, and her favoured captains were men such as Sir John Hawkins and Sir Francis Drake who were of humble origins and entirely dependent upon herself for their riches and status.[59] By the end of her reign, the nobility had been civilized and domesticated to a degree never seen before. At court, it was more important to be able to pen a telling tract or sight-read a madrigal than to be a member of the peerage. In the country, domestication was even more pronounced. As Thomas Sackville, Lord Buckhurst explained to Gilbert Earl of Shrewsbury,

> [...] Your lordship must remember that in the policy of this Common Wealth, we are not over ready to add increase of power & countenance to such great personages as you are. And when in the country you dwell in you will need enter in a war with the inferiors therein, we think it both justice, equity and wisdom to take care that the weaker part be not put down by the mightier.[60]

In other words, bullying tactics would not be tolerated. It was a long time since a peer had been subjected to actual punishment by the courts – not since Lord Dacre of the South had been hanged for murdering a gamekeeper in 1556 – but direct punishment was not necessary to make the point; the humiliation of seeing such punishments inflicted on their agents and clients was normally enough. Many years ago, Laurence Stone described this policy as 'flabby', but he admitted that it was effective.[61] Lord Keeper Williams could remark in 1626: '[I]n ancient times the record of the Court of Star Chamber were filled with battles and riots so outrageous, whereas now we hear not one in our age.' He was exaggerating, but not greatly so. In the reign of Henry VII, sixty-five per cent of the cases before the court had involved violence, but by the 1620s it was twenty-three per cent and the violence was less serious. Peers, like other men, had learned to turn their attention to the more sophisticated methods of fraud, forgery and perjury.[62]

Elizabeth was not hostile to her peers in any personal sense. She counted a number of them, and their womenfolk, among her close friends, but she was not much concerned to defend their status, either social or political. She created only some half-dozen Earls in the course of her forty-five-year reign, differing markedly from her father in that respect. By the end of her reign there were only some fifty-five peers, thirty-six of whom were Barons, and this was the lowest figure since 1509, when the effects of Henry VII's parsimony were at their height. After the death of the Marquis of Winchester in 1572, she did not employ anyone above the rank of Baron in high office. Lord Burghley, Lord Buckhurst and her kinsman Henry Carey, Lord Hunsdon were high in her confidence, but were not further promoted. Most of her key servants were knights or gentlemen like Sir Robert Cecil. Nor, in spite of the favours which she bestowed upon him, did she allow the Earl of Essex any control over official patronage. Indeed, her unwillingness to promote his clients was one of the grievances which festered in his mind in 1601, because he attributed that unwillingness to the machinations of Sir Robert Cecil.[63] In fact, it was the Queen's own will that it should be so, because much as she liked Devereux at a personal level, she never had any faith in his political judgement – and events were to prove her right.

The sustained policy of the Tudors over more than a hundred years had reduced magnates to the status of subjects – and subjects who saw their chief honour in service to the Crown. The lineage and chivalric culture of the late fifteenth century was now little more than a memory. The lengthy processes of sixteenth-century lawsuits not only allowed time for tempers to cool, they also acted as lightening conductors for local violence. Peers, like everyone else, had learned that the monarch had a will to be obeyed, and could in the last resort override the will of any subject, no matter how exalted.[64] Not the least of the Tudor achievements was the domestication of the nobility.

Hampton Court ground plan

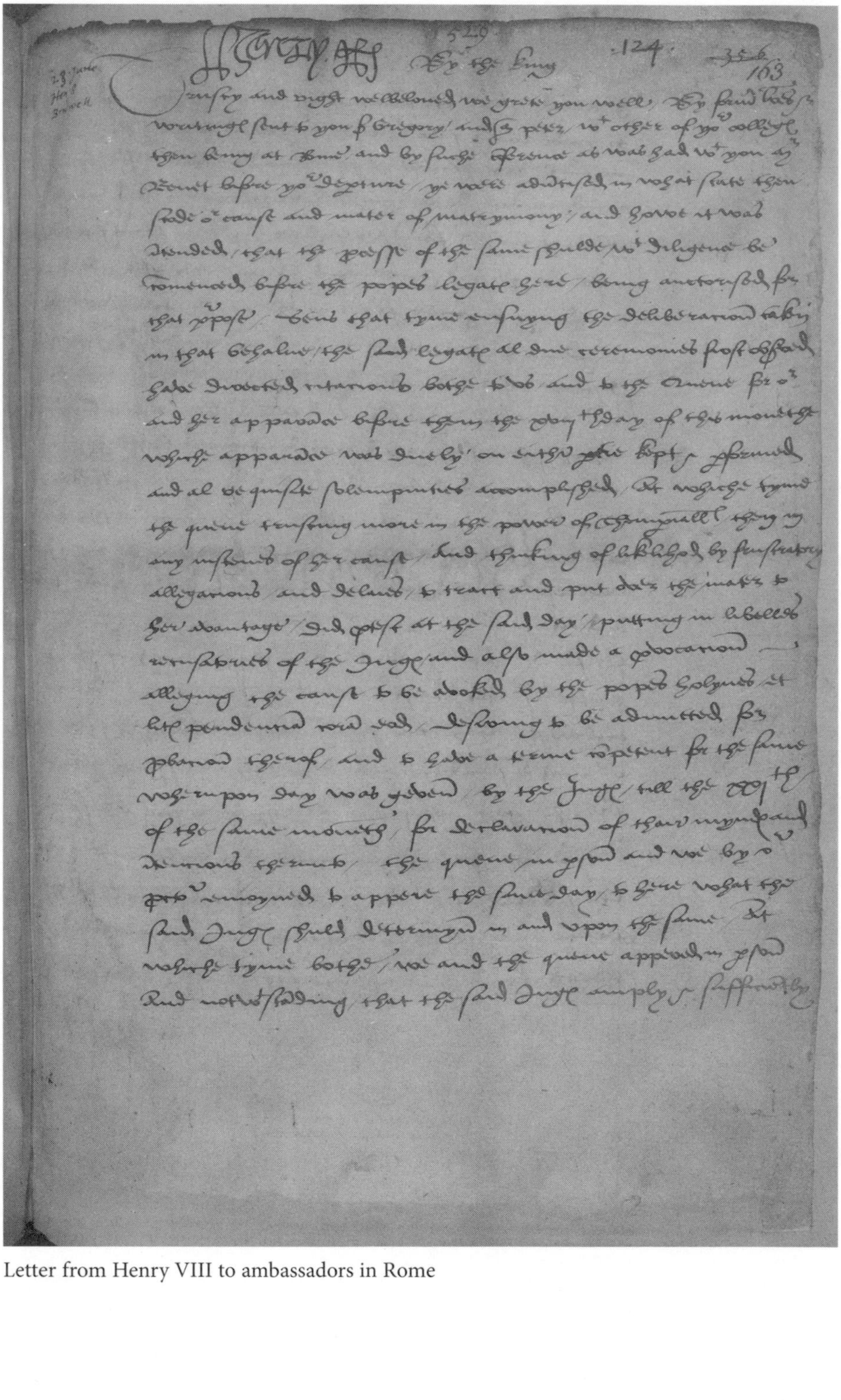

Letter from Henry VIII to ambassadors in Rome

Henry VIII, Edward VI, & the Pope

Jane Dudley [Grey]

Mary Tudor and Charles Brandon

Burning of Cranmer

The Tudors and Their Neighbours

At the end of the middle ages, England was not a great power. The reputation which her bowmen had earned her on the fields of Crécy, Poitiers and Agincourt had long since been dissipated in humiliating defeats – in Normandy in 1450 and in Gascony in 1453. Since then, the English had turned their swords upon each other and had slipped out of contention in the advance of military technology.[1] Only in relation to Scotland and Ireland could Henry VII be said to have inherited a dominant position, and each of those lands presented distinctive problems. Scotland was underdeveloped both socially and militarily, and her lawless borderers posed a constant threat. To be fair, the English borderers were not much better, and the continual raiding to and fro made for a prevailing state of tension between the two kingdoms. Richard III had only recently recovered the border town of Berwick, and James III looked on that loss with a jaundiced eye. He may have supported Henry at Bosworth, but that was more out of a desire to cause difficulties for Richard than out of any enthusiasm for the Earl of Richmond. Nevertheless, Henry pursued an active policy of peace in the north and signed a three-year truce with James in July 1486. Before that expired, the Scottish King had succumbed to rebellion and assassination, and in June 1488 was succeeded by his fifteen-year-old son, James IV.[2] This put the whole diplomatic situation on hold, but Henry continued to be well-informed about affairs in the northern kingdom by way of his contacts and agents. Soon after the Scottish King achieved his majority, Henry began tentatively to seek a marriage between James and his four-year-old daughter, Margaret. These negotiations moved ahead slowly in the hands of Richard Fox, the Bishop of Durham, but were rudely interrupted in September 1496 by the Scot's endorsement of Perkin Warbeck, and brief invasion of England. In spite of provoking a major military deployment on the English side, this turned out to be a storm in a teacup. By the end of the year James had dropped the pretender, who clearly had no support south of the border, and signed another truce at Ayton in September 1497. This was renewed two years later, and led on to the first full peace between the countries since 1328, also signed at Ayton in January 1502. This at last committed James to a marriage with Margaret, by then aged twelve, which took place the following year and led to a decade of amicable relations.[3]

In Ireland, the situation was more complex, because the whole Lordship was in theory subject to the English Crown. This meant that it was a domestic rather than a foreign problem, but since the greater part of the island rejected the English claim, and it could not be enforced, it is more realistically treated as an aspect of foreign policy. By the end of the fifteenth century, the King's writ ran only in the Dublin Pale, with a partial extension into the 'obedient lands', which were holdings of the great Anglo-Irish peers to the south and west of the Pale. The centre, west and north of the island was controlled by a miscellany of Gaelic tribes, which owned no allegiance except to themselves and were constantly at war both with each other and with their settled neighbours.[4] These 'wild lands' formed a challenge which successive Tudors were to struggle in vain to overcome. The Chief Governors, who ruled over the Pale, were normally absentee English magnates, and their Deputies (who did the actual work) were clergy or senior civil servants. Real power, however, rested in the hands of the Fitzgerald Earls of Kildare, and it was Gerald, the 8th Earl, who welcomed and supported Lambert Simnel in 1487. Yorkist sentiment had been strong in Ireland since the Duke of York had been Chief Governor there in the 1450s, and 'Edward VI' was generally well received. The battle of Stoke, however, put an end to his pretensions and left the Earl exposed to the royal vengeance. Revenge, however, was not in Henry's mind. He sent Sir Richard Edgecombe with a small force and the express intention of receiving into the King's peace all who submitted themselves. There being no realistic alternative, Edgecombe had an easy task, and Kildare's position was confirmed until he was replaced by the young Duke of York in 1494.[5] Since the Duke never went to Ireland, Kildare remained in effective control until he was replaced by his own son in 1513. He was summoned to England and attainted for his alleged role in the Warbeck conspiracy in 1495, but was quickly pardoned and restored to office. Henry was more concerned with the form than with the substance of power in Ireland. He appointed Sir Edward Poynings as Deputy in September 1494, who caused a Parliament to be convened which sat from December 1494 to April 1495. This Parliament passed over forty acts for the better government of the colony, including that known as 'Poynings' Law' which declared that no Irish Parliament should in future be recognized unless it was called by the King 'under his Great Seal'.[6] Poynings was recalled in December 1495 and, although his military expeditions had made little or no difference to the lawless state of the 'wild Irish', the King was well satisfied with his work. Provided that his authority was generally recognized in the Pale and the Obedient Lands, he was content to allow the Anglo-Irish to run their affairs in their own way. Although that involved a good deal of feuding among the noble families, it did not affect their professions of allegiance to the English Crown, and Henry was satisfied with that.[7]

Perkin Warbeck flies like a bird of ill omen through the foreign policy of the middle years of the reign, disrupting relations not only with James IV, but also with Charles VIII of France and with the Emperor Maximilian, both of whom were tempted for a while to give him countenance. However, it was before Warbeck came on the scene that Henry fought his only continental war – a brief invasion of France which was concluded by the treaty of Etaples in November 1492. This had arisen out of a conflict of interests and obligations, because whereas the King was duly grateful to Charles VIII for his support in 1485, he owed many years of safe refuge to Duke Francis II of Brittany. By 1488 the Duke was aged and infirm, and Charles was threatening to take over the Duchy when he died. This Francis resisted to the best of his ability, but his forces were defeated at St Aubin du Cormier in July 1488. In August he capitulated and in September he died.[8] That should have been the end of the matter, but Henry had his own reasons for wishing to guarantee Breton independence, and in February 1489 signed the treaty of Redon with the regency government of the twelve-year-old Duchess Anne, whose wardship the King of France was claiming. Neither the military gesture of a force under Lord Daubeney nor an alliance with the Emperor were sufficient to deter Charles from his purpose and early in 1491 he married the Duchess by proxy. The French had so far ignored Henry completely, and it was not in his interests to allow them to get away with it, so he revived his claim to the French throne and invaded with a substantial force in October 1492. How serious his intentions were must be a matter of some doubt. It was very late in the year for serious campaigning, and he allowed himself to be bought off within a matter of weeks.[9] However, he had honoured his obligation under the treaty of Redon and with that he was, apparently, content. Charles VIII's attention was thereafter diverted to Italy, where he invaded in 1494, and when he died in 1498 Henry made not the slightest attempt to prevent his wife from being transferred to his successor, Louis XII. Warbeck caused the merest ripple in the amicable relations which prevailed after November 1492.

With the Emperor, the situation was slightly less straightforward because of the independent actions of the Dowager Duchess of Burgundy, Margaret, who was the sister of Edward IV and implacably hostile to Henry. She recognized Warbeck and she had recognized Simnel, and in November 1493 introduced him to Albert, Duke of Saxony, who took him to Vienna and introduced him in turn to the new Emperor, Maximilian, who recognized him as the rightful King of England.[10] This could have led to a serious diplomatic breach, but Maximilian did not propose to do anything about his recognition, which was done largely to placate the Duchess, and renewed his predecessor's treaty with England soon after. When it came to the point, he made no difficulty over dealing with Henry as *de facto* King, and seems to have been quite unembarrassed by Perkin's exposure in 1497. Much the most serious of Henry's diplomatic engagements during the early and middle years of the reign was with Ferdinand and Isabella of Spain. Ferdinand had been rightly identified at the outset as being not only the holder of one of Europe's most prestigious thrones, but also a useful ally should relations with France become difficult. In addition, he was the father of an available daughter, Catherine, born in 1485, who would in due course make an excellent partner for Prince Arthur, born in 1486. Ferdinand was equally interested in an alliance with the strategically placed King of England, who was also *persona grata* with the Pope, and negotiations were opened as early as March 1488.[11] Agreement had been reached by July, and on 28 March 1489 the treaty of Medina del Campo was signed, whereby the marriage was agreed in principle and various commercial concessions were granted to English traders. This marriage treaty was renewed in 1496 and confirmed in 1497. On 19 May 1499 the wedding took place by proxy, accompanied by another treaty of alliance, and in October 1501 the Princess arrived in England for the ceremony to be repeated in person.[12] Alas for great expectations! Within six months Arthur was dead, and in the following year both Henry and Ferdinand became widowers. This circumstance strongly influenced their relations, not only with each other but also with the other powers. Henry was apparently seriously interested in Ferdinand's niece, Joanna, the recently widowed Queen of Naples, and by the summer of 1505 had received offers from both Maximilian and Louis XII of France.[13] However, it may be seriously doubted whether he had any intention of remarrying, and he contented himself for the time being with the betrothal of Catherine of Aragon to his second son, Henry, a match on which Isabella had been particularly keen. After Isabella's death in November 1504, on the other hand, the Castillian succession caused a shadow to fall between them. Isabella's heir was her daughter, Juana, married to Philip of Burgundy, the son of Maximilian. Henry backed Philip and Juana, while Ferdinand opposed them, being anxious to retain a role for himself. In the summer of 1505 Henry caused his son to repudiate his agreement to marry Catherine, and early in 1506 entered into a firm alliance with Philip, who then went on to secure his position in Castile. In the summer, Ferdinand patched up his relations with Louis XII and married his kinswoman Germaine de Foix, signalling a realignment of political forces which pitted Ferdinand and Louis against Henry and Maximilian.[14] Then in September 1506 Philip died, leaving Juana in an exposed position, and Ferdinand regained control of Castile with aristocratic backing. There was nothing that Henry could do about that, but he could draw closer to Margaret of Savoy, Maximilian's daughter, who was Regent of The Netherlands for her young nephew, Charles. A marriage treaty between Charles, then aged seven, and Mary, Henry's younger daughter, was proposed in December 1507 and ratified in October 1508, so at the time of Henry's death in April 1509 the Habsburg alliance seemed secure, and relations with Ferdinand were in cold storage.[15]

The advent of a new King dramatically changed that situation, because Henry VIII was set on war with France, and war required allies. He may have been in love with Catherine of Aragon, a rather woebegone figure since her rejection in 1505, or he may simply have identified Ferdinand as a more promising ally than the hard-up Emperor. In any event, his almost immediate decision to marry her transformed the diplomatic situation. Relations with France became deliberately distant, while those with Spain waxed cordial. Then, in 1511, Louis made the mistake of falling out with the Pope, and Julius put together a Holy League, which Henry joined in November, linking up with Ferdinand and the Venetians. In 1512 he went to war, ostensibly in defence of his claim to the French throne, but really in the hope of emulating Henry V by winning battles in the fields of France.[16] In that, he was moderately successful. Although the army which he sent to Guienne came back with its tail between its legs, his navy retained control of the Channel throughout that year, and in 1513 he took Therouanne and Tournai in the north eastern corner of France. His navy was slightly less successful in that year, but had grown into a powerful fleet.[17] More significantly, James IV had been unable to resist the temptation to exploit Henry's absence in France and declared war on his brother-in-law in August. Less than a month later, his army was crushed and he himself killed by the English under the Earl of Surrey at the battle of Flodden. This was far more important than the King's winning of 'ungracious dogholes' in France and led to the protracted minority of James V, who was barely a year old, and to the complications caused by his widow Margaret's remarriage to Archibald, Earl of Angus – a marriage contracted as much in self-defence as for any other reason. In spite of being gratified by the enthusiastic alliance of Maximilian, by early 1514 Henry was deeply disappointed in his main ally, Ferdinand, who had not only double-crossed him over the Guienne expedition, but had then proceeded to sign a separate peace with Louis in direct contravention of his treaty obligations. Pope Julius II had died in February 1513 and the heart had gone out of the Holy Alliance, so in spite of mobilizing purposefully early in the year, by the time the summer of 1514 arrived the King decided to cut his losses and make peace also. By that treaty he retained possession of Tournai and gave his eighteen-year-old sister Mary in marriage to the fifty-two year-old Louis – a union which lasted only a matter of weeks, as Louis died at the beginning of January 1515.[18] The only person to be thoroughly disillusioned by this outcome was the Archduchess Margaret, who pointed out that Henry, no less than Ferdinand, had bound himself not to make peace without consulting the Emperor, which had not been done. Such was the nature of renaissance diplomacy.

Leaving no direct heir, Louis was succeeded by his energetic young kinsman, Francis of Angoulême, who immediately made his mark by winning the battle of Marignano against the Imperialists in Italy. This victory made Henry green with envy, and for some time there were serious discussions about the possibility of renewing the war.[19] However, that diplomatic situation was defused by Henry's new man of business, Thomas Wolsey. For a variety of reasons, Wolsey was committed to a policy of peace, and although he had risen in the King's confidence by organising the logistics of the 1513 campaign, he now steered Henry in that direction. By the end of 1515, he was Lord Chancellor and Archbishop of York, and in September of that year Leo X was persuaded to create him a Cardinal. No one's influence with the King could equal that of Wolsey, and in 1518 he managed to hijack a papal initiative for a crusade to bring about the Treaty of London. This was in some ways the high-water mark of Henry's international reputation. Forgetting the crusade, all the great (and many of the lesser) powers of Europe came together in London to pledge themselves to universal and perpetual peace. Embedded within this hopeful declaration was a new Anglo-French treaty committing Henry's two-year-old daughter, Mary to a marriage with the even younger Dauphin.[20] Her aunt, also Mary, was by this time off the market, having married Charles Brandon, Duke of Suffolk about four months after King Louis' death. However, the good intentions embodied in the treaty lasted barely a year, because early in 1519 the Emperor Maximilian died, and the contest to succeed him very nearly undid all the good that had been done. Maximilian's grandson, Charles (King of Spain since Ferdinand's death in 1516), Francis I of France and Henry VIII all entered the lists. Henry never had much chance, but the other two were serious, and when Charles emerged victorious in the summer of 1519 the implications were important. Charles now controlled lands on three sides of France, and a resumption of conflict was more or less inevitable.

Both the potential antagonists began to angle for English support. This was less because Henry was a great military power than because of his strategic position on the fourth side of France. By the terms of the Treaty of London, Henry was committed to a personal meeting with Francis, and this duly happened with great pomp and circumstance at the Field of Cloth of Gold in June 1520. Wolsey had been at great pains to make this encounter a magnificent occasion, which it was, but politically it was not a success. The two young Kings were too alike, and their competition quickly turned to emulation, and almost to hostility.[21] The meeting was sandwiched between two less-heralded encounters with the Emperor, and at the end of the day Henry came down on Charles's side. By September 1521, hostilities had been resumed between the two main protagonists, and Henry committed himself to entering the war on the Emperor's side in 1522, provided no agreement had been reached by then. The Emperor, in turn, committed himself to marry the six-year-old Princess Mary when the time should come. However, when 1522 came, Henry was less than enthusiastic. This was partly due to his poverty, and partly to the influence of Cardinal Wolsey, but the military effort of that summer was virtually confined to a raid out of Calais by the Earl of Surrey in September. By 1523 his poverty was no less acute, but the treason of the Duke of Bourbon, who revolted against the King of France, presented an opportunity which could not be ignored and in the autumn he launched a large force led by the Duke of Suffolk into northern France, ostensibly to link up with Charles and Bourbon, who were supposedly advancing from the south and east. However, neither of these allies materialized, and Suffolk's expedition was a failure.[22] Disillusioned by this outcome, and desperate for money, the King did nothing in 1524, although the state of war in theory continued. Then, early in 1525, Francis was defeated and captured at the battle of Pavia and Charles was left in complete control of the situation. Rediscovering his enthusiasm, Henry immediately proposed an ambitious scheme for the partition of France, but the Emperor was not to be drawn. His aims were far more limited, and if Henry wanted to conquer France he would have to do it for himself. Thoroughly disgruntled by this response, Henry allowed Wolsey to commence negotiations with the regency government of Louise of Savoy, and in August 1525 peace was signed at the More, Wolsey's residence in Hertfordshire.[23] By the terms of this treaty, the King effectively changed sides, and committed himself to a diplomatic offensive to persuade the Emperor to settle with his enemy on reasonable terms. Charles, in short, had become far too powerful.

Francis was eventually released by the terms of the treaty of Madrid in January 1526, but soon revealed that he had no intention of abiding by its terms. He quickly put together a league to oppose the Emperor, which England eventually joined, Henry having been further alienated by Charles's repudiation of his treaty obligation to marry Princess Mary, although that can hardly have been unexpected in view of the disparity in their ages.[24] The Princess was duly transferred to the Duke of Orleans, Francis's second son. Meanwhile the King was on a collision course with the papacy over the annulment of his first marriage, and a preoccupied Cardinal almost missed the peace negotiations which were taking place at Cambrai in 1529. England was eventually included in the treaty through some fast footwork on Wolsey's part, but it was almost his last hurrah, because after the fiasco of the Blackfriar's court he fell from favour and power in October of that year.[25] For most of the next decade, relations with the Emperor continued to be frosty on account of the King's matrimonial problems, but they never broke down, because it was not in Charles's interest to make another enemy. At the same time, Henry attempted to rely (vainly, as it turned out) on Francis's diplomatic support in Rome. The most that the French King was able to do for his 'brother' was the postponement of the sentence of excommunication against him in 1536. In 1539 Francis and Charles briefly patched up their differences at the Treaty of Nice, and Henry feared a joint crusade against him. He armed and fortified his kingdom, but he need not have worried. Within a year the pair had fallen out again and were once more competing for his alliance. Meanwhile, the King's position in Ireland had been fraught with difficulties, largely because first Wolsey and then Thomas Cromwell were dissatisfied with the 'hands off' approach which had been sufficient for Henry VII. Their reforming policy commenced with the Lieutenancy of the Earl of Surrey from 1520 to 1522 and consisted largely in the introduction of 'new English' officials. It was, however, characterized by weakness and the unwillingness to expend sufficient money to achieve a military supremacy. It also failed to resolve the continual feuding between the Butlers of Ossory and the Fitzgeralds of Kildare.[26] Repeated commissions and small-scale interventions failed to solve this problem, and when the Earl of Kildare was summoned to London to give an account of himself in 1533, his son, 'Silken Thomas', rose in revolt. Ostensibly this was in resistance to the Royal Supremacy, but its roots were entirely Irish. Lord Ossory appealed for Imperial support and divided the Anglo-Irish community by appealing to the Gaelic Clans. At length, this produced an adequate military response under Sir William Skeffington and the revolt was suppressed. However, apart from the execution of Thomas Fitzgerald and his uncles and the future exclusion of Kildare, this victory achieved nothing.[27] The government struggled on, with mounting distrust between the Anglo-Irish of the Pale and the new English officials, until a new initiative was attempted with the arrival of Sir Anthony St Leger as Lord Deputy in 1540. This was an attempt to incorporate the Gaelic chieftains by persuading them to accept titles under the English Crown, or rather the Irish Crown, because Henry erected the lordship into an autonomous kingdom in 1542. This looked for a while as though it might succeed and led to a period of comparative peace and stability at the end of Henry's reign.[28]

Alarmed by his isolation in 1539-40, by 1542 the King was again hankering after an Imperial alliance, well aware that this would probably mean a further war against France. Charles, released from his obligation to Catherine of Aragon by her death in 1536, was willing enough to embrace Henry as an ally, and a new treaty was signed. Mindful of what had happened in 1513, the King this time decided to take the Scots out first and deliberately provoked a Scottish invasion in November 1542, ambushing and destroying the Scots army at the battle of Solway Moss. A fortnight later, King James V died and left his crown to his week-old daughter, Mary, a situation Henry tried to exploit by bullying the regency government into accepting a marriage between the infant Queen and his own son, the six-year-old Edward.[29] This they ostensibly did by the Treaty of Greenwich in the summer of 1543; however, in December the Scots Parliament repudiated the treaty, and meanwhile the King had missed his cue for an invasion of France. Henry was angry for both reasons, and in April 1544 launched a punitive strike against the Scottish lowlands. The Duke of Norfolk did immense damage and ruined Anglo-Scottish relations for the foreseeable future, but completely failed to reinstate the Treaty of Greenwich. Then, at last, the King launched his long-delayed strike against France in support of the Emperor. However, he sensibly confined his ambition to the taking of Boulogne, which was not Charles's idea of a co-operative campaign, and on the day the town fell the Emperor signed a separate peace, leaving Henry to defend his conquest as best he could. Isolated again, he outfaced a massive attempt by Francis I to recover the town in the summer of 1545, both by confronting his fleet at Portsmouth and by successfully supplying the fortress from the sea.[30] Realizing that he would be unable to achieve his objective without the command of the sea, which he could not see his way to obtaining, Francis made peace in the following year, leaving Boulogne in English hands, with a face-saving clause for its later redemption. When he died, therefore, in January 1547, Henry was in a precarious peace with France, a chilly stand-off with the Emperor, and an unfinished, undeclared war with the Scots. The massive efforts of his foreign policy over thirty-seven years had achieved remarkably little either in terms of territorial expansion or general security. Thanks to his unremitting aggressiveness, he actually had more enemies and fewer friends at the end of his reign than he had had at the beginning.

By comparison with the ducking and weaving in which the old King and his ministers had indulged for so long, the foreign policy of Edward VI's minority was straightforward. The Emperor remained passively hostile, not even acknowledging the boy's accession until he was certain that Mary would not put in a counter-claim. He became even more hostile as the minority regime lurched towards Protestantism in its religious policy, and declined to extend the defensive league of 1543 to cover Boulogne.[31] Francis I followed Henry to the grave in April 1547, and his son and successor, Henry II made no secret of his desire to recover that town, so a showdown there was very likely. However, at first the Lord Protector, the Duke of Somerset concentrated his attention upon Scotland. The Treaty of Greenwich was manifestly unfinished business, and in September 1547 he invaded, winning a crushing victory at Pinkie Cleugh on the 10th. An attempt to consolidate this victory by establishing garrisons across the lowlands was, however, a failure and merely provoked the intervention of the French, who landed six thousand troops at Leith in the summer of 1548. By the treaty of Haddington, Mary was whisked off to France and betrothed to the Dauphin, leaving Somerset's policy dead in the water.[32] He was too obstinate to give up, and planned another major incursion in the summer of 1549. However, before that could happen he was distracted by rebellions in the south of England, and in the midst of the confusion Henry II declared war. Henry undoubtedly expected to recover Boulogne by force of arms, but found it unexpectedly well defended, and was eventually only too glad to take advantage of the desire of Somerset's successor, the Earl of Warwick, to bring the war to an end. By a treaty signed at the end of March 1550, he was constrained to buy back his own town for 400,000 crowns, an outcome which was derided by the military faction in England, but in fact represented a remarkably good deal by the minority council.[33] Thereafter, keenly aware of the hostile signals which continued to emanate from Brussels, Warwick's policy was to become closer to the French, while endeavouring to protect London's trade routes to The Netherlands. It was a delicate balancing act, which helps to explain his enthusiasm for the diversification of trade represented by the Willoughby/Chancellor voyage in search of a north-east passage to China in 1553.[34] In 1551 Edward was betrothed to Princess Elizabeth, Henry's daughter, and there was an exchange of orders of chivalry between the two monarchs which delighted Edward's boyish enthusiasm, but when hostilities were resumed between France and the Empire in 1552, England remained studiously neutral.[35] This was undoubtedly a disappointment to Henry II, but made perfectly good sense in view of England's fragile domestic and financial position. When the young King died in July 1553, the Duke of Northumberland (as Warwick had then become) looked hopefully to France to endorse Jane Grey's claim, but his position collapsed too swiftly for any such support to be forthcoming. Instead, Henry was confronted with a new Queen,

Mary I, whose antecedents were entirely Imperial. It remained to be seen what action he would take.

Mary's foreign policy was defined by her marriage. She had been, in a sense, a Habsburg dependent since the early 1530s, and committed her choice of husband to her cousin the Emperor. Improper as this may have been in a ruling Queen, it produced an immediate response, and by the end of 1553 she was espoused to his son, Philip of Spain.[36] This naturally put relations with France into serious difficulties, but Henry II was not disposed to make a bad situation worse, and confined himself to making threats, although he would probably have supported the Wyatt rebellion if it had continued much longer. In the event, in spite of its unpopularity in England, the marriage duly went ahead in July 1554 and cemented England to the Habsburg cause for the rest of the reign. This settled orientation had its advantages, in that it resolved any potential disputes with London's main trading partner, Antwerp. It also led to a mending of fences with the papacy, from which England had been estranged since 1534. Julius III had appointed Reginald Pole to be Legate to England as soon as news of Mary's accession reached him, but it was not until the end of 1554 that the twenty-year schism was resolved and England returned to the papal obedience, thus ending one of the longest diplomatic stand-offs of the century.[37] Although Mary's council, in framing the marriage treaty, had been at pains to exclude England from participation in the war then ongoing between Charles and Henry, it was always likely that she would be sucked in eventually, and so it proved. Although the council at first opposed involvement, such decisions did not rest with them and in June 1557 Mary joined her husband in fighting the French. At first this intervention appeared to be successful, but in January 1558 it resulted in the loss of Calais, a humiliation which is supposed to have affected the Queen deeply, and the English war effort was generally derided by Philip's advisers as being both too little and offered with a bad grace.[38] Peace negotiations were already in hand when the Queen died in November 1558.

As well as being generally (and unfairly) blamed for the loss of Calais, Philip's reign had an adverse effect upon relations between the Council and the City of London. The merchants there complained bitterly at being excluded from the trade of the New World, and protested that every time they had a dispute with the Flemings (which was often), the King invariably sided with their opponents, irrespective of the merits of the case – a charge which he virtually admitted by explaining the importance of the wealth of the Low Countries to his revenues.[39] In Ireland, Mary's advent resolved one problem, because the introduction of Protestantism by Edward's council had been bitterly resented there and had made little progress against almost universal opposition. However, she could not redeem the failure of St Leger's conciliatory policy with respect to the Gaelic chieftains, and when the Lord Deputy was replaced by Thomas Radcliffe, Lord Fitzwalter in 1556, a fresh and eventually disastrous expedient was attempted. In order to frustrate tribal raids on the Pale, it was decided to plant the lands of Offaly, to the west of the Pale, with English settlers. In 1556 these plantations duly came into existence as King's County and Queen's County, and the settlers were discharged soldiers, making a permanent quasi-military presence and displacing the Irish landholders.[40] This created a malign precedent which was to bedevil English policy in the colony for the next hundred years. Ironically, in due course the Irish were to appeal to King Philip, then Philip II of Spain, to redress these wrongs, an enterprise which proved to be beyond his will or resources. In theory, Scotland should have joined France in its war against England, but in fact it had no will to do so, and attempts by Mary of Guise, the Queen Mother and Regent, to stir the aristocracy into action eventually backfired into rebellion, so Scotland was not a problem as Mary's reign drew to a close.

Elizabeth therefore inherited a war with France, but no conflict with Scotland. The key story of her reign, however, is one of increasing estrangement from Spain, culminating in a war which lasted for eighteen years and determined every other relationship of the period. At first, Elizabeth and Philip were allies, and might have been partners if she had accepted his proposal of marriage in January 1559. But she had no desire to commit herself, and the war was clearly coming to an end. Friends they might be, but nothing closer, and even that became problematical as Elizabeth began to encourage seamen such as John Hawkins into trading ventures which the Spanish regarded as piracy.[41] Within a decade, relations were strained almost to breaking point when Elizabeth authorized the seizure of that Genoese treasure which had been intended for the payment of the Duke of Alba's army in the Low Countries in December 1568. By the time that crisis arose, a number of other things had happened. First, the Scottish lords, calling themselves 'the Lords of the Congregation of Jesus Christ', who were in rebellion against the French-supported and Catholic government of Mary of Guise, appealed for Elizabeth's support. Elizabeth hesitated, but allowed herself to be persuaded by William Cecil into sending limited military assistance. This turned out to be sufficient to tip the balance. Mary died and the French agreed to withdraw, which they did by the terms of the Treaty of Edinburgh, signed in the summer of 1560. The Queen, as it turned out, had struck the right note in Scotland by abandoning her father's claim to suzerainty and proclaiming herself instead the Protector of the Liberties of the Kingdom.[42] Once the Lords were established in control, she grace-fully withdrew, and relations between the two realms continued to be mainly friendly thereafter. Even after Mary's return in August 1561, Elizabeth confined herself to the offering of good advice, and merely tut-tutted when Mary chose Henry, Lord Darnley as her husband in 1565. She was disturbed when the Scots deposed Mary in 1567, but did not hesitate to recognize the government of the young James VI. In 1568 Mary became her problem, but that did not seriously disrupt the amicable relations which prevailed between the two kingdoms.[43]

France presented a different challenge as it collapsed into civil war following the death of Henry II in 1559. There was no need for Elizabeth to become involved at all, but she allowed herself to be persuaded (probably by Lord Robert Dudley) that it would be in her interest to support the Protestants, and possibly to regain Calais thereby. She signed an agreement with the Prince of Conde, and committed troops, which were sent in to garrison Le Havre, offered as a cautionary town for the return of Calais. Unlike Scotland, this campaign went seriously wrong almost from the beginning. The Protestants came to terms with their opponents and turned on their erstwhile allies. Plague broke out in Le Havre and the commander, the Earl of Warwick was forced into a humiliating surrender. Elizabeth insisted that she had not been at war with France, but was nevertheless forced to sign the Treaty of Troyes in 1564, whereby she surrendered all claim to Calais.[44] She had burnt her fingers badly, and was not disposed to intervene again. Instead, she concentrated on maintaining good relations with the Crown of France, which, through the minority of Charles IX and on into his personal rule, was struggling to maintain its authority against the warring factions of Catholic and Protestant. As relations with Spain deteriorated, it began to seem increasingly important to establish good relations with France, and in spite of the vicissitudes of French politics and the failure of the Anjou marriage negotiations, these came to fruition in the Treaty of Blois in 1572. The treaty survived the St Bartholomew's Day massacre of that year, and remained a key to Anglo-French relations down to the assassination of Henry III in 1589, an event which brought the protestant Henry IV to the throne and prompted Philip II to intervene on the Catholic side as the League struggled to establish their anti-king, Charles X.[45] That, in turn, drove Henry into open war with Philip and led Elizabeth to dispatch forces to support him, even after Henry converted to Catholicism in 1593 – a move which caused the majority of Frenchmen to accept him – and transformed the Catholic League into a gang of Spanish pensioners. Henry withdrew from his war with Philip in 1598, and the Queen withdrew her remaining forces from his dominions.

The key to understanding Anglo-Spanish relations during Elizabeth's reign lies in the Low Countries. Philip had not been popular there when he had had visited at his father's behest in 1549, and his rating had not improved during his residence from 1555 to 1559, when he had demonstrated a conspicuous failure to understand the essentially commercial and bourgeois culture of the wealthy Netherlands towns. Philip was altogether too Spanish for their taste, unlike his father, who had understood the region.[46] When he departed for Spain, he left behind him Margaret of Parma as Regent, ostensibly supported by a council of local nobles, but with secret instructions to pay attention only to Cardinal Granvelle, her hispanophile chief minister. Philip had an agenda for The Netherlands, which he desired to bring into a centralized monarchy on the Spanish model. This started with a scheme to rationalize the bishoprics into three archbishoprics, corresponding to the political boundaries of the seventeen provinces.[47] Suspecting his intentions, the nobility resisted and set up a movement, misleadingly called 'the Compromise', to demand the retention of their provincial liberties and a measure of religious toleration. Elizabeth was not directly involved, but her subjects made their sympathies abundantly clear, and in 1566 Margaret embargoed their trade. This did more harm to Antwerp than it did to London, and was soon withdrawn, but the Regent had made more concessions than Philip liked, and he replaced her with the Duke of Alba, who had orders to crush all opposition.[48] That he proceeded to do, arousing in the process the strongest alarm and suspicion in London. Fugitives scattered in all directions, many of them ending up in England, where they were (on the whole) warmly welcomed. It was this suspicion which led Elizabeth to 'borrow' the Genoese money which was on its way to pay his army in December 1568, a move which led to a fresh trade embargo and generally worsening relations. Then, in 1572, while Alba's forces were deployed in Flanders and Hainault in anticipation of a French invasion, Elizabeth expelled those Dutch pirates known as the 'sea beggars'. Whether this was intended as a conciliatory gesture towards Parma or not, we do not know, but the beggars promptly crossed the North Sea to Brill in Holland, which they seized. This reignited the revolt in the northern provinces to a degree that Alba was unable to suppress, and he was recalled.[49] His replacement, the King's half-brother, Don John, was faced with a rebellion which for a time embraced all the seventeen provinces. However, by 1579 the southern provinces had come to terms with his successor, the Duke of Parma (Margaret's son), leaving the seven northern provinces, the signatories of the Union of Utrecht, to continue the war alone.[50]

Again, Elizabeth was not directly involved, but her subjects volunteered in significant numbers to serve in the forces of the United Provinces, and this aroused Philip's further ire. In 1584 William of Orange, the leader of the rebellion, was assassinated, and the Queen, who had declined an offer of the sovereignty of the provinces in 1581, was driven to open intervention. The revolt was in serious danger of collapse, and in 1585 Elizabeth signed with the Estates General an agreement at Nonsuch committing forces to their support in a manner which clearly implied open war with Spain. War was never formally declared, but Philip's seizure of such English traders as he could lay his hands on, and Drake's retaliatory raid on the Caribbean in the autumn of the same year, marked the beginning of hostilities.[51] By 1586, the King of Spain had determined on a massive strike against England, reckoning that he would never be victorious in the Low Countries as long as Elizabeth remained a belligerent. This enterprise, known as 'the Armada', was assembled at Lisbon and Cadiz during 1587, and, in spite of Drake's disruptive raid on Cadiz, was ready to sail in May 1588. It had been immensely expensive, and only sailed at all thanks to the administrative genius of the Duke of Medina Sidonia, who had taken over control in February 1588 when the original commander, the Marquis of Santa Cruz, died.[52] Although battered and further disrupted by storms, the Armada entered the Channel in good order at the end of July. It was then shadowed and attacked by the English fleet, but held its formation well and arrived at Calais with only minimal losses about a week later. There Medina Sidonia discovered to his alarm that the Duke of Parma, who was supposed to be supplying more than half his army, would not be ready for another week. Lacking a deep-water port capable of sheltering his fleet, he had no option but to stay where he was, in the open roadstead.[53] The English Admiral, Lord Howard of Effingham, sent in the fire ships and broke up the formidable formation, before attacking with his whole fleet off Gravelines the following morning. The battle that followed was a massacre. The English guns fired far more rapidly than their Spanish counterparts, inflicting terrible casualties. Only about three ships were actually sunk, but several others were rendered unseaworthy and their crews decimated, before a change of wind direction enabled the Armada to escape into the North Sea. Howard pursued them for a way, but the danger of invasion was now past and, with plague on board his ships, he returned to port and demobilized as quickly as possible.[54] It had been a great victory, which the English government was quick to attribute to the mercy of God. *Flavit deus et dissipati sunt* (God blew, and they were scattered) declared the memorial medal, doing rather less than justice to Lord Howard and his men. Both sides claimed Divine approval, and the English apparently had the better case.

The war, nevertheless, went on, with varying fortunes. The English failed in 1589 both to take Lisbon and to destroy the remains of the Armada, but succeeded spectacularly in capturing Cadiz in 1596.[55] Two further, but smaller, Spanish armadas were dispersed by storms in 1596 and 1597, but the English Islands voyage of 1597 was a failure, as was Drake's final raid on the Caribbean in 1595. After barely surviving with English help, the Dutch at last discovered a leader of genius in the person of William's son, Maurice of Nassau, and after the death of the Duke of Parma in 1593 made steady progress against his less talented successors. During the early 1590s the main theatre of operations switched from the Low Countries to France, particularly Normandy and Brittany. Having learnt a sharp lesson from the 'Gran Armada', Philip decided to strike at England from closer range, and in 1592 attempted, with the support of the Catholic League, to establish a base in Brittany. This was, of course, resisted by Henry IV, and Elizabeth was prompted by the imminent danger to send a force to his aid, led by Sir John Norris. Taking advantage of the surge of royalist support following Henry's conversion to Catholicism in 1593, Norris was successful in dislodging the main Spanish garrison from Crozon in 1594, a victory which was less celebrated than it should have been, given the formidable reputation of the Spanish army.[56] Philip rebuilt his Atlantic fleet after the Armada fiasco, and the English never succeeded in capturing the *flota*, or treasure fleet, from the New World, which remained an objective of naval policy until the war finally came to an end in 1604. By that time both Philip (1598) and Elizabeth (1603) were dead; the France of Henry IV had re-established itself as a major power; and the Dutch had consolidated their hold on the northern Netherlands. There was no clear-cut victory for either side, but Spain was financially exhausted, and the war party in the English council was reduced to a minority. England was no more a Great Power than she had been in the reign of Henry VIII, but her navy was second to none, and her soldiers could acquit themselves well when the occasion required. She could expect to be taken seriously in international diplomacy.

The failed armadas of 1596 and 1597 had been aimed at Ireland rather than England, and it was probably there that Philip missed his best opportunity of striking at Elizabeth. Years of abortive rebellion, of plantations, and of persistent religious strife had culminated in 1595 in the great revolt of the Earl of Tyrone, known to the Irish as the Nine Years War or the First War of Independence. Tyrone had succeeded to an unprecedented degree in bringing unity and discipline to the Gaelic tribes. His army defeated the English army under Henry Bagenal, the Marshal of Ireland at Yellow Ford in August 1597, and forced Elizabeth to commit major forces to the island at a time of great hardship and financial stress, but Philip, although appealed to, did not respond.[57] He was old and sick, and his resources were already overstretched. The Queen at first entrusted her response to her favourite, the Earl of Essex, but he made a disastrous mess of it, and made way for a professional soldier in the person of Charles Blount, Lord Mountjoy. When Philip III's belated and inadequate intervention failed at Kinsale in 1601, Mountjoy gradually gained the upper hand and brought Tyrone to the point of surrender in the last days of Elizabeth's life, in March 1603. She died before the news reached her. So Ireland was, in a sense, pacified. Its government was now organized on English lines by counties, and the major land-holders were either English or Anglo-Irish. But Gaelic loyalties were not eradicated, and found a powerful rallying point in the Catholic missions, which were much more successful in Ireland than they were in England. By 1600 the native Irish were a Catholic people in a sense which they had not been fifty years before, and the attempts of the English to impose Protestantism were largely responsible. The more the reformed faith was associated with the English ascendancy, the stronger the Gaelic-Catholic alliance became, until it burst out into renewed rebellion in 1641.[58]

Of Scotland, by contrast, there is little to be said. The English council was perturbed when the fourteen-year-old James took his French cousin, Esmé Stuart, into his favour in 1579. Esmé succeeded in bringing about the fall of the Regent, the Earl of Morton, in September 1580, and his execution the following June. However, in spite of being created a Duke in 1581, James awakened fears of a Catholic revival in Scotland, and the Protestant peers combined against him, forcing him to return to France in 1582.[59] Elizabeth had not been required to intervene, although her agents and representatives were active, and the council could breathe easily again. James made correct noises when his mother was executed in February 1587, but soon made it clear that he did not intend to do anything. After all, he had not seen his mother for nearly twenty years and they had little in common least of all their religion. Elizabeth made it clear that Mary's death had not affected her transmission to him of her claim to the throne, and for the next fifteen years he concentrated on keeping the right side of his formidable cousin in case she should change her mind. The Queen never explicitly acknowledged him to be her heir, but he was so recognized by the political establishment of England.[60] In spite of Henry VIII's last Succession Act, there was no realistic alternative and, although unrepealed, the act was effectively ignored. Scotland and England were about to be united under a single crown, so Henry and Somerset's ambition was realized at last, although not in the way that they envisaged – or would have wished.

Tudor diplomacy was immensely complicated and was carried on both by resident ambassadors and by special missions. Henry VIII maintained envoys in all the major courts of Europe, except France in time of war, and Rome after 1534, but still conducted treaty negotiations by way of special embassies, both sent and received. Diplomatic despatches, particularly those of Eustace Chapuys, form one of our principal sources for a knowledge of his reign, although they must be used with caution because of their author's special agenda.[61] Edward's council continued these practices, including the estrangement from Rome, but ran into difficulties when the ambassadors accredited to the Imperial court sought leave to have religious services according to their own usage. The Imperial ambassador in London had his Mass, but reciprocity was not conceded, further taxing an already strained relationship. After the first year of her reign, Mary maintained no embassies either in Spain or the Low Countries, and that in France was closed in June 1557. She did, however, resume diplomatic relations with the Pope, and entertained special envoys from her husband while he was absent – such as the Count of Feria, who came to her in 1558. Elizabeth, like her father, maintained a full set of embassies (again excepting Rome), but also her councillors, especially Sir Francis Walsingham and Sir William Cecil, kept agents and spies in all the countries with which she did business. This was especially true of Scotland and France, both countries where complex internal tensions needed to be constantly monitored.[62] Ambassadors, of course, retained their own spy networks, especially among the French Huguenots, and Spanish ambassadors in England, particularly de Spes and Mendoza, were in regular contact with the English Catholics, as well as having informants within the court. One of the principal tasks of a Renaissance Prince was to maintain his (or her) own honour, and the interests of his realm, in the face of foreign competition, rivalry and hostility. This meant that foreign affairs occupied an immense amount of time and energy in each of the Tudor reigns, feet often paddling furiously beneath the apparent calm of a secure relationship, and diplomacy was one of the sure routes to royal favour. From Sir Thomas Boleyn to Sir Nicholas Throgmorton, fortunes were to be made in foreign embassies.

The Trouble With God

In the late fifteenth century the English were celebrated for their piety. According to one Italian account, great ladies habitually went to Mass accompanied by pages bearing their liturgical books. We know from the works of Eamon Duffy that parochial cults, such as that of St John of Bridlington, were flourishing, and that the *ars moriendi* concentrated the minds of the faithful on the last rites and on the doctrine of purgatory.[1] Dissent, known as Lollardy, did exist, but it was confined to a small minority, mainly in London and the Home Counties. The Lollards, although sustained by a network of 'known men', lacked both intellectual and social leadership, and appeared to pose no threat to the established order. Their rejection of transubstantiation was particularly mocked by the orthodox:

> The bread is flesh in our credence,
> The wine is blood without doubtance,
> They that believe not this with circumstance,
> But doth themselves with curious wit enhance,
> To hell pit shall they wend …

wrote Thomas Ashby, an Augustinian canon, in his commonplace book.[2] Nevertheless, all was not well with the Church. Absenteeism was a perpetual problem, and although few followed the doctrinal teachings of John Wycliffe, his attacks on clerical wealth and greed prompted a more positive response. It would be an exaggeration to describe this as anticlericalism, because respect for the sacramental functions of the priesthood was undiminished, but it did mean that regard for the 'clerical proletariat' of those in minor orders was undermined, and that the laity were inclined to look with a jaundiced eye upon clerical claims to moral superiority. This was particularly true of the religious orders, whose function of maintaining the *opus dei*, or constant fount of prayer to God, had gone out of fashion by the end of the fourteenth century. Withdrawal from the world ceased to be seen as a way of remedying its ills, and the great monasteries found it hard to make up the numbers which they lost to plague and indifference after about 1350.[3] Houses like St Peter's at Gloucester, which held many properties within the town, found themselves constantly at odds with the urban authorities over their management policies and leasing structures. The Abbey was also regularly at loggerheads with the Mayor and aldermen over matters of jurisdiction, and feelings occasionally ran high, even escalating to violence.[4] This had nothing to do with the teachings of the Church – indeed, when the protagonists came to make their wills, they were mostly conspicuous for their orthodoxy – but it did have quite a lot to do with suspicions that the community was not well served by its clergy. Within the towns, and especially in London, there was also the issue raised by improving lay education. Sometimes this led to a demand for the Bible to be in English, but more often to a kind of contempt for the average parish priest or curate. There was no recognized scheme of clerical training, and very few had advanced beyond the most basic of schooling. They were literate to the extent of being able to read the Latin services, but had no theological or biblical learning. This meant that they had no ability to answer the kind of questions which spiritually aware laymen were increasingly inclined to ask, except by repeating the formulae of ecclesiastical authority. This was a practice which the laity found increasingly irritating.[5] There were, of course, learned clergy, trained in the universities, but they were seldom to be found in ordinary parish cures. They were for the most part deans, prebendaries and archdeacons, and although they might hold several livings, probably did not reside in any of them. Their preaching abilities were mostly tested in the cathedrals, and sermons were rare at parish level, unless they were supplied by Franciscan or Dominican friars.

There were, therefore, tensions within the Church when Henry VII came to the throne. There had always been tensions between the higher clergy and the lower, between the different styles of piety they represented, and between clergy and laity over tithe payments and other dues. However, to these were now added educated discontent with popular piety and dissatisfaction with the clergy who offered it. This was largely due to the materialistic emphasis which much of that piety had acquired, based on what was called 'works theology'.[6] This involved the accumulation by each individual of sufficient good works to outweigh their sins on judgement day – a credit balance in the heavenly ledger. Such works could be very varied in their nature, from acts of mercy and sheer kindness to attendance at Mass and making large offerings to the Church. This inevitably created the impression that the well-off could buy their way into heaven, a notion which was anathema to the educated, both laity and clergy, but also gave the humble an opportunity to earn their salvation by their own pious efforts and those of their friends and kindred. Since receiving the sacraments were 'good works' in this sense, the clergy held the keys to heaven, and woe betide the cross-grained individual who found himself excommunicated. The priest had a high calling, and Church leaders were uneasily aware that many of their humbler colleagues failed to live up to that calling. It was this unease which lay behind John Colet's famous sermon, delivered to convocation in 1511.

> Wherefore I came hither today, fathers, to warn you that in this your council, with all your mind, ye think upon the reformation of the church. But forsooth I came not willingly, for I knew mine own unworthiness. I saw beside how hard it was to please the precise judgement of so many men ...[7]

By reformation, Colet meant education and discipline, but it is significant that, even so, there were murmurings of 'heresy' among those who might find themselves in the firing line. It was easy to brand every critic a heretic, no matter how positive his intentions. Popular piety might well be flourishing, and church building programmes running at a high level. Shrines and other centres of cult observances were also doing well, but the Church was nevertheless divided against itself in a manner which was to be highly significant when it came under real attack, first from the King and then from the Lutherans.[8]

Henry VII had no trouble with God, or with the Church. His personal piety was conventional and active, although he did have a tendency to fund his new foundations by diverting the revenues from decayed ecclesiastical institutions rather than out of his own pocket. He established new houses for the Observant Franciscans at Canterbury, Newcastle and Southampton, as well as three others for the Conventuals, and built the Savoy hospital in London for one hundred poor people. He also encouraged his mother, and others, in their pious benefactions, allowing the Lady Margaret considerable influence over Episcopal appointments. Relations with the papacy were exemplary. Innocent VIII, for a variety of reasons, was anxious to bring an end to the political confusion in England which had resulted from the deposition of Edward V, and hastened to recognize the victor of Bosworth. When appealed to for a dispensation for the King's marriage, he not only granted it, but declared an anathema against any who challenged his title.[9] His successors, Alexander VI (1492–1503) and Julius II (1503–13) were equally anxious to retain the support of the King of England in their attempts to confront French or Spanish aggression in Italy. As a result, they turned a blind eye to his modest infringements of ecclesiastical privileges, such as the curtailment of sanctuary and the removal of benefit of clergy from those in minor orders, actions which gratified the laity at no expense to himself.[10] He also sanctioned the persecution of heretics under the existing ecclesiastical laws, even earning credit for orthodoxy by intervening personally to convert a priest burned at Canterbury, 'so he died as a Christian'. About seventy persons were tried and convicted for heresy in the course of his reign, although only three were actually burned.[11] Of course, the King did not have much option over these convictions, which were carried out under the canon law, but he did sanction the capital punishment by issuing writs *de haeretico comburendo*, which he appears to have shown no reluctance to do. The Pope was happy enough to endorse Henry's collaboration with Cardinal Morton over Church matters, and the King supported Alexander's jubilee indulgence of 1501, allowing it to be preached throughout the kingdom. Both his sons were brought up in the humanist intellectual tradition, which privileged Bible reading and had no time for the banalities of popular religion, but that is the only sign that his religious views were not entirely conventional, and even in that he did not transgress the fashion prevalent in Rome at the time. He did not, however, repeal the Act of Provisors and Praemunire, and his attitude towards papal jurisdiction was more ambivalent than might at first appear.[12]

Although dramatic in some respects, the advent of Henry VIII made no difference to this relationship. Morton was dead by that time, but the council continued to be dominated by Archbishop Warham and Bishop Richard Fox until these made way in 1512 for the King's almoner, Thomas Wolsey. Wolsey was a priest by force of circumstance rather than by vocation, and never let his clerical status stand in the way of his service to the King, but it did mean that he could be rewarded with benefices rather than lands. He became Bishop of Lincoln in March 1514 and was translated to York in September of the same year, following the death of Cardinal Bainbridge. In September 1515, yielding to persistent pressure from Henry, Leo X created him Cardinal.[13] By that time, the King of England was well established as *persona grata* in the curia. He had joined Julius II's Holy League against France in 1511, and made peace (against his inclination) when earnestly bidden to do so by Pope Leo in 1514. At this point, his personal piety seemed to be as conventional as his father's. He went on pilgrimage to Walsingham to celebrate the birth of his son in January 1511, and offered scores of pound to the shrines of Our Lady of Pew, St Edward the Confessor, St Bridget of Sion and several others.[14] He made no bones about allowing one papal official to be replaced by another in the see of Worcester in 1522, and in 1521 wrote (at least partly) the *Assertio Septem Sacramentorum*, a defence of the seven sacraments against Luther, which roundly asserted the papal authority over all such matters. The clouds on this sunny horizon were no bigger than a man's hand. Parliament had in 1512 approved a further measure against benefit of clergy, which prompted a response from Pope Leo in the form of a decree that no priest should be subject to lay jurisdiction on any issue whatsoever. Three years later, when the anti-clerical Londoners were pursuing the Bishop's officers over the death of Richard Hunne, the King was appealed to and set up a disputation on the extent of ecclesiastical jurisdiction, in the course of which Abbot Richard Kidderminster of Winchcombe argued that the King had no right to touch the Lord's anointed priests, while Dr Henry Standish denied that any papal decree upholding the immunity of those in minor orders had any validity in England.[15] For this opinion he was summoned before convocation on a charge of heresy, and convocation was in turn accused by the King's judges of a praemunire. A first-class row seemed to be in prospect, but neither side had any will for a breech, and Wolsey was able to cobble up a compromise, whereby the clergy apologized to the King without conceding that he had been right, and Henry made a vague declaration about recognizing no superior authority on earth, without specifically denying the papal claims. Although this jurisdictional issue did no go away, it remained dormant, and relationships were apparently back to their best when Henry set out to secure the annulment of his marriage to Catherine of Aragon.[16]

He was undoubtedly relying on his reputation as a good Christian prince to secure this divorce, and that was one of the reasons why he was so insistent on the biblical argument from the Book of Leviticus. Unfortunately he miscalculated, and the Pope was not amused at being instructed in biblical exegesis by a mere laymen, even if he was a prince. There were, of course, other factors. Catherine was the Emperor's aunt, and Charles, who was powerful in Rome, was determined that his family honour should not be besmirched. The marriage had been properly dispensed by Pope Julius II, and Clement VII was not minded to allow his predecessor's judgement to be called in question.[17] The issue also raised in an acute form the question of the limitations of canon law. Was this a canonical matter, as the Pope's lawyers argued, or was it a matter of the law of God, as Henry insisted? For all these reasons the King's cause was delayed, postponed and sidelined for nearly five years, as Clement hoped against hope that the King would change his mind or go away. Enraged and frustrated, by 1530 Henry was determined to secure a solution from the courts within his own realm, and by 1532 was prepared to break with the papacy altogether in order to secure that. He had lashed out, first at Wolsey and then at the clergy in general, with charges of praemunire, which they had bought off first with money and then with an equivocal submission, so that by 1533 he was reasonably sure that no clerical opposition within England would be effective against him.[18] He then allowed his chief minister, Thomas Cromwell, to introduce into Parliament the Bill in Restraint of Appeals, and to follow that with a Bill of Supremacy in 1534. By becoming acts, these measures severed the jurisdictional links between England and Rome, taking the English Church into schism. Although claiming to be reinstating an ancient tradition, these acts also created the Royal Supremacy, replacing the authority of Rome not with that of Canterbury, but with the secular power of the Crown.[19] Although an anointed prince, the Supreme Head was a layman.

In spite of his reliance on biblical arguments, Henry always insisted that he had no quarrel with the doctrines of the Church, and on the whole he was correct. He had always believed that it was the right, and the duty, of all Christian men to read the Bible, a belief he had absorbed at an early age from his Erasmian tutors. Although there is no evidence that he thought much about it before the 1530s, in due course this conviction was to lead him to the important endorsement of an English translation. Although conservative clerics cried heresy, there was actually nothing in the official teaching of the Church which forbade such translations, even after the Council of Trent. It was, however, an ancient tradition that the scriptures should be available only in Latin, which gave the literate clergy a controlling say in all questions of exegesis. In other words, the appearance of the Bible in English was a blow against a clerical monopoly rather than against the doctrine of the Church.[20] Henry claimed that his power extended only to the *potestas iurisdictionis*, and did not touch the *potestas ordinis* – in other words, he could not exercise the priestly function of administering the sacraments – in spite of which he took it upon himself to decide what constituted true doctrine, and how the Church should conduct its worship. He did this in three (or perhaps four) stages: the Ten Articles of 1536; the Bishops' Book of 1537 (which did not carry the King's authority); the Act of Six Articles of 1539; and the King's Book of 1543. None of these documents is heretical, although all are cautious on such matters as the doctrine of purgatory, the use of images, and the honour due to saints. The last two are more 'conservative' in that they place great emphasis on transubstantiation in the Mass, and insist on clerical celibacy and on the observation of vows taken in religion.[21] However, these fairly subtle changes of emphasis do not represent significant changes in the King's attitude. It is the fact that the first two are known to have been influenced by Thomas Cromwell and Archbishop Cranmer which have caused them to be regarded as more 'reforming'; whereas the latter two, influenced by the Duke of Norfolk and Bishop Gardiner of Winchester, are thought to represent a reaction in the King's thinking. In fact, Henry remained more or less consistent in his doctrine, and his reforming agenda was confined to matters such as the English Bible, the pruning of the calendar (removing some of the more luxuriant growth of saints' days) and, of course, the dissolution of the monasteries, none of which were affected by the alleged conservatism of the period 1539–43.[22]

Henry had never had much time for monks. Even in his comparatively thoughtless youth he had not endowed or founded religious houses, or made significant contributions to their revenues. In that, he was a true follower of Erasmus, who spent most of his adult life trying to escape from the fact that he had been professed in his youth. Most of the Abbots and Priors had accepted the Royal Supremacy with little fuss, but Cromwell knew that papal supporters lurked in the cloisters of England, and that the wealth of the monasteries hung upon the emaciated frame of the religious life like an overlarge coat. For both these reasons, a drastic pruning was called for, and when the King ordered a stock-taking of the Church in 1535, the *valor ecclesiasticus* gave him a chance to assess the scale of the task.[23] At first it seems that a pruning was all that was intended, and when commissioners were sent out to assess the state of the religious houses in 1536 they were given fairly neutral instructions. However, attitudes quickly hardened, and soon the commissioners were left in no doubt that their brief was to find fault, which they did with imaginative enthusiasm. Armed with these results, Cromwell then turned to Parliament to pass a Dissolution Act. Even so, there seems to have been no intention of bringing the religious life to an end, but rather to dissolve the smaller houses and transfer their inmates to 'the great solemn monasteries of the realm, wherein, thanks be to God, religion is right well kept and observed'.[24] What changed this attitude was probably the small number taking up the offer of transfer – most preferred a faculty to return to the world – and the enthusiasm with which the laity began to petition for grants of the newly acquired property. This last factor changed Cromwell's mind, and from intending to create a new endowment of Crown property, he decided that Henry's political interests would be better served by creating instead a large body of men committed to the Royal Supremacy by the purchase of former monastic lands. Pressure began to be applied to the 'great solemn monasteries', and over the next three years they surrendered one by one. By the spring of 1540 the last had gone, and a thousand-year-old way of life had come to an end.[25] The monks may have been drones, and were frequently at odds with their local communities, but there were many who regretted their passing and that northern demonstration known as the Pilgrimage of Grace was, partly at least, raised in their defence. The friars, however, were not drones; they worked in the world, preaching and caring for the sick, and were generally well regarded. Nevertheless their houses went down in 1538 with surprisingly little fuss, either from the friars themselves or from their communities. Perhaps the relatively easy transition from a friar's habit to the secular priesthood was a factor there; certainly most of the ex-regulars were readily absorbed into the parochial system. The ease with which these dissolutions were achieved and the lands sold off must raise questions about the prevailing religious climate of the country, which is generally supposed to have been conservative, and where reforming buds were tender shoots. It argues a robust materialism in the assessment of profit and loss and a lack of sentiment about ancient institutions.[26] In that, the King seems to have been at one with his subjects. When Henry came to make his will at the end of 1546, it was, in religious terms, strictly conventional, endowing thousands of Masses for the repose of his soul. The King knew that he had a problem with the Church, but not with God, whose representative on earth he claimed to be.

Henry remained consistently hostile to Martin Luther, whose views on Justification and on the nature of the Divine presence in the Eucharist he found abhorrent. Anyone embracing such opinions in public was liable to share the fate of John Lambert, burnt on the King's personal insistence for Eucharistic heresy in 1538.[27] Nevertheless there were those about Henry who were much more ambivalent, and these were known as Evangelicals, or, more straightforwardly, reformers. They shared the King's Catholic reforming agenda, but were privately prepared to admit some merit in the Lutheran position. Because these Evangelicals were strongly committed to the Royal Supremacy, Henry tended to favour them in the last five years of his life, and gave them a majority on the body of executors which he set up to implement his will. They were also favoured by his last Queen, Catherine Parr, and dominated the Privy Chamber. After the fall of Thomas Cromwell in 1540, this party was cautiously led by Archbishop Thomas Cranmer, who, as Cromwell had once noted, seemed to be able to disagree with Henry in a way which nobody else dared to do.[28] It should therefore have come as no surprise that Cranmer's Homilies, issued in the summer of 1547, contained several quasi-Lutheran propositions, or that Parliament should have repealed the Act of Six Articles at its first Edwardian session in December of the same year. For the next eighteen months, the Church in England had no standard of orthodoxy beyond its well-recognized estrangement from the papacy, and Bishop Stephen Gardiner found himself in prison for insisting on the traditional doctrine of the Mass. The same session of Parliament which repealed the Six Articles also dissolved the chantries, which were foundations designed to offer prayers for the dead, and represented another step in the Evangelical programme.[29] Then in 1549 came two developments which marked the transfer to Protestantism, both, significantly, implemented by Parliament rather than convocation. The first was the imposition of a vernacular liturgy, known as the *Book of Common Prayer*, which not only replaced the traditional Latin liturgy, but abolished the Mass in favour of a communion of the people. Although the book was based on the Sarum rite, this represented a major change in parochial practice and was much resented. There was general grumbling, riots in some places, and a major disturbance in Devon and Cornwall.[30] English people might be happy with the Royal Supremacy, but not when it was used to deprive them of the Mass, which was an ancient and much-respected rite. The second development was the abolition of the rule of celibacy for all those in major orders, a change of lifestyle which had been a subject of acrimonious debate between conservatives and Evangelicals for a generation.[31]

Although no doctrinal code had yet been issued, the English Church by the summer of 1549 was moderately but firmly Protestant. Most of the bishops either supported this move or acquiesced in it, only Gardiner of Winchester, Edmund Bonner of London and Cuthbert Tunstall of Durham being deprived for their opposition. The most vociferous objector was the Princess Mary, the heir to the throne. She greeted the implementation of the new liturgy at Whitsun 1549 by causing the Mass to be celebrated with especial splendour in her chapel at Kenninghall and promptly appealed to the Imperial ambassador for his support. Charles welcomed this opportunity to put pressure on the English government and instructed his ambassador, François van der Delft, to demand assurances.[32] Mary's protest was based not so much on the defence of the true faith as on the protection of her father's settlement, which, she argued, should not be touched until Edward came of age. The ambassador ignored that qualification and made his demands as instructed. A compromise was eventually reached, because (as the council pointed out) no licence could be issued to defy the King's laws. The council agreed to tolerate her mass in private, and she agreed not to welcome the general public to her chapel. It was an uneasy arrangement, but the Princess had made her point, and the Emperor was not prepared to take the matter further.[33] By 1550, Protestantism was strong in the council and the court, and the young King was emerging as a committed radical whose views were closer to those of the Swiss reformers, Martin Bucer and Hienrich Bullinger, than they were to Luther. This radical movement was led at court by the Scots reformer John Knox and in the country by the controversial Bishop of Worcester, John Hooper. Its members were dissatisfied with the 1549 Prayer Book as being insufficiently Protestant, and in 1552 they succeeded in persuading Archbishop Cranmer to issue a replacement, cutting out all prayers for the dead and every mention of the intercession of the saints. The Eucharist was also simplified and its communion aspect strengthened.[34] Conservatives seem not to have bothered to protest against these revisions, since they had lost the Mass, which was central to their devotions, in 1549, and one heretical liturgy was much like another. In 1553 the Protestant reformation was in a sense completed by the issue of a doctrinal statement in Forty Two Articles, which made clear the rejection not only of traditional Catholicism but also of the radical innovations of Anabaptism, which were infiltrating the 'left wing' of the reformation. Genuine Protestants were a small minority in the population at large, but they were strong at the top, and led enthusiastically by the King. So, by the summer of 1553 the Church of England was thoroughly reformed by law, the Parliament having been a willing instrument in all these changes – or apparently so.[35]

When Edward died in July 1553, he left instructions that he was to be succeeded not by his lawful heir, Mary, but by his Protestant cousin, Jane Grey. This change was not at all to the liking of the political nation, and even the Protestants were divided, so when the Duke of Northumberland attempted to uphold the King's wishes, he was defeated, and Mary came to the throne. She had, apparently, made her religious position abundantly clear, and most people, at all social levels, liked what they saw. She was committed to the Mass, to the traditional ceremonies of the Church, and to 'religion as King Henry left it'.[36] It turned out that she was equally committed to the papal authority and to the Church of the 1520s, but that was not at once apparent. She started cautiously, issuing a bland proclamation on 18 August, expressing her devotion to the 'old faith', without explaining exactly what that was, and proceeded to repeal the Edwardian statutes in the second session of her first parliament. By 20 December the Mass was back, the clergy were again supposed to be celibate, and the ecclesiastical clock had been turned back to 1546.[37] Mary had no desire to be styled Head of the Church, which was a part of her official title, and took refuge, like Elizabeth, in an 'etc' clause. Quite apart from theological objections, it was a title which no woman could hold. Nevertheless she exercised its powers, conducting a royal visitation in March 1554 aimed at removing Protestant – and particularly married – clergy from their cures. Several bishops, including Holgate of York and Hooper of Worcester, and many hundreds of incumbents fell victims to this purge. Having thus restored the sacraments to their proper place in the Church order, Mary then proceeded to marry that good Catholic Prince, Philip of Spain, in July 1554, Bishop Stephen Gardiner of Winchester conducting the ceremony in his own cathedral on the 25th of the month. Gardiner had been appropriately but secretly dispensed for this purpose, but the realm was still in schism, a fact which Philip and his entourage blandly ignored.[38] The task of restoring the Church to the Roman obedience was then effectively entrusted to Philip, who had the right kind of influence in the Curia, and he began negotiations with Julius III. The main obstacle from the English point of view was that Parliament had dissolved the monasteries and most of their property had been sold on to the aristocracy. It was only when Julius consented to waive the Church's right to those lands that agreement was reached, and Cardinal Pole was able to return and issue the official dispensation. Even so, the lawyers insisted on including the text of the dispensation in the Act of Repeal, thus ensuring that the restored Roman Church was by 'law established', just as its Edwardian predecessor had been.[39] Mary was not happy with this compromise, but became convinced of its necessity, and yielded to her husband's judgement – as, eventually, did Cardinal Pole.

The English people, on the whole, did not care very much about the papacy. They had been happy enough with Henry's supremacy, but they did like the return of the traditional sacraments, particularly the Mass, and were content with what were called 'the Queen's proceedings'. However, they needed re-educating as a Catholic flock, and many of the clergy (particularly the younger ones) needed retraining for their new role. Pole and his team devoted a great deal of attention to this problem, through visitations, 'goodly sermons', and the publication of such pastoral guidance as Edmund Bonner's *Profitable and Necessary Doctrine* and Thomas Watson's *Holesome and Catholic Doctrine concerning the Seven Sacraments*.[40] The results were patchy. In some places, particularly the universities, 'devotion was well restored', but in others such as London there was more reluctance. Pole decided that 'sermon gadding' was not an answer as far as the capital was concerned, and concentrated on the discipline of observing ceremonics, on the ground that good habits would translate into pious obedience. He may not have been right, but he could not have known that his time would be so short. It had been likely, since the failure of Mary's pregnancy in the summer of 1555, that the Catholic regime would be confined to her lifetime, but there was no means of knowing that that would be so limited. Criticism of the priorities of Mary's Church on the grounds of a lack of urgency are thus beside the point. The infrastructure was well restored, Episcopal authority refurbished, and Catholic piety encouraged.[41] However, the Pope was not popular, and the fact that he had been restored through the agency of Mary's even more unpopular consort did his cause no good whatsoever. It would be an exaggeration to say that Pole and his bishops were swimming against the tide, but the ghost of Henry VIII nevertheless loomed large over the Church between 1553 and 1558. Nor was everyone happy with the restored Mass. Protestants may well have been more numerous than the prevailing atmosphere of conformity would suggest. In towns such as Norwich,

Gloucester and London there were many – most of whom kept their heads down when the political tide turned against them. However, there were some who felt called upon to 'testify', and others at loggerheads with their neighbours who were only too happy to denounce them. Altogether some eight hundred fled into exile abroad, and an indeterminate number sought refuge in quieter parts of England.[42] Well over a thousand ended up before the ecclesiastical courts on charges of heresy – usually the denial of transubstantiation – of which nearly three hundred were executed. The severity of this persecution has cast a cloud over Mary's Church (and her reign) ever since, but it has to be seen in context. The burning of recalcitrant or relapsed heretics was a duty imposed upon Catholic princes, and one which Mary took with particular seriousness. It was necessary to purge the land of their contaminating presence, lest others be infected.[43] This was a responsibility which the Queen at first envisaged as involving the removal of a few leaders to force the rest into submission, but this turned out to be a mistake, and as the rank and file went to the stake also, the leading bishops drew back. Some lay magistrates were keen persecutors, however, and kept up the pressure, urged on by the Queen's conscience. In the circumstances it is easy to see why this minority of defiant Protestants created such a problem, and why the authorities reacted as they did, but their actions were not well received. Most Englishmen did not regard heresy as a serious crime, unlike theft or murder, and although most of the crowds which turned up to witness burnings were motivated mainly by curiosity, it was often not difficult for fellow believers to set up a demonstration in sympathy with the victims. These demonstrations were an embarrassment to the authorities, because they indicated the limits of the Church's evangelical success, but they never threatened to get out of hand and alarmist reports to that effect were exaggerated.[44] Significantly, the Queen's death stopped the persecution dead in its tracks, long before there was any certainty what Elizabeth's policy would be. In spite of all the exonerating circumstances and the positive achievements of her Church, it was the persecution which earned Mary the sobriquet 'Bloody' – and not without reason. Mary believed that she was God's agent for the restoration of His truth, but the old traditions of the Church turned out to have a dark side.

Elizabeth, likewise, believed that she was on a mission and directly responsible to God. Her Protestantism may have been eccentric by Edwardian standards, even old-fashioned, but it was genuine enough; her private collections of prayers and meditations make that abundantly clear.[45] On her accession she made no demonstration of allegiance, but those who were expecting her to restore the reformed faith were not disappointed. 'I am very much afraid', the

Count of Feria wrote on 14 November 1558, 'that she will not be well disposed in matters of religion', and he noted that all those most favoured by her, including William Cecil, were heretics.[46] On her entry into London, and ahead of her coronation, she sent out coded messages to the same effect, embracing the English Bible and walking out of Mass at the elevation. Consequently no one was particularly surprised when the Bills of Supremacy and Uniformity came before Parliament in January 1559. The bishops resisted both in the House of Lords to the best of their ability, but they were depleted in numbers because Philip's quarrel with the Pope had resulted in English business being neglected in the Curia in 1557 and 1558, with the result that there were a number of vacancies.[47] Resistance was unavailing against the Bill of Supremacy, where only a few lay peers supported them, but it almost prevailed against the Bill of Uniformity, which re-established the Protestant liturgy Only by consigning two bishops to the Tower during the Easter recess was the measure passed by the slenderest of margins. Both bills passed the Lower House with only insignificant resistance, and Elizabeth took the hint that, in this respect, the Lords were more representative than the Commons. Having got her way over the ecclesiastical establishment, she abandoned the title of Supreme Head in favour of Supreme Governor, and set up an ecclesiastical commission to run the Church in her name. Although she believed passionately that God had entrusted her with the responsibility for running His Church, she was canny enough to see that that would be better done indirectly.[48]

These attitudes dictated her dealings with the Church for the rest of her life. A royal visitation in the summer of 1559 got rid of the Catholic bishops, some of whom were imprisoned and some of whom fled abroad, but she was reluctant to allow their Protestant successors the freedom to enforce conformity in the way that they wished. She knew perfectly well that the majority of her subjects, had they been allowed to vote on the matter, would have opted for religion 'as King Henry left it', and hoped that a 'softly softly' approach would induce conformity where there was little enthusiasm. At first, it was thought that marriage to a Catholic prince, such as the Archduke Charles, would modify her religious settlement, or at least introduce an element of toleration. These hopes were disappointed, and Elizabeth evaded an invitation to send representatives to the Council of Trent, but before 1570 there were plenty of Catholics and crypto-Catholics in public life and, to the indignation of her more zealous bishops, the Queen did nothing about them.[49] What changed that situation, at least in part, were the events surrounding the Northern Rising of 1569. The constant threat presented by Mary, Queen of Scots as the Catholic claimant to her throne awoke the Queen to the danger of 'popish conspiracy', and made her realize that it was no longer possible to turn a blind eye to the danger presented by the Roman obedience. This was emphasized by the appeal which the rebels made to the Pope, and by his response in the form of the bull *Regnans in Excelsis*, which declared her excommunicate and deposed and freed her subjects from their allegiance. This was a declaration of war, and meant that henceforth anyone recognizing the authority of the Pope was a potential traitor.[50] Fortunately from Elizabeth's point of view, it also concentrated the minds of her subjects, who realized that they must now make a choice. The overwhelming majority chose their allegiance to the Queen, no matter how conservative their religious views might be, and that left the papists as a defined minority, henceforth known as 'recusants'. Recusancy remained a problem, particularly after the arrival of seminary priests (after 1575) and Jesuit missionaries (after 1580) stiffened the faith of many waverers. The Jesuits in particular condemned the practice of occasional conformity, or 'Church popery', in unequivocal terms, and although such priests as Edmund Campion disclaimed any political objectives, they became actively involved in conspiracies against the Queen's life.[51] It was one such, fronted by a foolish young man named Anthony Babington, which cost the Queen of Scots her life in 1587. By that time England was at war with Spain, and recusancy became even more associated with treason, although most Catholics, even the more extreme ones, hastened to assert their temporal loyalty to Elizabeth, thus denying the papal deposing power and throwing the Catholic camp into some confusion. There was even a movement among some secular priests to frame an oath of temporal allegiance to the Queen, which they would be prepared to take, but that was roundly condemned in Rome and never came to fruition. [52]

Although her attitude towards Catholics was no longer equivocal, her House of Commons was not satisfied with the zeal which she displayed in the cause of 'godliness'. There had been from the beginning a number of members, who would later be known as Puritans, who believed that the Church settlement was incomplete and who looked for further reform. Against these Elizabeth constantly set her face. It was not just that she disapproved of what they were trying to achieve, she disapproved even more strongly of being told what to do. While these members confined themselves to anti-Catholic measures after 1570, she was acquiescent, and allowed the bills against Bulls from Rome (1571), against Reconciliation with Rome (1581) and against Jesuits and Seminary priests (1585) to pass unhindered.[53] However, when they began to press for further reform, as with Strickland's bill in 1571, or Cope's Bill and Book in 1587, she called them out of order. By the 1580s this minority had become Presbyterian, looking for a system of government by a hierarchy of

Synods rather than by the Crown, and Elizabeth took this to be a direct attack upon her authority. Fortunately a majority in the Commons took the same view, and the Presbyterians shot themselves in the foot with the Marprelate Tracts of 1587. These were scurrilous (and amusing) attacks on the Episcopate, which derided their authority in terms which rang alarm bells with the secular authorities. If bishops could be so derogated, might not temporal lords be next? The establishment closed ranks against Martin Marprelate, and Presbyterian political influence declined.[54]

As the Church of England settled down into a fairly conservative conformity in the 1590s, radical Protestants began to seem as big a menace as the Catholics. In some way they were worse, because recusants could be identified by their refusal to come to church, whereas very few radicals went so far as to withdraw their membership. The danger lay in the priority which they gave to scripture, which prompted many of them to place their own interpretation of the Bible ahead of that prescribed by the Church; in other words, they were advocating the sovereignty of their own consciences. This was an idea which no government, either Catholic or Protestant, could accept, and prompted the Parliament in 1593 to pass an Act against Seditious Sectaries condemning all those who 'advisedly and purposely practice or go about to move or persuade any of her Majesty's subjects or any other person within her Highness's realms or dominions, to deny, withstand and impugn her Majesty's power and authority in causes ecclesiastical united and annexed to the Imperial Crown of this realm'[55] to indefinite prison 'until such time as they shall conform and yield themselves'. This drastic measure effectively, if temporarily, killed off Puritanism as a political movement, until it was revived by the sympathetic reaction of James I to the millenary petition.

By the end of her reign, it could be said that Elizabeth had made peace with God on her own terms. England was a Protestant nation, thanking God for deliverance from the Armada, and Francis Drake was reading selections from Foxe's *Acts and Monuments* to his hapless Spanish prisoners. Indeed, the first four editions of this great work in a sense chart the fortunes of the Elizabethan Church.[56] At the time of the first edition in 1563, optimism was high. A godly Queen was upon the throne, and the Catholic beast had been vanquished. Elizabeth was hailed as the New Constantine, and the triumph of the reformation was celebrated. However, by the time that the second, greatly enlarged edition appeared in 1570, much of that triumphalism had waned. The Queen's Protestant allegiance was not in question, and she had not (so far) succumbed to the blandishments of a Catholic marriage, but her godliness was open to serious question. She had resisted all attempts to persuade her to embrace further reform, and Catholics had not been driven from public life. The dedication to the New Constantine was quietly removed. This was the edition which convocation ordered to be set up in cathedrals and other major churches, but while the emphasis upon the sacrifice of the martyrs remained, doubts had clearly begun to intrude as to the worthiness of the their successors.[57] The third edition in 1576 was intended as a cheaper version of the 1570 edition, and although that makes a point about demand for the work, the agenda was not much advanced. Doubts remained. The last edition for which Foxe was personally responsible, that of 1583, was altogether more relaxed. England had weathered many storms and the possibility of a Catholic marriage for Elizabeth had now vanished. Foxe was also getting older and less inclined to look on his contemporaries with a jaundiced eye. The Catholic threat remained, and needed to be fought with all the weapons which God provided – particularly the printing press – but perhaps the Queen's cautious approach to godliness was justified. Certainly the antics of the Puritans, both inside and outside Parliament, lent credibility to her stand. Stability appealed more to the older Foxe, which the Queen had delivered for over a quarter of a century. The edition was also brought up to date with some more recent atrocities from France. England had a lot to be thankful for. Foxe did not live long enough to see the defeat of the Armada, but he would no doubt have rejoiced in that further great testimony to the fact that God approved of the Church of England, and of the Queen who had brought it about and guarded it so carefully.[58]

'God is English', Hugh Latimer had proclaimed at the time of Prince Edward's birth in 1537, and that sense of special providence prevailed throughout the Tudor period. Not greatly invoked in the reign of Henry VII, it nevertheless helped the Englishman to decide that he was not French (thank God!) or Scots (mercifully), but a true-born son of Albion. Under Henry VIII it supported that magnificent young man and his beautiful Queen with suitable piety, and it was national sentiment rather than theological understanding which caused so many of his subjects to accept his break with Rome. He had defied those interfering foreigners the Pope and the Emperor, and if the cause was personal to himself, it could easily be made to appear in the interests of England. Edward was the Godly Imp, the second Josias, and England the first realm in Europe to cast off the obscurantist tyranny of the Catholic Church.[59] National sentiment worked against Queen Mary and her Spanish husband, especially the latter, and both the religious persecution and the fall of Calais were blamed on Philip, although he had had nothing to do with the former and had done his best to prevent the latter. Elizabeth, significantly, was proclaimed (and proclaimed herself) to be 'mere English', and worked the patriotic ticket assiduously throughout her reign. By the time of the Armada, nationalism and the Protestant faith were synonymous.[60] The liturgy and the Bible had long been in English, and it was obvious that God approved of the way in which 'his Englishmen' were conducting themselves. John Foxe did not, in fact, describe England as the 'Elect Nation', but he did concede that it was an elect nation, along with the other professors of the reformed faith, and the idea that England was the 'new Israel' was widespread among the godly by the end of the century. Elizabeth had been specially protected during the perilous years of her sister's reign, so that she might emerge as Deborah 'taking counsel for the people of the Lord'. Even her virginity was hailed as a particular sign of Divine protection. Patriotic Catholics and Protestant radicals were alike disenfranchised by this prevailing sentiment, which identified the Queen as a unique agent of God. The wheel had come full circle. Henry VII and the young Henry VIII had been regarded by their subjects as especially favoured, because of the peace and unity which they had brought. For more than a generation after 1530 the country had been divided and confused by religious ideology and the conflicting claims of monarchy, but after a long struggle, Elizabeth brought the Crown, the Church and national sentiment again into line. By 1600 it was seditious to challenge the divine credentials of the Queen, a sentiment which James I was to try in vain to exploit.

Merchant Matters

There was no such thing as a Gross National Product in medieval England. Economic activity took place at a local level, and most traders looked only to their immediate hinterland for their business. Insofar as there were exceptions to this, they occurred mainly in international trade, the export of wool and the import of wine. By 1400 Bordeaux was exporting nearly 100,000 tuns of wine a year, the bulk of which was coming to England, but it was arriving in a number of different ports and was not controlled by any single company. The merchants of Bristol, Southampton and London were making a good profit out of the wine trade, but it was not co-ordinated in any way, and royal agents were also importing directly for the tables of the court. The export of raw wool can be partly tracked through the customs records, which begin in 1275. At that date something like 30,000 sacks (each of 250 fleeces) were going out every year, but they too were going through a number of different ports and the trade was not in any sense co-ordinated.[1] Then in 1343 a change took place with the creation of the Staplers' Company. This company was granted a monopoly of all trade in raw wool to the Low Countries, which was the major market. The Merchant Staplers were not confined to any single town, although the headquarters was in London and the main drive came from the capital. The Staplers' control did not extend to wool being exported to other destinations, and for some time a flourishing business continued to be conducted with Spain and Italy, but the lion's share went to The Netherlands, where a Staple, or export control, was established at Bruges.[2] This appears to have been the first time that the Crown had involved itself in any commercial enterprise, and the intervention was almost certainly undertaken on the initiative of the merchants themselves. Towards the end of the fourteenth century, however, an increasing quantity of English wool was being spun and woven at home, as sheep took over the holdings left vacant by the black death and landlords strove to increase their profits. English cloth finishing was small-scale and primitive by comparison with the major continental centres and an export trade grew up in unfinished cloth, which rapidly assumed significant dimensions. In 1407, again in response to a petition from the merchants, a company similar to the Staplers was established to control this trade. It was called the Merchant Adventurers, and was again based in London.[3] The same rules applied: the company was open to merchants of other towns, and controlled the trade only to the Low Countries. However, the demand for unfinished cloth was negligible elsewhere, and the Merchant Adventurers soon acquired a monopoly in the full sense.

Unlike his predecessors, Edward IV had adopted a very 'hands-on' approach to the merchant community of London. He knighted Aldermen and invited them (and their wives) to court, in the interests of maintaining the political allegiance of the capital, which meant a lot to him.[4] He also traded extensively in his own right, using his own factors, many of whom were Italians.

> This same king in person, having equipped ships of burden, laded them with the very finest wools, cloth, tin, and other products of his realm, and like a man living by merchandise, exchanged good for goods, both with the Italians and Greeks, through his factors...[5]

wrote the (somewhat scandalized) Crowland chronicler. He even waged a confused and intermittent war with the Hanseatic League between 1568 and 1573 in defence of the privileges of the Merchant Adventurers. The Hanse enjoyed the right of trading Baltic goods to England, and had been using that status to export cloth to the Low Countries in defiance of the Adventurers' monopoly. By the Treaty of Utrecht, which brought that war to an end, all privileges were confirmed, and the English were promised a reciprocal arrangement which would give them access to the Baltic ports. That never happened in practice and friction between the Adventurers and the Hanse continued into the sixteenth century. However, merchants were good tax-payers, and the Crown regularly provided 'wafters' or escorts, not only for the Icelandic fishing fleet, but also for the annual convoy of ships bearing the cloth which had been gathered at Blackwell Hall in London to its finishing market in Bruges, Ghent and Antwerp.[6] By the time Henry VII succeeded to the throne, it was a regular practice to pass Acts of Parliament regulating matters of trade and manufacture, but these were nearly always enacted on the initiative of the merchants involved, often by way of petition, and should not lead to the assumption that the Crown had a commercial policy. Often such measures would be repealed in the next session at the instance of some rival group whose interests had been adversely affected. The King was interested in trade in the general sense that the customs of the port of London were a significant item in his annual income, but he did not on the whole concern himself with detailed matters of regulation. Bristol merchants occasionally ventured out into the Atlantic, and seem to have got as far as the Canary Islands (with a little Portuguese help), but with that the King had nothing to do. He confined himself to maintaining friendly relations with the elite of London.

At first, the accession of Henry VIII made no difference to this situation. The balance of power between the Staplers and the Merchant Adventurers had changed by then. Having peaked at 45,000 sacks in 1355, the former's exports had shrunk to about 10,000 sacks by 1480, while the Adventurers by the same date had advanced to 60,000 broadcloths, a figure which was still rising.[7] This change was partly due to the Crown's taxation policies, because raw wool had been (and still was) taxed at a much higher rate for customs purposes. In addition, the Staplers were supposed to maintain the garrison at Calais when the wool staple was moved there from Bruges on account of political troubles in the Low Countries during the 1490s. Henry was concerned to defuse conflict within the merchant community, and insisted that no acts concerning merchandise should infringe the privileges of the Hanseatic League. This frustrated the Merchant Adventurers, who were trying to do just that, but it was in the interests of the King's foreign policy rather than any sensitivity to their commercial needs. He did, however, move to settle a dispute between the Staplers and the Adventurers in what was a purely economic matter. The Staplers' trade had shrunk to 7,500 sacks a year between 1491 and 1497, and some of them were trying to recover their prosperity by trading cloth, which was an infringement of the Adventurers' monopoly.[8] They were doing this by using their own staple at Calais, which they argued did not touch their rivals' rights in the Low Countries, but when access to Flanders and Brabant was barred by a political embargo, as happened from time to time, the Adventurers also used Calais, which caused endless confusion. In 1497 the King decided to legislate a solution. The relevant act did not address the issue directly, but rather authorized the Adventurers to set an entry fine of 10 marks (£6 13s 4d) for freedom of their fellowship. This was less than they were wont to charge, but had the great advantage of giving them statutory authority to admit or exclude whomever they wished. It also extended their monopoly to cover all outlets for unfinished cloth.[9] This should have clarified the legal position, but unfortunately it did not, and in 1505 the parties were again in dispute before the King's Council. The council then ruled, without reference to the statute, that members of each company were free to trade in the other's commodity, provided that they submitted their disagreements to the jurisdiction of the appropriate court. Shortly after, the Staplers came back complaining that their rivals had seized cloth belonging to their members in order to force them to become free of the Adventurers also. In spite of the fact that the statute clearly authorized such action, the council instructed the Adventurers to return the cloth and to cease their campaign of harassment.[10] The dispute rumbled on into the next reign, and must have been linked to the Staplers' steadily weakening position. Between 1503 and 1509 their exports sank to no more than 5,000 sacks. The King appears to have had no understanding of the intricacies of the wool trade, but was earnestly concerned to prevent his two most prestigious merchant communities from feuding. In 1505 he erected by Letters Patent a Governor and Court of Assistants for the Merchant Adventurers in London, bringing them into line with the Staplers, but he also stipulated that the outports must be represented on this Court, in an attempt to defuse another long-running dispute and impose some unity on what was by then England's largest export trade by a considerable margin.[11]

Similarly, he gave his merchants a ride on the back of his foreign policy. It would be a mistake to assume that either the treaty of Redon or that of Medina del Campo in March 1489 was negotiated for commercial purposes; the first was to guarantee the independence of Brittany and the second to secure a marriage between Prince Arthur and Ferdinand and Isabella's daughter, Catherine. However, each contained trading clauses, the latter being particularly favourable to the English. The merchants of both countries were to receive reciprocal rights in respect of customs duties, which were fixed at the rates prevailing thirty years before. This was before the era of inflation, so the rates would not have been very different, but the clause did have the effect of depriving the Spaniards of the preferential rates conceded by Edward IV (much to the indignation of the Londoners) in 1466.[12] These privileges were confirmed and amplified in a further treaty of 1499 which again was primarily a treaty of amity and alliance. Similarly the *magnus intercursus* of 1496, which was mainly about political co-operation with the Emperor Maximilian, contained many clauses favourable to English merchants, which were extended still further (much to the indignation of the Low Countries men) in the *malus intercursus* of 1506, which was signed with Philip of Burgundy and signified a shift in Henry's foreign policy.[13] The main purpose of the latter treaty was to indicate the King's support for Philip in his bid for the Crown matrimonial of Castile in the wake of Isabella's death. The Navigation Acts of 1486 and 1489 were also aspects of foreign policy at least as much as commercial promotion. They required all trade coming to or going from English ports to be carried either in English ships or in vessels belonging to the immediate trading partner – in other words, to cut out the carrier. They were aimed primarily at the Venetians, with whom several skirmishes were being fought at that time. In 1490 Henry signed a treaty with the Florentines making their port of Pisa the staple for English wool in

Italy, which was another political move against Venice.[14] The Navigation Acts were also aimed to promote English shipbuilding, in the interests of having a reserve of large vessels which could be called up for naval service should the need arise. The King also paid bounties to owners commissioning large ships, on the understanding that they would be available to the navy when required.[15]

Unlike Edward, Henry did not trade extensively in his own right, nor did he invest in commercial enterprises. His one venture in that direction was more in the interests of his image as a patron and promoter than it was to secure commercial advantages. There were persistent rumours in Bristol that ships from the town had made a landfall on the other side of the Atlantic. The absence of any corroborative detail means that this was probably wish-fulfilment, or a distorted memory of a visit to the Canaries, but it was sufficient to attract the attention of John Cabot, a Genoese by origin but a citizen of Venice, when he was looking for support for a voyage of discovery in 1495. Cabot had a hunch that the north Atlantic offered the quickest route to China, and there were those in Bristol who agreed with him. He must have been well informed, because he latched onto this interest at once and bypassed London, which would have been a more obvious place to start looking for money. He received the promise of at least one ship and a modest level of investment before he approached Henry. The King was sufficiently impressed to grant him Letters Patent authorizing him to undertake a voyage in the name of England, using not more than five ships, and to claim whatever lands he might find 'previously unknown to Christian people'. He was also granted 80 per cent of any profits accruing for the voyage (20 per cent was to go to the King) on the condition that he met the whole cost of the enterprise himself.[16] This was hardly generous, and Cabot may have found some difficulties, because although the patent was granted in March 1496, it was May 1497 before he set sail, and then he had only one small ship. However, he made a landfall, probably on the coast of what is now Maine, and dutifully hoisted an English flag before returning to report. He was back in Bristol by 6 August. Henry was sufficiently impressed to award the explorer an annuity of £20 in December 1497, which was obviously a retainer to keep him in English service, and on 3 February 1498 issued Cabot with fresh Letters Patent. This time he was authorized to undertake a voyage with up to six ships, of which the King would supply one. The others were financed by merchants of Bristol and London, who also seem to have been convinced by his first discovery. Early in May 1498, John Cabot set sail with his modest fleet and completely disappeared.[17] It is possible that one ship may have returned, but there is no firm evidence; the one thing that is certain is that John Cabot himself died.

Somehow, by 1501 Henry knew that whatever it was Cabot had discovered on the other side of the Atlantic, it was not Asia, and did not appear to be particularly rich. This knowledge indicates that one ship at least did return, but the information it carried was so disappointing that all interest in the enterprise evaporated. Presumably Henry had paid only one instalment of John's annuity! Cabot's son, Sebastian, did his best to keep the venture alive, and a company in which he was involved was granted further patents in 1501 and 1502, setting out regulations for colonies as well as trading privileges.[18] However, all this was so much wishful thinking. The King remained benevolent, but strictly non-participatory, and Sebastian struggled. A further patent was granted in 1506 to a 'company of adventurers to the New Found Lands', but investors were few, no trade resulted, and as far as we know the patent remained a dead letter. Apart from a modest flicker early in 1498, Henry had more important things to think about than the remote projects of over-ambitious merchants.

Henry VIII was only intermittently interested in commercial matters. His concentration span was short, and although he could be stirred to enthusiasm, it was normally of brief duration. He was far more interested in building a navy to fight the French than he was in long-distance voyages of uncertain outcome. Like his father, he gave his assent to a large number of mercantile bills in Parliament, but this does not indicate any serious level of concern, and he made no attempt to arbitrate merchants' quarrels in the way the older Henry had done. Nor were the London merchants particularly willing to risk their capital in such ventures. The Merchant Adventurers' trade to Antwerp was flourishing, and the Staplers no longer presented a serious challenge. The number of broadcloths going down that route had reached about 112,000 by 1547, and although there were periodic alarms of a political nature because of fluctuating relations with the Emperor, a series of local commercial agreements prevented any serious breakdown of trade.[19] The most important (and richest) group in the capital thus had no incentive to seek diversification. At first, such ventures as were proposed were encouraged mostly by Cardinal Wolsey. In 1517 John Rastell, Sir Thomas More's brother-in-law, set up an expedition which seems to have been mainly in search of new fishing grounds, although it also included some vague intention of colonization. Apart from being armed with royal letters of commendation, obtained by Wolsey, this was an entirely private venture and it got no further than Waterford in Ireland.[20] By this time Sebastian Cabot had got the message and taken himself off, first to Venice and then into the service of the Emperor Charles V, where he was to remain until 1548. In 1521 Wolsey tried more seriously to set up an expedition to search for the North-West Passage, and offered Cabot (then in Venice) a large reward to come back and lead it. However, Cabot was not to be drawn, and Wolsey was forced to press on without him. In this he seems to have been encouraged by an outburst of enthusiasm on the part of Henry, who was temporarily engaged by the prospect of a really large-scale enterprise. Reality was not far away. When the Cardinal canvassed the London merchants and held a meeting with them at Drapers' Hall, they did not want to know either, and in spite of a sharp intervention by the King, the Mayor remained unmoved.[21] Perhaps he appreciated the ephemeral nature of Henry's interest, and the whole scheme came to nothing.

Rather more was achieved by two ships which set out without any kind of official encouragement in May 1527. One was lost, but the other reached Hudson's Straits before returning, having at least proved that Cabot's landfall thirty years earlier had not been a chimera. William Hawkins of Plymouth, with no more than a nod of encouragement from the Crown, set up a voyage to Brazil, which must have produced some return because he repeated the exploit two or three times over the years following 1530. According to Richard Hakluyt, writing much later but within the lifetime of William's son John, 'he made three long and famous voyages to the coast of Brazil, a thing in those days very rare, especially to our nation'.[22] By that time Wolsey was off the scene, but in 1536 apparently a Mr Hore of London led two more ships to Newfoundland, although whether they did anything more than catch fish is not apparent. According to Hakluyt he was supported by fifty gentlemen in his enterprise, who presumably put up the money, but the whole episode is obscure.[23] Since 1521, and no longer inspired by the Cardinal, Henry's interest seems to have evaporated entirely, and when Sebastian Cabot offered to return to England in 1537 his proposal was ignored. In 1541 there was talk of renewing the quest for the North-West Passage, which got as far as the council, but in the absence of any enthusiasm from the King the whole matter was dropped and nothing happened. Robert Thorne, an English merchant based in Seville, had written to Henry in 1526, urging him to buy an interest in the Spice Islands that Charles V was reported to be willing to sell, but the King had no money at that point and nothing was done. Thorne himself invested money in a venture which Sebastian Cabot (then in Spain) set up at about the same time, but beyond the fact that two of his English friends, Roger Barlow and Henry Latimer, went on the voyage and gained valuable experience, no advantage accrued to England.[24] Viewed from the perspective of subsequent developments, the whole reign of Henry VIII looks like a time of wasted opportunities. The Levant trade collapsed after the capture of Rhodes by the Turks in 1522, and the cloth trade of the outports dwindled in the face of London competition, being down to 14,000 a year by 1547. Other local trades appear to have stood up well, but they are hard to quantify in the absence of official interest, and of course the London/Antwerp cloth trade, which was the hallmark of England's commercial prosperity, went from strength to strength.

After Henry's death in January 1547, the new reign brought new circumstances. Relations with Charles V, which had always been erratic, took a turn for the worse as the Protectorate regime began to move towards Protestantism, and this inevitably cast doubts on the security of the Antwerp market. More importantly, Henry VIII had begun to debase the coinage in an effort to pay for his last war with France, and that unsettled the exchanges.[25] As the value of the pound sterling began to decline against the Flemish pound, English cloth became 'good cheap'. At first this led to a boom, which stimulated production at home, and the export figure nudged up towards 150,000. The market became saturated. Then the government in England, determined to tackle the crisis in the exchanges which had declined from 26 shillings Flemish to 13, in 1551 devalued the currency, bringing the shilling down to nine pence.[26] As a result, the price of English cloth shot up and the saturated market could not cope. Piles of unsold English cloth accumulated at Antwerp, production stalled and weavers were laid off. Quite apart from the social dislocation which this caused, there was alarm in the City of London, and suddenly the Merchant Adventurers began to show an interest in markets elsewhere. Before any of this happened, and for reasons which remain obscure, in 1548 Sebastian Cabot gave up his position as Pilot Major to the Emperor and returned to England. He may have been hankering to do this for some time and had certainly kept in touch with his English friends. Now his ideas for the development of long-distance trade seemed especially relevant, and he was given an annuity of 200 marks (£166 13s 4d) by the council in 1549.[27] This time, probably at the instance of the council, he stayed in London. On 4 June 1550 he was granted an exemplification of the Letters Patent which he and his father had received in 1496, and seems to have been working towards the establishment of a London-based Cathay Company, this time seeking a passage to China around the north of Asia – the North-East Passage. In January 1551 the Imperial Ambassador reported that he was working with a certain Jean Ribault, a Frenchmen, and a number of Englishmen 'to discover some islands or to seek a road to the Indies',[28] and early in 1553 this scheme came to fruition. A company was established with the unprecedented number of 240 shareholders, each paying £25, to raise a capital of £6,000. Not only was the size and funding of this company unusual, so was the composition of its support, because in addition to the normal merchants (mostly London-based) there were Privy Councillors, Courtiers and other royal servants. Individual councillors and officials had done business in the city for many years, but collaboration on this scale was new. The young King was alleged to be interested, even enthusiastic, but the real driving force behind this innovation was almost certainly the President of the Council, John Dudley, Duke of Northumberland. It may well have been Dudley who commended Cabot to the attention of the council in the first place. Cabot himself was appointed Governor, and instructions were drawn up for the government and operation of the enterprise. These were dated 9 May, although probably drafted earlier, and on the 10th a fleet of three ships under the command of Sir Hugh Willoughby set off from the Thames bearing letters of commendation addressed to any potentate they might encounter and written (hopefully) in Latin.[29]

Meanwhile, relations with the Hanseatic League had reached breaking point. In 1547 the Hanse were still trading under the privileges granted by the Treaty of Utrecht, and recently they had begun surreptitiously to increase the number of undyed cloths which they were shipping to Hamburg. This had not mattered while the Merchant Adventurers' trade was booming, but by 1551 it constituted serious – and most unwelcome – competition. There were various diplomatic incidents involving naval support for the Scots and the seizure of an English ship in Dantzig, and in January 1552 the Adventurers presented a comprehensive list of grievances to the council, prominent among which was the lack of that reciprocity which had been promised under the Treaty of Utrecht. On 9 February the matter was adjudicated and the Hanseatic privileges were withdrawn.[30] The League continued to trade and its London headquarters, the Steelyard, went on functioning, but they were now on the same footing as all other alien merchants and paid the alien rates of customs duties. The reasons for this move may have been partly commercial, but were primarily political. The Duke of Northumberland needed the support of the City more than he feared the enmity of the Hanse or the diplomatic fall-out from the Emperor, whose subjects most of the merchants were. Relations with Charles were already at rock-bottom, but Northumberland rightly calculated that he would not risk war over a 'merchant matter' while he was still locked in a military struggle with the French. The cancellation of the Hanseatic privileges, like the official support for the Cathay Company, was part of a bridge-building exercise between the government and the City of London, and helped to ensure that the livery companies would underwrite the council's borrowings in Antwerp. This was an essential aspect of the financial security of the regime, and assisted greatly in the restoration of England's credit rating, as the pound sterling gradually recovered its value on the Bourse.[31] It was not accidental that the agent whom Northumberland eventually employed in Antwerp was that well-respected London merchant and banker, Thomas Gresham.

Any goodwill which may have been generated by these means proved unavailing when Edward endeavoured to alter the succession in the summer of 1553. Dying before he achieved his majority, the young King, with Northumberland's support, attempted to bar the lawful heir, his half-sister Mary, in favour of his cousin Jane Grey. In spite of strong Protestant influence, London did not support this move, and when a divided council proclaimed Mary on 19 July there was universal rejoicing.[32] As Mary established herself, however, the city became divided. This was particularly true over her proposal to marry Philip of Spain. The city elite was at first happy with this move, anticipating not only a secure future for the Antwerp trade, but also access to Spain's extensive colonial empire in the New World. The rank and file, however, were unhappy with the prospect of a foreign King, and when Sir Thomas Wyatt rose in rebellion in January 1554 the city militia, the Whitecoats, which had been mobilized against him, deserted *en masse* – a move for which they paid a severe price when the rebellion was suppressed.[33] When Philip eventually reached London after his wedding in August 1554, the livery companies did their best to give him a warm welcome, but the population was unenthusiastic. The new King, moreover, did nothing to build on the potential goodwill which existed. Mary's council had already restored the Hanseatic privileges as a placatory gesture toward the Emperor, who was Philip's father, and the Merchant Adventurers were not amused. An anonymous memorandum drawn up in December 1554 spoke of 'the discommodity and hindrance [to] this realm, and the subversion of the laudable trade and traffic of English merchants...' which had resulted from the restoration.[34] The King absolutely forbade any English access to the markets of the New World, on the grounds that this was a Castilian monopoly in which even his Aragonese subjects did not share, and did his level best to discourage London ventures to the west coast of Africa, on the grounds that this infringed the rights of the Portuguese 'which narrowly concern me', although in what way he did not specify.

Mary was acutely sensitive to her husband's concerns and did nothing to mitigate the severity of his negative attitude, with the result that the London merchants complained bitterly that whenever a dispute arose between themselves and the Flemings (which was often) the King invariably sided with his Low Countries subjects, irrespective of the merits of the case.[35] It was only when Philip's interests were not involved that she was prepared to be flexible. Sir Hugh Willoughby had perished in Lapland in the course of the voyage which had started so hopefully in May 1553, but his colleague Richard Chancellor had made in round the North Cape to Archangel, and thence to the Court of the Tsar in Moscow. In the summer of 1554 he returned, bearing offers of extensive

trading privileges throughout Ivan's wide realms. Russia was not China, nor the
Spice Islands, but it was on offer, and the prospect was eagerly embraced. As a
result the Muscovy Company was established early in 1555, with a consortium
of investors headed by the Lord Treasurer and eleven other Privy Councillors.[36]
It did not match the size of the Cathay Company, having ninety-seven investors
in all, but its composition was similar, and it had Sebastian Cabot as its first
Governor. Cabot died in 1557, and the volume of trade conducted by the
company was not large, but it was a beginning in that process of diversification
which London now earnestly desired. Nor was this all, because another enter-
prising Englishman had been probing around the Near East on a similar quest.
This was Anthony Jenkinson, who had left London in 1546 and spent about
eight years wandering in the Ottoman Empire looking for opportunities. In
1553 he secured an audience with the Sultan, and Sulieman proved surprisingly amenable to the prospect of trade with distant England. However, when
Jenkinson returned in 1555 or 1556 he found England ruled by Sulieman's arch-
enemy, Philip, and nothing came of his initiative for a number of years. Instead,
Jenkinson joined the Muscovy Company, and when its first major fleet set out in
1557 bearing English broadcloths to Russia, he was in command.[37] Mary, notori-
ously, had no foreign policy of her own, and when she joined Philip's war against
France in 1557 the London merchants were disgusted, losing at a stroke all the
profitable lines of communication which they had established with that kingdom
over the previous decade. It was, however, some consolation that the Antwerp
trade recovered its buoyancy, and after a fitful decade exports from London were
back to 120,000 cloths in 1559–61.[38] Mary's short reign had been one of hopeful
beginnings rather than solid achievement, but at least the momentum estab
lished under Edward VI was continued, in spite of the poor relations engendered
by Philip's attitude. Thomas Gresham was able to continue using the cloth credits
to underwrite government loans, and the exchange rate recovered fully.

Elizabeth, according to the Count of Feria, relied primarily upon 'the
people' for her support, and nowhere was that more true than in London.
The elevation of the well-connected William Cecil, who had been Principal
Secretary in the latter years of Edward's reign, to a position of power
was a long step in the right direction, and the Queen's interactive performance during her pre-coronation entry into the city also enhanced her
popularity.[39] Cabot had gone, but the outward-looking strategy which he
had represented was well sustained by Stephen Borough, who had visited
the *casa de contratacion* on Philip's invitation, by Richard Eden and by the
polymath John Dee, cosmographer and soothsayer.[40] A close relationship
developed between these men and the officers of the navy, particularly

William Winter and Benjamin Gonson. Although they were operating in a private rather than an official capacity, these officers were nevertheless able to make ships and guns available for a London venture to the west coast of Africa sent out by William Garrard and William Chester in 1562–3, such protection being necessary in view of the hostility of the Portuguese authorities.[41] The 1560s were a turbulent decade in England's maritime trade. When the English became overly sympathetic to the protest movement in The Netherlands against Philip's policies there in 1565–6, an embargo was imposed by the Regent, Margaret of Parma. This was a nuisance, but far more damaging to Antwerp than it was to London, and was lifted after about a year. Then Margaret was replaced by the Duke of Alba, who had orders to suppress all dissent, a policy which was very ill-received by the Queen, who seized the opportunity to divert the Genoese money intended to pay his army into her own coffers. This took place in December 1568 and resulted in another trade embargo.[42] By the time this came to an end in 1573, the London merchants had made other arrangements to sell their cloth in places such as Emden and Hamburg, which were less convenient but safer. After 1573 the staple was never fully restored, and following the sack of Antwerp by a mutinous Spanish army in 1576, the English withdrew altogether. The bulk of English cloth continued to go into northern Europe, but through a variety of different ports. The 1560s were also adventurous in another sense, because Elizabeth herself entered the equation. She did not do this in the old fashion by trading in her own right, but by contributing ships and money to what were otherwise private enterprises. This began with John Hawkins' Carribbean voyage of 1564, which, although thinly disguised as an orthodox trading venture, was in fact devoted to a mixture of slave raiding and piracy.[43] Hawkins had had a trial run for this exploit in 1562, using entirely private money, and the profit returned had caught the royal eye. The syndicate set up for 1564 therefore comprised not only the Queen, but also Cecil, the Earl of Leicester, Lord Clinton and the 'navy board group' already noticed. In fact Elizabeth did not invest money, but rather one large ship, the *Jesus of Lubeck*, fully armed and victualled. What was new about this arrangement was that the Queen did not rent the vessel out to the entrepreneurs, but rather let it stand as her contribution, and her entitlement to a share of the profits. The results were encouraging and she used the same system in 1568, on which occasion she also turned a blind eye to Hawkins' claim to hold a royal commission when it suited his purposes. This time she burned her fingers when the *Jesus* was lost at San Juan d'Ulloa and Philip waxed indignant at such incursions into his empire.

Hawkins seems to have believed that he had a special understanding with the King of Spain, but the origin of this belief is obscure, and certainly Philip's agents on the ground in the colonies knew nothing of any such arrangement. They did, however, need the slaves he brought, and therefore connived at his illegal activities in a manner which probably encouraged his belief. Certainly, after losing the *Jesus*, Hawkins had the nerve to go to Spain and try to recover his losses through the Admiralty court. Needless to say, he had no success.[44]

After 1570, perhaps fearful of the consequences of further provocation, Elizabeth drew back from such direct involvement. She did not, however, cease to give her blessing to the piratical adventures of men like Francis Drake, who in May 1573 set off on what looks like a private war against the Spanish colonies. On this occasion, after a fruitless attack on Nombre de Dios, he joined forces with a French pirate called Le Testu to ambush a silver train in the vicinity of the town and came back with as much bullion as his ships would hold. After this exploit he went off to serve in Ireland for a spell, only to be recalled in 1577 when the Queen herself had a major enterprise in mind.[45] This was not intended to be a trading voyage. If anything, it was an exploration, although whether of Terra Australis Incognita or of the west coast of South America is not clear. Primarily it was a statement – a declaration that English ships could go wherever they wanted in the world; and it was timely. For the best part of a century, English seamanship had been overshadowed by that of the Iberians, who had established colonies from Goa to Peru and appeared to rule the world's oceans. Now the English were ready to compete. It was in that same year that John Dee published *The Perfect Art of Navigation*, which not only demonstrated that the English had caught up, but even postulated the idea of a British Empire.[46] This expedition was intended to demonstrate that such ideas were practicable. The Queen did not wish her involvement to be known, but the composition of the syndicate put together to support it pointed inevitably to her influence: the Lord Admiral, the Earl of Leicester, Sir Francis Walsingham and Sir Christopher Hatton were all shareholders, as were John Hawkins and the Winter brothers. With Hawkins just taking over as Treasurer of the Navy, Drake was the obvious man to lead such a venture, and he duly sailed from Plymouth on 15 November 1577 with four ships.[47] The resulting epic is one of the best-documented ventures of the century and shows both the best and the worst of Francis Drake. Before reaching Cape Horn he had fallen out with his second in command, Thomas Doughty, framed him on charges of insubordination, and had him executed.[48] Perhaps as a result of this ruthlessness, one of his ships turned back before reaching the Magellan Strait. Another turned back in the strait, and a third was wrecked, so only the *Pelican* eventually made it into the Pacific. 'Annoying the King of Spain' was probably an objective from the beginning, and Drake had his shareholders to consider, so he raided the unsuspecting west coast colonies and made off with a substantial booty. He then coasted north as far as California, perhaps looking for the mythical Strait of Anian, before crossing the Pacific to the Moluccas, where he reprovisioned and careened his ship. From then on, the journey was as uneventful as such exploits can ever be. He reached Sierra Leone on the west coast of Africa in July 1580 and re-entered Plymouth Sound on 26 September with a lot of loot and about half the men he had set off with.[49] The Spanish Ambassador was speechless with indignation, but Elizabeth was delighted, both with the lavish presents he gave her and also with the statement he had made in circumnavigating the globe. She caused him to bring his ship round to the Thames and knighted him on the deck. Although he had found no new lands and opened no trade routes, his exploit had served notice to the Spaniards that they no longer ruled the waves, and Philip was seriously annoyed. Consequently he was already contemplating war before Elizabeth's intervention in the Low Countries effectively forced his hand in 1585.

Drake's circumnavigation may not have discovered any new markets, but it certainly helped to broaden mercantile horizons. The Hanseatic privileges had been whittled down again after 1560 until they no longer mattered, and the Steelyard was eventually closed in 1598.[50] The declining power of the League had, in any case, opened the Baltic markets to English merchants well before that, and an Eastland Company was established in the 1570s to take advantage. Most English trade at this time was in the hands of small unincorporated groups of merchants who shared the risks on a day-by-day basis, but where the capital required was greater, or the risks more substantial, a regulated or joint stock company might be established to formalize the investment and to take the strain if things went wrong. A company also provided an administrative and judicial structure if disputes should arise, and a mechanism for negotiating with rulers or with other trade organisations to preserve the merchants' integrity – and profits.[51] Apart from the Muscovy and Eastland companies, there was a Levant Company, set up in 1581 to exploit a reviving trade with the Middle East, where convoys were a necessity because of the activity of the Barbary corsairs; a Guinea Company to cope with the erratic hostility of the Portuguese authorities; and eventually, in 1603, an East India Company. All these companies were chartered by the Crown, and conferred monopolistic rights to trade. They were therefore, in a sense, aspects of royal policy, but Elizabeth was more concerned to encourage commercial activity than to place any kind of restraints upon it. Politics inevitably played a large part in determining commercial development, but very seldom deliberately so. It was standard practice to give and receive trading privileges in the course of treaties of amity between states. Such privileges normally had the effect of improving conditions for exporters to the country concerned, while frustrating attempts to restrict imports. More importantly, the companies formed a ground of common interest upon which merchants, gentry and nobility could meet with something approaching equality. Theodore Rabb has identified more than thirty such companies established between 1575 and 1630, most of them before 1603.[52] Altogether they had nearly 5,000 shareholders, of whom 3,800 were merchants and 1,200 nobles and gentlemen. This was an important political and sociological fact, because the noblesse of France or Spain did not sully their hands with business, whereas the English aristocracy recognized a hierarchy of wealth, and freely intermarried, particularly with the Aldermanic families of London. They were in more than one sense in partnership with the Tudor government, because not only did they pay taxes and run the county administration as Justices of the Peace, they also supported the Crown through investment in trading companies which paid a noble share of the customs dues, not only in London but also in outports such as Hull and Southampton. 1577 was the first 'good year' for the companies because over 380 members were admitted, and 1581 ran it close with 307 admissions. Of course, some enterprises failed, but there were always others to take their place. The number of new companies grew faster than the failures, and that sector of the economy was expanding steadily in the later part of Elizabeth's reign.[53]

The Ottoman Sultan was always on the lookout for Christian powers opposed to his arch-enemies the Habsburgs. In the 1530s the Turkish fleet had wintered in Toulon, and in 1553 Suleiman had been willing to give trading concessions to the English. It was a long time before this offer was taken up, but by 1580 diplomatic relations had been established and two London merchants, Sir Edward Osbourne and Richard Staper, obtained a *firman* from Murad III, granting full rights and privileges to English merchants throughout his empire. This time there was no delay, and within a few years the Levant Company had established depots at Aleppo, Damascus, Tunis, Alexandria and many other places.[54] Here the demand was not for heavy broadcloths, but for the lighter kerseys, made mostly in Hampshire and Devon, where manufacture was greatly stimulated by these new outlets. At the same time, between 1579 and 1582, one John Newbury, another London merchant, was travelling by way of Persia to India, and laying that foundation of contacts which was eventually to produce the East India Company.[55] Like her grandfather, Elizabeth was always quick to perceive the foreign policy implications of trade, and like him, used the one in the service of the other. However, Henry had been playing only on a local stage. Not only were his treaties with France, the Emperor and the King of Spain, the reach of his merchants was, apart from the Mediterranean, confined to northern and western Europe. He was primarily concerned to keep on the right side of the Hanseatic League and the rulers of the Low Countries, and encouraged his merchants as agents in that quest. He occasionally leased out the ships of his navy for commercial purposes, but was never proactive in that connection. Elizabeth was quite different. Thanks possibly to William Cecil's experiences with the Duke of Northumberland, she was keenly aware of the desirability of becoming involved. The building of partnerships with her subjects was always a feature of her policy, and her partnership with the maritime community was one of her most successful.[56] She had a lot to offer in return for their commercial and financial expertise; not only money, but ships, guns and diplomatic support. Through most of her reign she was playing cat and mouse with Philip II, and merchants who were also pirates (and pirates who were also merchants) were ideal agents in that game.

Whereas at the beginning of the period the only large-scale foreign trade was that in wool and undyed broadcloths to The Netherlands, by 1603 England's commercial reach was worldwide and diverse. Although unfinished cloth was still exported in large quantities, it now went to Russia and the Baltic as well as to the Low Countries and northern Europe; lighter cloths had been developed with the aid of immigrant workmen from Flanders, the Rhineland and France. These families had usually come as religious fugitives, from the Duke of Alba or the massacre of St Bartholomew, but they had brought their skills with them and were only too willing to impart them in return for hospitality.[57] These kerseys and worsteds were sold in the Levant, West Africa and the New World, as well as even further afield in Persia, India and the Indies. The customs rates had been revised in 1507 and again in 1558, bringing them more into line with financial reality, and at the end, as at the beginning, the customs formed a significant element in the Crown's ordinary revenue.[58] What had changed was that the merchants, and the seamen with whom they were in partnership, were now at the sharp end of England's relations with the outside world. From being an offshore island of secondary significance, the country had become a global maritime power, and would shortly have an Empire to match.

Elizabeth in Parliament

Elizabeth, William Cecil, Francis Walsingham

Robert Cecil

Mary Queen of Scots

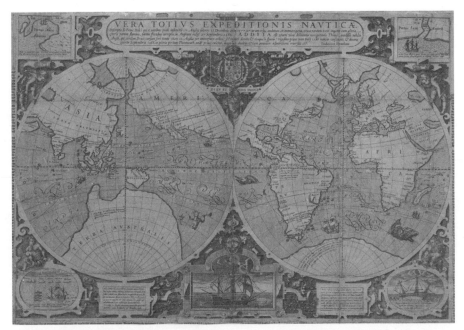

Drake's world voyage

Drake crowned by Indians

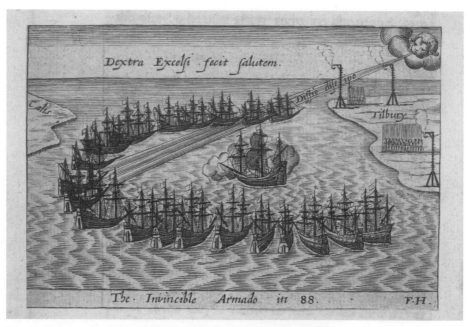

The Armada

Elizabeth

The Good Lord and His Servants

Medieval society was hierarchical, structured partly by wealth and partly by status. It was overwhelmingly (more than 80 per cent) rural and based originally on the military system of feudal tenure. At the top was the nobleman, a tenant-in-chief of the King, who held many honours, comprising scores of manors. Below him were his principal vassals, who might be knights or minor nobles, and who held one or two honours. Below them again were their sub-vassals, esquires and gentlemen, holding a handful of manors, or perhaps a single manor. The tenements into which these manors were divided were worked by unfree labourers or villeins, who also provided the infantry when the system was mobilized for war. Notionally one or two villages and their lands made up each manor, and a group of contiguous manors made up the honour.[1] Reality, however, never corresponded to this tidy model. In the first place, a manor was a jurisdictional unit, not a topographical one, so that a single village might comprise more than one manor, or tenants in a number of villages owe suit to the same court. Similarly, the lands of an honour might be dispersed over several counties, and intermingled with the lands of other honours in a most confusing fashion. At the same time, a village community was not simply an undifferentiated mass of 'peasants'. In the first place there were the craftsmen, the blacksmiths and cartwrights, who were free men and not serfs, and who sold their services to lord and labourer alike. More important were the yeomen, free workers often of some substance, who held their lands under the common law and were not subject to suit of court.[2] As time went on, and particularly during the demographic problems of the late fourteenth century, lords often found it advantageous to 'manumit' their serfs – that is, to grant them their personal freedom – which meant that although the lands which they held might continue to be unfree and to be held of the manor, the men themselves were free to move as economic or personal circumstances dictated, and were subject to the jurisdiction of the King's courts rather than those of the feudality.[3] At the same time, as more tenements came into fewer hands, there also developed a class of landless labourer or cottager, who survived by selling his labour, and who probably lived in a house built without technical permission on what should have been common land. In other words, the late medieval village was a complex community, where the offices of churchwarden or constable were held by substantial yeomen, and where these officers worried about the behaviour of the rootless poor, whose children might become a drain on the resources of the parish.

The relationship of such a community with its lord varied with the circumstances. If he was resident, and behaved reasonably, there would be a warm sense of loyalty, not conditioned by service obligations but by respect for his status. His household would be drawn from the community, and that generated an additional sense of dependence. If, as was usually the case, he was an absentee, then his steward supplied his room. But a steward was a member of the community rather than set apart from it, and the loyalty generated was rather different. A steward was also more likely to see his relationship in terms of cash, of income generated for his employer, and that could damage the harmony. The same would be true, of course, if the lord was ecclesiastical – a bishop or a religious community – where the sense of personal involvement would be even less. Many manors had been granted to the Church over the years, and monasteries were seen as particularly impersonal lords, with whom relations were often bad.[4] By the end of the fifteenth century one of the principal problems was caused by the tendency of many lords to protect their income by enclosing lands for sheep farming. While the population was low, the conversion of arable holdings in this fashion was often carried out with the permission of the manor court and was not controversial. However, when the number of potential tenants began to increase again, sharp practice might be resorted to, and grievances created. By 1518, depopulating enclosure had become an issue which Cardinal Wolsey felt it necessary to address, and by 1549 had become a major source of social dislocation.[5] This, in turn, led to an anti-gentry animus in some parts of the country which Marxist historians have interpreted in terms of class war, but which was in fact less ideological than pragmatic. Respect for the gentry, and indeed for the wealthy merchants who were seen as their allies, depended less on their social status and more on their behaviour. A proper sense of traditional values was becoming necessary to preserve traditional loyalties.[6]

The 20 per cent or so of the population which could be classed as urban followed rather different rules of engagement. In the first place, many towns were small, with no more than two thousand inhabitants, and these resembled villages in their social and jurisdictional structure. If they were not incorporated, the main difference may have lain only in the proportion of craftsmen and traders living in them, and in the fact that 'burgage tenures' were usually free in origin. They would be subject to the authority of the lord's steward and have no rights of self-government. If they were incorporated, either by their lord or by the Crown, then the situation was rather different. In the case of an ordinary town, its charter of incorporation probably conferred upon its mayor and councillors a limited jurisdictional autonomy, authorized them to hold markets and a market (or pie powder) court, and granted its merchant company exclusive control over its trade.[7] If the incorporation was from the Crown, the mayor might become an *ex officio* Justice of the Peace, and the corporation be authorized to elect two members to sit in the House of Commons. In such cases the elite of the town would form the merchant guild, provide the councillors and control elections to the office of mayor. At the same time the urban craftsmen would form themselves into guilds, usually after the nature of religious fraternities or friendly societies. Such fraternities might control a second council (if there was one) and ensure that no outsiders trespassed upon the trading rights of their members. A handful of major cities such as Norwich, York, Bristol and – above all – London constituted counties in their own right, with their own sheriffs and commissions of the peace.[8] They had the same commercial privileges as their less exalted neighbours, and were similarly represented in Parliament, but enjoyed a higher degree of autonomy, and London returned four MPs.

Although gentlemen, and even noblemen, might have town houses, they were not normally resident there, and did not form a part of the urban hierarchy, where authority was determined by function rather than by status. The merchants who formed the town's elite were drawn from a closely knit group of wealthy families who had no pretensions to aristocratic status. They were rich traders who closely guarded their privileged and exclusive position. Below them came the craftsmen, whose guilds might give them access to the lower reaches of urban government, and who equally guarded their positions as masters with jealous care. Below them again came the journeymen and apprentices, who were attached to the guilds but not full members, and at the bottom of the social pyramid those casual labourers who had no security of employment, but who nevertheless formed the unenfranchised majority of the town's population.[9] Below the bottom, in both town and country, and out of reach of everything except charity and punishment, came those rootless drifters known as vagabonds. Sometimes these had been displaced by economic or personal disaster, sometimes they were discharged soldiers or seamen without the proper paperwork which they were supposed to carry, and sometimes they were 'sturdy rogues' who had deliberately chosen a life of wandering and crime. How numerous they were we have no means of knowing, but they were perceived as a growing social threat as the sixteenth century advanced. It was not until 1536 that a statute began to distinguish the unfortunate (who were worthy of charity) from the criminal (who were worthy of nothing but a whipping).[10] A series of Elizabethan Acts, culminating in the Poor Law of 1601, put this distinction on a regular basis and organized local communities to provide the necessary relief. Although the Crown was prepared to acknowledge a responsibility for this provision, it did not extend to any financial assistance.[11]

'Good lordship' was an aristocratic concept which did not extend to such social depths. It indicated a level of mutual obligation and respect which was set out originally in the relationship between a lord and his vassal. At the highest level it was an expression of cultural solidarity between the King and his nobles. The noble owed his monarch service, loyalty, and obedience – up to a point. The monarch, in return, provided patronage and leadership, especially in war. He was expected to listen to the advice of his nobles, and not to require of them any obedience which was derogatory to their honour – such as ordering them to commit a crime in his interest. It was a breach of good lordship if a King governed through favourites, excluding a significant section of his nobles from his council, and it was worse if he concentrated his favours on those same favourites so that many of his vassals were excluded from his bounty. It was behaviour of this sort which weakened the ties which bound Henry VI to his nobles and caused a significant proportion of them to declare against him when Richard of York raised his counter-claim to the throne.[12] A similar relationship existed between a noble lord and his gentry dependents. He provided them with patronage and protection in troubled times – even protection against the law if they had offended – and they in return served him. This service might be of an intimate nature, within his household, or it might be in their capacity as tenants and retainers. When times were difficult, as they were in the mid-fifteenth century, many gentlemen would 'commend' themselves to a lord, offering loyalty in return for protection where no closer tie existed. These were known as his 'well-willers', and formed a significant penumbra around the core of his servants proper.[13] A similar bond might unite a gentleman and his dependants, but did not extend further down the social ladder. The relationship between a master craftsman and his apprentices would be of a similar nature, but would not be so described. At that social level the concept of good lordship blended with that of natural authority. It was a part of the order designed by God that a householder commanded the obedience of his servants, a master that of his pupils, or a husband that of his wife and children.[14] A woman was supposed to be inferior, both morally and intellectually, to a man, and an unmarried woman was subjected to the authority of her father or brother, who might also control her property, if she had any. Upon marriage she became subject to her husband, who acquired a life interest in her property, and only when (and if) she became a widow did she become *une femme seule* in the eyes of the law, and hence an autonomous person. The discipline of a household was delegated to its head, who was expected to exercise 'reasonable correction' upon its members, including servants, for whom he was deemed to be responsible. In the old days, householders had been placed in groups of ten, known as 'tithings', with mutual responsibility for each other's actions, but the advance of the King's laws had made such a system obsolete long before the fifteenth century.[15] Nevertheless the concept of the 'masterless man' lingered on as a pejorative term, and was applied particularly to vagabonds and others who had slipped through the nets of social constraint.

Natural authority and good lordship were both part of that divinely ordained structure of good order which was supposed to guarantee the smooth functioning of human society. As Thomas Cranmer's Homily on obedience put it in 1547,

> Almighty God hath created and appointed all things in heaven, earth and waters in most excellent and perfect order. In heaven he hath appointed distinct orders and states of archangels and angels. In the earth he hath assigned kings, princes, with other governors under them, all in good and necessary order.[16]

Obedience to constituted authority was thus in accordance with the will of God, and Divine punishment awaited the transgressor, in addition to the penalties inflicted by the law. That, at least, was the theory, and every aspect of a man's (or woman's) life was supposedly encompassed within this structure of control. If a man robbed or murdered his neighbour, he had broken the King's peace and came within the jurisdiction of the King's courts. If he had cheated in his business, he could find himself before the municipal court; and if he had committed fornication or defaulted on his tithes, then he was answerable to the Archdeacon.[17] However, habits of obedience were harder to generate. Urban courts only extended as far as the authority of the corporation, and although in principle everyone, high and low, was subject to the jurisdiction of both the King and the Church, in practice that was not the case. A gentleman could use his status to avoid an appearance before the Archdeacon, and a nobleman could employ his retinue to overawe the Assizes. In the latter case, a lot depended upon the effectiveness of the King. In times of royal weakness a nobleman could not only escape the consequences of his misdeeds, but actually use the courts as an alternative weapon of aggression. As Jack Cade complained in 1450, the law

was perverted to serve factional ends – a situation which caused his desperate
followers to take up arms.[18] Neither Edward IV nor Henry VII were weak in the
sense that Henry VI had been weak, and the worst abuses were over by 1461,
but both Kings used their council to adjudicate disputes between men deemed
too powerful for the ordinary courts – a system which evolved under the latter
into the Court of Star Chamber.[19] By the time of Henry VIII, respect for the
royal judges of Assize had been fully restored, and commissions had been used
to extend the King's authority into every corner of the disciplinary system, with
the exception of the Courts Christian. After 1534, these courts also became part
of the royal jurisdiction and the Archdeacon exercised an authority delegated
ultimately from the Crown. Under Elizabeth, that authority was wielded by the
Court of High Commission, but the commissioners were left in no doubt about
who was ultimately in control. Social discipline thus became merged in an
obedience to the Crown which was supposed to be unconditional. If the King
commanded something contrary to established tradition, then he was responsible to God for the aberration (if aberration it was) and no subject was entitled
to judge his actions. Parliament was the voice of the realm in that respect,

> For every Englishman is intended to be there present, either in person or by procu-
> ration and attornies, of what pre-eminence, state, dignity or quality soever he be from
> the prince (be he king or queen) to the lowest person in England. And the consent of
> the parliament is taken to be every man's consent ...[20]

and every pronouncement of Parliament must be taken and obeyed as law. No
custom, tradition or private conviction whatsoever could lawfully stand against
such acts, or against any action taken by the King with the consent of the estates.

This ideology of obedience, which was strongly emphasized by all the
Tudors, was thus intended to cut the ground from beneath all other value
systems, whether chivalric (in the case of the nobility) or religious (in the
case of the clergy). It was a political statement, and the enforcement of the
King's laws, whether secular or ecclesiastical, was only the tip of the iceberg.
The hanging of Lord Dacre of the South for the murder of a gamekeeper was
similarly a political statement aimed at the whole aristocracy rather than the
punishment of an individual offender.[21] There was only one snag with this
ideology. The King was supposed to provide 'good justice', not as part of a
bargain with his people, but as an aspect of the duty which he owed to God.
If he failed to do that, the royalist argument ran, then it was up to God to
impose sanctions. However, in practice there were always those who thought
that they knew better and who censured the King (or Queen) for failing in

this aspect of his (or her) obligation. This opposition was not engendered by any failure to impose penalties for felony or heresy, but in response to policies formulated by the Crown, which might vary from demands for direct taxation to the establishment of the Royal Supremacy.[22] Consequently, in spite of (or perhaps because of) the ideology of obedience, there were frequent riots, and occasional demonstrations or rebellions of a more general nature. Some of these forced concessions from the Crown, others required coercive force to suppress, and in a realm with no police force or standing army this could cause problems. The Tudors, as we have seen, were suspicious of the military pretensions of the aristocracy and preferred to rely on levies raised from the county militias, but this could be difficult if a whole region was disaffected and troops had to be brought in from outside.[23] It says a lot for the effectiveness of Tudor propaganda that this never proved to be physically impossible, and as a result, no revolt against Tudor rule was ever successful. These revolts had a number of different agendas, from regime change to protests against social policy, and appealed to different constituencies, but none of them combined popular force with effective leadership in such a way as to challenge the security of the throne.

At first – and before the Tudor ideology became effective – these rebellions were hangovers from the civil wars. Thomas Stafford and Viscount Lovell at Easter 1486 aimed to replace Henry, probably with the Earl of Lincoln, who had been Richard III's designated heir, but they commanded little support and were easily suppressed. Lincoln was not a direct kinsman, and few were prepared to treat the late King's will with that degree of respect.[24] Similarly those who believed, or pretended to believe, Lambert Simnel's claim to be Edward, Earl of Warwick were harking back to a Yorkist claim that most were happy to see relegated to the background of political life. In spite of the disturbance which he caused on the international scene, Perkin Warbeck's claim to be Richard of York generated even less enthusiasm in the 1490s. Although backed by his 'aunt', Margaret, and by James IV of Scotland, he failed to find significant support either in Ireland or the north of England or Cornwall, and ended up by confessing his imposture as a prisoner in the Tower of London. If it had not been for Sir William Stanley's somewhat mysterious involvement in a conspiracy on his behalf, he would have had little more than nuisance value.[25] Indeed, his incursions probably had the effect of strengthening loyalty to the King, particularly in the Anglo-Scottish borders, where anything coming in with Scots support was liable to arouse ancestral hatreds. Paradoxically, the largest and most dangerous rebellion against Henry VII did not aim to depose him in favour of any rival, real or imagined, but was a protest against his demands for taxation. In January 1497, Parliament voted Henry a subsidy, on the grounds that it was needed to

defend the Northern Marches against the Scots.[26] The Cornishmen, who had
no sense of national priorities, objected forcibly, but had no agenda beyond
demanding the withdrawal of the tax. Nevertheless they swept across the south
of England like a storm, attracting few recruits but also meeting no effective
resistance. The King's army was deployed in the north, and had to be recalled
in haste. On 17 June Lord Daubenny encountered the rebels at Blackheath and
comprehensively defeated them. Two or three of the ringleaders were executed,
but in truth it had come nowhere near shaking Henry Tudor's crown, and it is
interesting to speculate what might have happened if Daubenny had not arrived
when he did. Probably the King would have placated them with concessions,
and might even have exempted Cornwall from the tax. The most interesting
feature of the rebellion, in many ways, is the indication which it gives of the
effectiveness of Henry's campaign to demilitarize the nobility.[27] The speed of
the rebels' advance wrong-footed everyone, and there were no available military
retinues to stand in their way. When Warbeck arrived in Cornwall shortly
after, hoping to take advantage of the discontent, he met with a very negative
reception and was quickly captured by the royal forces which had, by then, been
sent to the area. The Cornish rebellion was a warning to Henry not to take the
loyalty of his subjects for granted – at least when it came to getting money out
of them – but it was scarcely a warning which that security conscious-monarch
needed.

Henry VIII was aware of the discontent which these fiscal policies had
caused, and had no desire that it should mar the magnificence of his accession.
So he cancelled many of the obligations which had been owed to his father,
and promptly disposed of his two principal enforcers, Sir Richard Empson
and Edmund Dudley, so that for the time being no hint of protest spoiled the
smooth passage of his opening years.[28] It was not until 1517 that his *laissez faire*
attitude provoked riots, and then they were not aimed against the King. His
relaxed attitude to international trade had resulted in many foreigners living
and doing business in London, and in that year a mixture of xenophobia and
economic self-interest provoked riots against them in the city. No one was
killed, but property was damaged and many dignities were upset. The Mayor
lost control of the situation, and it was only when the council brought troops
into London that order was restored.[29] This was a warning of the limitations
of urban self-government, and the Mayor was threatened with the loss of the
city's privileges. Some dozen people were executed and over four hundred
pardoned in simultaneous gestures of severity and munificence, which satisfied
the needs of good lordship and suitably enhanced the images of the King, the
Queen – and Cardinal Wolsey. It was, however, as nasty little episode, which

alerted the authorities to the need for constant vigilance in the imposition of social discipline.[30] The same is true of that confrontation between the King and his subjects known as the Amicable Grant, which occurred in 1525 and which harks back to the events of 1497. Henry had fought two wars against the French, completely emptying his coffers for no tangible gain whatsoever, and that had caused hackles to rise among his wealthier mercantile communities. In 1523 Wolsey had tried to cajole a double subsidy out of the House of Commons, and had been constrained to settle for a single one.[31] So, aware of the resistance but hoping to bypass it, he tried to raise a substantial grant without recourse to Parliament on the basis of the assessments made three years earlier in connection with the military survey. Demands were duly made, and commissioners for the collection appointed, but those assessed refused to pay. Anxious consultations resulted between Wolsey and his council colleagues, and various unsuccessful attempts were made to soften up the opposition. However, as the tense situation began to move towards violence in some place – 'almost a rebellion' it was called – the government drew back. The demands were first modified and then withdrawn altogether, and the King was left facing a humiliating climbdown which he was quick to blame on Wolsey.[32] No law had been broken, and the King's position had not been challenged; nevertheless, as an act of political defiance it had been completely successful. There were clearly limits to Henry's authority, which were unarticulated in any contemporary theory, but nonetheless real. The King could not dispose of his subjects' property without their consent, which was a custom rather than a law, and it remained to be seen whether there were any other similar pitfalls in the way of that exercise of sovereign authority which Henry believed to be his as part of his compact with the Almighty.[33]

The most complete expression of that partnership was, of course, the Royal Supremacy over the Church. Drafting the relevant acts in Henry's name, Thomas Cromwell represented that authority as being not only consistent with the ancient constitution of the Church, but also with the will of God. The authority of the Pope was a human invention no more than a few hundred years old, and his canons and decretals a matter of political power and money which had nothing to do with the propagation of the Christian Faith.[34] Cromwell was able to take advantage of long-standing discontents with the exercise of priestly power, and of a more recent upsurge of anticlericalism in the House of Commons, to get these acts passed into law, but nevertheless there was widespread opposition. This came not only from the clergy but also from many influential laymen, who were now confronted with a conflict of principals. It was a religious duty to obey the King in all temporal matters, but also to obey the

Pope in spiritual matters. Was it possible to obey the King in spiritual matters also – and did ecclesiastical jurisdiction constitute a spiritual matter? Yes, said the Pope; no, said the King.[35] Coercive power rested with the latter, and it was not difficult to convince oneself that the King's stand was a mere temporary expedient, designed to enable him to change his woman. Once that had been accomplished, and a son born to the union, a deal would be struck and the high-flown rhetoric would be forgotten. It was unnecessary to run the appalling risks of high treason to resist a brief aberration. So many important men grumbled and accepted the changes, only realizing when it was too late that Henry was in deadly earnest about his supremacy, and had no intention of surrendering it, no matter how much his circumstances might change.[36] Consequently, outright resistance to the supremacy was confined to a few individuals – More, Fisher and the Carthusian priors, who paid a terrible price for their opposition – and to those (mostly clergy) who grumbled loudly enough for their discontent to come to the ears of Cromwell's informants. Nearly all the latter submitted when faced with the dire alternative, and the fact that Cromwell was never short of information should warn us against assuming that they represented a majority of the community. [37] In fact, the Royal Supremacy was accepted by most men, both high and low, and it was only when it began to be used to affect changes in the ancient usages of the Church that effective resistance crystallized.

The Pilgrimage of Grace, which began in Lincolnshire in the autumn of 1536, was in many ways a radical movement. When its demands were formulated in the Pontefract Articles of November, they constituted a complete indictment of royal policy over the previous decade. They requested that the recently dissolved monasteries should be reinstated, that the Royal Supremacy Acts should be repealed, and that base-born and heretical councillors such as Cromwell and Cranmer should be dismissed and punished. They were based on the traditional (but fictional) assumption that the policies objected to were the work of 'evil councillors' who had misled the King. What they did not propose was that the King had broken his coronation oath, and thereby forfeited his crown.[38] In fact, they had no sanctions to implement at all, beyond, presumably, using their armed force to impose their will. They professed loyalty to the King, and a desire to recall him to the 'good old ways' of government. One of the leaders, Lord Darcy, spoke in terms of honour; the King had dishonoured himself and his peers by his recent actions, and needed to remember the old code of his nobility. They did not see themselves as rebels at all, but as loyal subjects protesting against the King's ill-considered actions.[39] Although they demanded that Princess Mary be restored to her place in the succession, they did not propose to advance her in her father's place. Nor were the leaders united. Some of the more radical wished to use the fact that they had 20,000 men under arms to press on south from Doncaster, taking advantage of the fact that Henry had no adequate force to oppose them. Others wished to accept his offers of concessions, and settle for what they could obtain without resorting to violence. This, they argued, would be more consistent with their professions of loyalty. It was the latter group who prevailed, and the rebel army dispersed without ever coming to blows.[40] The King offered a general pardon, but had no intention of honouring his concessions, and a secondary outbreak in Yorkshire in January 1537 gave him an excuse to forget the pardon also. One hundred and thirty-two rebels were executed, including most of the leaders, and this act of official terrorism seems to have deterred any further expressions of discontent.[41] Although there were many reports from the south of England of sympathy for the 'northern men', the rebellion did not spread, and the magnates to whom the insurgents had looked for support – the Duke of Norfolk, the Earl of Derby and the Earl of Shrewsbury in particular – all declared for the King. The Royal Supremacy, and the actions which followed it, deeply divide the country, but most men, uncertain how to react, took refuge in the thought that it was Henry's responsibility to get his act straight with God, and the ideology of obedience prevailed.

Henry's death at the end of January 1547 removed his awesome personality from the scene and left the supremacy in the hands of a child. Edward's council nevertheless decided to pursue a 'forward' policy and embraced a moderate form of Protestantism. One of the reasons for this was to protect the supremacy against any possible conservative backlash following Henry's death, but its implementation was complicated by the fact that the reformed faith was only embraced by a very small proportion of the population.[42] The introduction of the first Prayer Book at Whitsun 1549 was therefore greeted with widespread complaint, with rioting in Oxfordshire and with a full-scale rebellion in the South West. The latter, which was inspired and partly led by conservative clergy, like the Pilgrimage of Grace, professed loyalty to the King, but was clearly directed against the minority council. Its demands were not formulated in the same respectful language as those of the Pilgrimage, being characterized by the refrain 'we will have…'. Interestingly, it did not demand the repeal of the supremacy, but was rather focused on its use in a conservative sense.[43] The council was under no illusions that this was a rebellion, but although it commanded a good deal of support in Devon and Cornwall, it did not spread much outside those counties, and was put down after a hard-fought campaign in which the use of German mercenaries featured largely. Levies were used from counties further east, but sparingly, as there were legitimate doubts about their reliability. The ideology of obedience was confused by the circumstances of the minority, but by and large it held, and when the council introduced a more radical Protestant book in 1552, it was accepted without resistance. In 1549, however, the issue was further confused by the coincidence of a rebellion of a different kind on the other side of the country. This was the so-called 'camping movement' in East Anglia, which was directed not so much against the council or the Lord Protector as against the local gentry.[44] The gentry were, of course, the agents of the government, but this protest was rather against their failure to implement official policy than against that policy itself. Since Wolsey's investigations in 1518, the Crown had set its face against 'depopulating enclosure' – that is, the conversion of arable land to sheep runs – and had directed a number of statutes and proclamations to that effect. The Protector himself was known to be sympathetic to this cause, and the grievance arose from the failure of the local gentry to implement a policy which was clearly against their economic interests.[45] The protest began with a riot at Attleborough, near Norwich, in July and spread rapidly across Norfolk and Suffolk. There was little personal violence and the demands of the leaders were reasonable enough, but the council had no option but to treat it as a rebellion. To challenge the authority of the Commissioners of the Peace was to challenge indirectly the authority of the Crown itself, and there seemed to be little point in negotiation. The conflict was sharpened when a military force sent down under the leadership of the Marquis of Northampton was repulsed from Norwich, with severe loss of life. However, Robert Kett, who was the effective leader, had no idea how to exploit his victory and merely waited to see what the government would do next.[46] It sent another force, led by a competent soldier (the Earl of Warwick) and consisting largely of mercenaries, which defeated the rebels decisively at 'Dussindale', near Norwich, and recaptured the city. Kett and a number of the other leaders were hanged, because the government had no option with those taken in arms against it, but no solution was proposed to the grievances which had provoked it, and discontent simmered on for a number of years. The gentry were reinstated and the one thing which was made clear was that the government regarded authority as a seamless web, which was not accessible to piecemeal challenge. The sacred authority of the King and the natural authority of the gentleman were equally embraced by the same theory of obedience.[47] It was perhaps significant that both in Devon and in Norfolk the natural authority of the nobility had recently been removed by Crown action, and perhaps the time had not yet come when the King was able to supply that leadership himself – not at least while he was a child.[48]

The advent of England's first ruling Queen, in the person of Mary, produced similar uncertainties. In a sense, a 'sovereign lady' was a contradiction in terms, and if Mary had been confronted by a man with a reasonable claim instead of by Jane Grey in July 1553, she might never have come to the throne at all. Henry had spent most of his adult life trying to forestall such an eventuality, but when Edward died without heirs, the accession of a woman was inevitable.[49] It was the old King who had secured her inheritance for her, both by being her father and by so designating her in his last will and testament. So the acceptance of Mary was an aspect of obedience to Henry VIII, and was generally seen as such. However, having made the imaginative leap required by the acceptance of a creature normally seen as weak and vulnerable in the position of supreme authority, the next question was – whom would she marry? As a single woman, Mary had been singularly free from male tutelage. Her father was dead and her brother was a minor, so she had grown to be a magnate in her own right before any question arose of her succeeding to the throne. There was, however, only one way to secure a legitimate succession and that was by marrying and bearing children, so marriage was hardly an option, and Mary tackled the problem at once. For a variety of reasons her choice alighted on Prince Philip of Spain, a widower with one son, and that immediately raised the spectre of a foreign King.[50] So while her council concentrated on negotiating a treaty which would give Philip as little power as possible, malcontents began conspiring to force her to change her mind. The result should have been a threefold march on London – an unstoppable demonstration of popular outrage – but the authorities were alert and what actually happened was a medium-sized rebellion in Kent, led by Sir Thomas Wyatt. Although briefly threatening, this collapsed in the face of the loyalty of the City of London, and Wyatt and about a hundred of his followers were executed.[51] Discontent rumbled on, but the marriage took place as planned in July 1554, and Philip accepted (although with no very good grace) the limited position which had been negotiated for him. There were those, particularly among the military-minded aristocracy, who welcomed him simply because he was male, and restored something of the right order to the structure of authority. Mary remained the focus of public loyalty, and although she lost popularity through her marriage, and through the religious persecution with which she endeavoured to solve the problem of a divided Church, she remained very much the lady in charge. This survived her failure to bear a child in the summer of 1555, and was enhanced by Philip's subsequent departure for the Low Countries and his unwillingness to return. Although this was a cause of much personal anguish to Mary, it simplified her position as the sole head of government. The King gradually lost interest in England and, apart from returning in the spring of 1557 to bring England into his war with France, he left the Queen very much to her own devices.[52] By the end of the reign there was a great deal of grumbling about Mary's rule, but her council did a good job of running the administration in her name and, in spite of some conspiracies, there were no further rebellions against her. By November 1558, despite Philip's somewhat erratic intrusion into the country's affairs, England had got used to the idea of a sovereign lady and had embraced that statute which declared her authority to be the same as that of any of the Kings, her predecessors. That had at least solved the vexed problem of having a *femme couvert* on the throne, and clarified that the realm of England was a public office not a private lordship, to be passed to her husband in full ownership for life. Although she found difficulty in coping with the concept, Mary was a sovereign first and a wife second.[53]

When her sister died in November 1558, Elizabeth thus found herself in a strong position. The teething troubles of female monarchy had already been overcome. Philip at first welcomed her accession on the ground that it guaranteed the stability of one of his key allies, and the people of England welcomed her as King Henry's only surviving child. She may have been helped by the fact that all her possible rivals – Margaret Clifford, Catherine Grey and Mary Stuart – were also female, but no resistance was raised on the grounds of her gender, even when that led to unpopular marriage negotiations.[54] Whereas Mary had regarded her sex as an embarrassment and a liability, Elizabeth regarded hers as an opportunity. She retained control by a mixture of bafflement and flirtation, so that she became, in turn, the unattainable damsel of courtly love, '*la belle dame sans merci*', and the mysterious virgin of Christian tradition. Partly for this reason, she also had a unique capacity for attracting loyal service, and her council was particularly efficient. The formula was simple. Where the action concerned was popular, as in the recreation of the Royal Supremacy, the Queen would take the credit; when unpopular, as with the negotiation of the Anjou marriage, it became the council's responsibility. The Queen liked divided councils, as they helped to keep her options open for as long as possible, and (with the possible exception of Robert Dudley) did not confer political benefits upon her personal favourites.[55] Emphasizing her parentage as being 'mere English', she showed from the start a special talent for generating loyalty, and faced only one rebellion in the course of her forty-five-year reign. This was the rising of the northern Earls in 1569, which posed no real threat to her crown and provided instead a forensic exercise in solving the problems of that part of the country.

It has been described as a 'feudal' rebellion, and in a sense that is true, but it was inspired less by baronial discontents than by objections to the Queen's religious policy. In 1568, Mary of Scotland, deposed by her own people, had sought refuge and support in England. Mary was the granddaughter of Margaret, Henry VIII's elder sister, and therefore in the eyes of Catholic Europe the true Queen of England. That was not an issue in 1568, but she did have a good claim to be Elizabeth's heir if the Queen should die childless, and there were many in England, not only Catholics, who wished to see that claim acknowledged.[56] A plan was proposed to marry her to the Duke of Norfolk, who was a conformist in his religion, on the not unreasonable assumption that that would diminish her Catholic credentials. Elizabeth would have none of it, and berated the Duke for his presumption. This caused some consternation among his supporters, among whom the Earls of Westmorland and Northumberland should be numbered. At the same time, a conspiracy was forming at the court against the overwhelming influence of Sir William Cecil. Cecil was blamed for the diplomatic fracas caused by Elizabeth's diversion of Alba's pay ships in December 1568, an episode for which he was held responsible, although the decision had undoubtedly been the Queen's. Thanks to the Earl of Leicester, the Queen got wind of this plot as well, and made it clear that her secretary enjoyed her full confidence.[57] The northern Earls had also been on the fringes of that plot, and by the summer of 1569 were feeling very vulnerable. Added to that, they were both conservative in their religious preferences, and objected both to the Royal Supremacy and to the way in which it was being exercised. Furthermore, the Earl of Northumberland had lost that favour at court which he had enjoyed under Mary, together with the wardenship of the East March, and felt that it was only a matter of time before Cecil moved against him. He seems to have been contemplating something like a pre-emptive strike, but he was not much of a leader and his moves were tentative. The Earl of Sussex, the President of the Council in the North, heard of these preparations and summoned Northumberland to explain himself. He appears to have been satisfied, but the Queen was not, and summoned both the Earls to court.[58] Fearing that this presaged their arrest, and stimulated by the redoubtable Countess of Westmorland, they ordered a general mobilization of their affinities, at first on the grounds that the Queen had ordered it. In spite of the confusion caused by this misinformation, the response was not overwhelming.

On the whole, the Neville and Percy affinities in County Durham and the North Riding answered the summons to Brancepeth, giving the Earls a reasonably large following, but the Percy retainers in Northumberland and those outside the immediate area held aloof, so that although the rising was a feudal one – or, at any rate, a bastard feudal one – the result was nothing like the private army which the Earls' grandfathers would have been able to raise. At first they enjoyed considerable success, largely because there was no royalist force mobilized against them. They occupied Durham and celebrated Mass in the cathedral before setting off south, not much augmented by their passage through the palatinate.[59] Nor was the leadership completely united, because although their professed aim was to free Mary, Queen of Scots from Bolton where she was being held and to force Elizabeth to acknowledge her as the heir of England, at the same time a more radical element among their following, probably led by Richard Norton, were seeking Spanish and papal help to depose Elizabeth and raise Mary in her place. By 25 November, when they reached Bramham Moor, near Leeds, it was obvious that the movement had run out of steam. The support they had sought from the rest of Yorkshire and from Lancashire had not materialized and the members of their original force were beginning to desert.[60] Rumours reached them of a royal army advancing from the south, and they began to retreat. In spite of enjoying a belated success in the taking of Barnard Castle a few days later, they went on retreating, diminishing as they went, until they arrived at Hexham in the middle of December. There the Earls dismissed what was left of their following and fled over the border into Scotland. A few days later, Lord Hunsdon arrived with a significant royal army, and the gentry of the area made haste to demonstrate their credentials of loyalty. The Duke of Alba had not wanted to know about so shaky an enterprise, and the papal response, in the form of the Bull *Regnans in Excelsis*, came only long after the rebellion had collapsed.

The rebellion of the northern Earls was thus less a threat to the Queen than an object lesson in how far central government had progressed. The ancient retinues of two of the country's most powerful and traditional nobles were exposed as feeble forces when directed against the Crown, and the allegiance of the north-eastern gentry, like that of the rest of the country, belonged overwhelmingly to the Queen. Placed in direct confrontation, the ideologies of Lordship and of Obedience resulted in a decisive victory for the latter. The earldom of Westmorland was broken up, and that of Northumberland severely pruned, while the inheritance of Dacre was also taken into the hands of the Crown by the attainder of the Duke of Norfolk.[61] Some of these lands were kept in the hands of the Queen, but the bulk were distributed among the loyal gentry of the neighbourhood, thus converting the northern shires of England from 'Indian territory' into counties like any other – well on the way to becoming the middle shires of the seventeenth-century kingdom. Elizabeth faced many more dangerous threats, but none of them involved any attempt to raise a part of the country against her. The Catholic conspirators who plotted against her life, from Ridolfi in 1571 to Babington in 1586, all proposed a great Catholic rising to take advantage of the confusion following her death, but none showed the slightest signs of putting such a rising in place.[62] Indeed, the great Catholic rebellion was a fiction with which the plotters comforted each other and sought to give substance to their plans. By 1603 there were no alternative structures of loyalty except among that minority which clung to the papal allegiance, and even they were doing their best to reserve their temporal obedience.

So by the end of the period, the Crown had established its claim to a monopoly of political authority, and national priorities had taken precedence over local ones. In 1601 an Act of Parliament 'for the government of the north parts' made it clear that the exercise of any private jurisdiction was illegal, and that rights of arrest and punishment belonged exclusively to the Queen's courts and commissioners.[63] About ten years earlier the Commission of the Peace had been revised, clarifying both the administrative and judicial functions of the office and its answerability to the Privy Council.[64] Symbolic of the shift in priorities which had taken place was the virtual disappearance of the offence of Petty Treason. It was High Treason to rebel against the monarch, to conspire against him (or her), or even to criticize the government. Innumerable statutes through the century had amplified or curtailed the offence, adapting it to changing circumstances. Petty Treason had been the commission of similar acts against one's lord or master. A gentleman taking arms against his overlord, or a wife seeking to poison her husband, would have been guilty of petty treason, because they were acting contrary to the obedience which they naturally owed. However, such a concept had virtually disappeared by the reign of Elizabeth, when such offences would simply have been treated as breeches of the Queen's peace – either felonies or misdemeanours. With the disappearance of 'bondmen of condition', which took place between the middle of the fifteenth and the middle of the sixteenth centuries, the whole structure of private justice was dismantled.[65] A villein or serf had only been answerable in his lord's court, no matter what his offence, but when such people no longer existed, the manor or honour court lost its jurisdiction, and the private courts were restricted to economic matters such as disputes over tenures or land use. Similarly, the disappearance of franchises following the Act of 1536 meant that the King's writ ran uniformly throughout the land. Franchisal courts had always administered the King's laws, but now they did so always in the King's name rather than in the franchise-holder's. By 1603 the Crown enjoyed a monopoly of criminal justice, just as it enjoyed a monopoly of physical force. The private criminal court, like the private army, was a thing of the past. The concept of natural order remained, but it no longer had jurisdictional teeth.

The Selling of the Monarchy

Henry VII was not a charismatic person, but he needed to project himself as King. The feeble nature of his hereditary claim, and the circumstances of his accession, meant that from the very first he had to work hard to convince his subjects of his royal credentials. He did this partly by acting the part, calling a parliament and ennobling his more prominent followers, and partly by showing exemplary piety and dignity. According to Francis Bacon (who at least knew what should have happened) he 'caused *Te Deum Laudamus* to be solemnly sung' while still on the field at Bosworth, and on reaching London went straight to St Paul's to 'make offertory' of his standards.[1] No one was to doubt that his victory had been conferred by God for the specific purpose of expiating his predecessor's crimes. What Henry's private religious views may have been we have no idea, but throughout his reign he was to display the warmest devotion to the Church. When he went on progress, he made pilgrimage to the shrines of the saints he encountered on his way and punctiliously celebrated every stage of his journey with offerings and thanksgivings. He founded religious houses, celebrated the Pope's jubilee, and built the splendid chapel which still bears his name at Westminster Abbey. He also built a magnificent royal palace at Richmond and borrowed from the Court of Burgundy a style of grandeur which was to be developed more fully by his successors. He spent lavishly on jewels, tapestries and pictures, and mounted tournaments with gilded armour and bejewelled trappings displaying the red and white roses which were the symbols of his rule.[2] He provided a glittering coronation for his Queen using the symbolism of the unity of the roses to emphasize the significance of their union, and encouraged the City of London to stage an ornate and learned pageant for the marriage of his son, Arthur with Catherine, the Princess of Spain. Display was fundamental to his style of monarchy, and applied not only to public events but also to his patronage of scholars, musicians and printers. Everything had to be of the highest quality.

Henry resurrected the ancient ceremony of crown-wearing on such feasts as Christmas, Easter and Whitsun, and also instituted a special rite for the ceremony of touching for the King's Evil, both things being designed to assert the sacral nature of kingship as he wished it to be seen.[3] It was with a similar end in mind that he pressed for the canonization of his Lancastrian predecessor, Henry VI, and caused a votive figure of himself in a devotional posture to be placed by Edward the Confessor's shrine at Westminster. Especially after 1503, when the Tudor succession hung on the single life of the young Henry, the King needed all the supernatural reassurance he could get. Nor did the politics of display stop with his own actions and self-presentation. The Revels Office and the council were busily concerned to ensure that his hosts on progresses got the message as well. This was clearly demonstrated when he went to York in the spring of 1486. The city had been strongly supportive of Richard III, and a new dialogue of authority was necessary – or, as Edward Hall put it, the King needed to 'purge the contentious smoke of dissention'.[4] With suitable guidance from the court, he was greeted with a pageant of six Henrys and a Solomon welcoming him as the 'most prudent prince' of all. David emerged to present him with the sword of victory, and Our Lady promised her special intercessions to ensure that God's grace would rest with the new sovereign. The encounter was a great success, and Henry left with the feeling that there, at least, a reconciliation had been affected. While there, he celebrated the Feast of the Garter with due solemnity, wearing his crown in honour both of the place and the occasion.[5] From York, the King conducted a stately progress to Worcester, Hereford and Bristol, where the city authorities likewise deployed the arts of praise in support of petitions for royal favour – the 'delicate tactics of counsel and instruction', as one scholar has called them.[6] Henry interested himself in every detail of this tour, realizing how important it was to establish the mutual obligations of King and subject. Even at this very early stage, and without any personal experience to guide him, the King showed a keen awareness of the importance of ceremony, of his own participation, and of the piety and dignity which he displayed at each venue and in the company of nervous local dignitaries. The delicacy of his situation was emphasized when, even as the progress went on, Viscount Lovell raised an insurrection in Worcestershire. It was an episode of no great significance and was easily suppressed, but it served as a warning to Henry not to take his victory for granted. More pageants of triumph and submission would be called for before his position could be described as secure. However, his marriage had reconciled many former Yorkists, and the prompt birth of Prince Arthur in September 1486 convinced other waverers that God was really on his side. Henry had no natural gift for the theatricalities of monarchy, but he was able to go through the motions with a convincing grace, and he clearly understood the need for royal display.[7]

Nevertheless, and despite the studied magnificence of his court, Henry's image did not altogether match up to reality. This was partly because he was not naturally a very public person. He knew how to enjoy himself, but it was mostly within the confines of his chamber. He played a great deal at cards and dice (losing substantial sums in the process) and generously rewarded those musicians, acrobats and other entertainers who beguiled his leisure hours. When he travelled on progress, which he did frequently, he spent much time in hawking and hunting, and in watching archery competitions. He gave generous presents, often on the spur of the moment to people who had no particular claim upon him, and spent large sums on rebuilding at Greenwich and Baynard's Castle, but it was all rather unsystematic.[8] Typically, he gave both his sons a first-rate humanist education, but there is very little evidence of humanist influence in his court as a whole, or that he himself shared such tastes. Nor did he take any part in the magnificent tournaments with which he entertained foreign ambassadors, even during the first ten years of his reign while he was still young enough to have done so. He was abstemious in his diet and retired early, even from the most sumptuous of banquets, kept no mistresses and never attempted to dance the night away. In Bacon's words: '[…] in so much as in triumphs of jousts and tourneys, and balls and masques, which they then called disguises, he was rather a princely and gentle spectator than seemed much delighted.'[9] Consequently there was an ambiguity about his image, which became more marked as the reign progressed. His nervousness about aristocratic pretensions, and the fiscal penalties which he imposed on his nobles for notional breeches of security, made him unpopular with precisely that constituency which he was trying to impress through his courtly splendour. This unpopularity had an adverse effect upon his image and caused him to appear grasping and acquisitive. There was a sense in which this was accurate, especially during the last five years of his life, but it was also extended to make him appear mean, which was never true. So, towards the end of his reign, Henry became rich (which he was), and prudent (which he was also), but also a grim old miser, which he most certainly was not. It was a grey and rather tired image which Henry VII bequeathed to posterity, the result partly of his failing health and partly of the of the 'apprehensions and suspicions' with which he was beset; but he did bequeath his crown to his surviving son, who burst on the scene like a sun in splendour in 1509.[10]

It was almost as though Henry had choreographed this succession. Henry VIII was as great a contrast with his father as could well be imagined. Polydore Vergil had described the old King as slender of body, 'his height above the average', but the young King was built like a tank and head and shoulders taller than his courtiers. He excelled in all physical sports and took part with great enthusiasm, whether it were tennis, archery or jousting. He inherited his physique from his maternal grandfather, Edward IV, from whom he also seems to have got his reddish hair and his appetite for life. His image could have taken care of itself, but it was fostered both by the King and by his council. He distanced himself, quite deliberately, from his father's fiscal policies, sending out the message that he was not interested in money but in glory. Being scarcely out of the schoolroom himself, he was able to pose as a patron of learning, and was immediately hailed as such by humanists eager to enjoy his bounty.[11] Although it was not explicitly acknowledged, sexuality was an important aspect of his general prowess, and although he could have had his choice of the ladies of the court, he chose to marry his beautiful sister-in-law, Catherine of Aragon, to whom he had been betrothed on and off for several years. Their wedding was a relatively quiet event, possibly because it was arranged in a hurry, but their joint coronation on midsummer's day was an event of great splendour, which kept the goldsmiths, tailors and embroiderers busy for weeks. As Edward Hall observed: '[…] of a surety, more rich, nor more strange nor more curious works hath not been seen than were prepared against this coronation.'[12] Henry's zest and his appetite were remarkable and he followed an enormous banquet by dancing until dawn, long outlasting his dutiful but exhausted spouse. Jousting and feasting occupied the next few days, and then merged seamlessly into an unbroken round of festivities, revels, disguisings and pageants. The King spent long days in the saddle, hunting and hawking, and long nights in dancing and making music. Catherine fell pregnant within weeks of their marriage, and Henry's image as the very model of a King was complete. The fact that the child was a girl and born dead may have damaged Catherine's credibility, but it did no harm to the King's at all, and when he took her off on progress in the summer of 1510 he kept up an extraordinary regiment of shooting, wrestling and casting of the bar, in addition to singing, dancing and playing on a variety of musical instruments. It was the sheer arrogance of youth which caused him to exclaim that the King of France dared not look him in the face.[13] When his aggressive policies led to war in 1512, Henry discovered that the real thing was not a tournament, and he was not particularly successful, but in the eyes of his subjects he was now a triumphant warlike prince, in addition to the other virtues with which he was so lavishly endowed.

Henry hankered after war, not because he was naturally bloodthirsty, but because it offered a short cut to that glory and reputation which he so craved. Where Henry VII had been cautious and prudent, husbanding his resources, Henry VIII was spendthrift, lavishing money on his army and navy and on developing the latest in big guns. Disillusionment may have caught up with him in the summer of 1514, or more likely Wolsey convinced him that his resources were exhausted, but the king yielded to papal pressure and made peace. However, the death of Louis XII soon after and the accession of Francis I led to more posturing, and a renewal of the war seemed likely – until, that is, Henry changed his mind again. Leo X's initiative for a crusade gave him his cue, and he decided to become the prince of reconciliation.[14] He had tried unsuccessfully to bully Francis; now he would upstage him by demonstrating that he was the true arbiter of Europe. Thanks to Wolsey's indefatigable diplomacy, by 1518 he was in a position to build a new Anglo-French agreement into a treaty of universal peace. Europe had never seen anything quite like it. Bilateral and multilateral treaties were common, and usually of short duration, but all the great powers and most of the smaller ones adhered to the Treaty of London, which was intended to last for ever. What had begun as a papal initiative for a five-year truce followed by a crusade had ended as a universal peace, brokered by the King of England.[15] A brief mention of a crusade in the preamble gave a nod in the Pope's direction, but otherwise he was included as a mere participant. Leo was chagrined but in no position to object to such a worthy process, so it met with universal acclamation. Henry's reputation soared. He had achieved by diplomacy a status which no amount of armed posturing could have equalled, and his image was gratifyingly enhanced. It did not last, of course. The very next year, the death of the Emperor Maximilian and the ensuing Imperial election reignited tensions, and Henry felt bound to enter the lists in order to maintain his reputation. He did not stand a chance and was humiliated by his rejection. By 1520, the successful candidate, Charles of Spain, and the French king were squaring up to each other and Henry's role as the arbiter of Europe had been reduced to that of makeweight between the two major protagonists. However, he was seriously short of money and in no position to do anything about it.[16]

Instead he turned his attention in a different (and cheaper) direction by writing and publishing a theological treatise against Martin Luther. Luther was a fair target for orthodox polemics, and it is very doubtful how much of the *Assertio Septem Sacramentorum* actually came from the King's pen. Nevertheless it achieved its desired objective, earning from the Pope the title *Defensor Fidei* and giving Henry a reputation for orthodoxy and for scholarship, neither of which was wholly deserved.[17] Henry VII had originally made use of the printing press as a vehicle for propaganda when Machlinia had printed a summary of Innocent VIII's Bull recognizing him as King of England, a proclamation which was issued on 13 June 1486. However he had not followed this up by printing subsequent proclamations, and Henry VIII had done so only infrequently. It was therefore a new departure when the *Assertio* was published by Wynkyn de Worde in the summer of 1521. It was something of a best-seller, translations into German and French as well as English appearing in about twenty editions in Antwerp, Rome, Cologne and several other places.[18] In spite of earlier brushes with the papal jurisdiction, by the mid-1520s Henry's reputation as a champion of the faith, and of the papacy, seemed assured. It was against this background that the King's famous falling-out with Rome occurred. As early as the summer of 1527 Henry was contributing to tracts written in defence of his cause, which were circulated to interested parties. These remained in manuscript, but the King was clearly directing the ideology of the debate long before Wolsey fell from power in the autumn of 1529.[19] The first of these controversial works to appear in print was the *Censurae academiarum*, published by Thomas Berthelet, probably in April 1531. This was a collection of the (favourable) pronouncements made by various universities upon the King's theological case, but did not appear in Henry's name, or with any obvious input from him. The *Censurae* was translated into English and published again in the same year, because there was no doubt that Henry was widening the debate to include the whole political nation as his own thinking moved towards a domestic solution to his problem. He was concerned to demonstrate just how unreasonable Clement was being in not acceding to his request. By this time, something of a pamphlet war had broken out. John Fisher's *De causa matrimonii serenissimi Regis Angliae*, published at Alcala in 1530, was only to be expected, but William Tyndale's *Practice of Prelates*, which appeared at Antwerp in the same year, was an unlooked-for blow. Henry had been expecting the reformer and Bible translator to support him against the Pope. The King struck back with *A Glasse of the Truth* in 1532, a work which, although not passing in his name, was nevertheless partly his work, and certainly represented his point of view.[20] By 1533 Thomas Cromwell was masterminding the King's publicity campaign, and polemicists such as Christopher St Germain and Richard Morison carried it to a new level of intensity. By this time also continental theologians were wading into the fray, mostly on the Pope's side, and the conflict had become a *cause célèbre*. When Henry began to use statutes to make his will effective, the preambles also became polemical statements, aimed not merely at the members of the Parliament but, in addition, at those educated laymen (lawyers for the most part) who bought copies of the printed Acts.[21]

The King's image therefore underwent a dramatic transformation between 1530 and 1535. From being a loyal son of the Church, and no worse than most in terms of his sexual morality, he became in the eyes of Catholic Europe a schismatic and lecherous tyrant, imposing his will upon his hapless wife and subjects in pursuit of his own lusts Of course, the image which he and Cromwell presented to the English people was very different. Henry was a true King, championing the law of God against a politicized Pope and his venal henchmen. He was also a true-born Englishman, standing up to the wickedness of foreigners, particularly the Pope and the Emperor, and doing his best to secure a lawful son to succeed him on his throne, thereby avoiding the risk of a foreign King. This polarization was exacerbated in 1535 by the executions of Fisher, More and the Carthusian priors. Henry became not merely a tyrant but a bloodstained one, a reputation made more infamous in 1536 by the beheading of his concubine, Anne Boleyn. 'Junker Harry', as Luther observed, 'means to be God and do as pleases himself.'[22] Outside England, his reputation continued to deteriorate, helped on by his repudiation of Anne of Cleves in 1540 and the execution of her successor in 1542. Henry was now a serial wife-killer as well as a heretic, and his subjects in exile, such as Reginald Pole, did their level best to enhance that image. Within England, some secretly shared this condemnation, but most accepted the King as he was presented to them – a God-fearing prince, executing justice on those who conspired against him. What better endorsement could his proceedings receive than the birth of his longed-for son, Prince Edward in 1537? This schizophrenic image long outlasted the King's own life. To Elizabethan Englishmen he was a great King who had established the Church of England, founded the Navy, and made England feared in the western world, while to Catholic exiles such as Nicholas Sanders and Robert Parsons he was the supreme egotist who had destroyed centuries of religious life in pursuit of his own personal and selfish goals and had left his country divided and isolated.[23]

Henry did not rely only on the written word to counter these damaging attacks. Deeds spoke louder than words and his will was effectively enforced both by Parliament and by the courts, while charges of heresy were refuted by the passage of measures such as the Act of Six Articles. He also commissioned portraits of himself, magnificently clad and in a posture of aggressive self-confidence. The best-known is that by his German court painter, Hans Holbein, which shows him in about 1537, with his arms akimbo and his codpiece very much to the fore. This has survived endless reproductions, both at the time and since, to become the classic image of triumphant monarchy.[24] How many people outside the court would ever have seen this image is another question. The representations of Henry in the widest circulation were those on his coins and his seals, which show him in a conventional pose, and that on the title page of his Great Bible, which shows him as Solomon handing down the Word of God to the temporality and the clergy. Henry relied heavily upon the Old Testament imagery of Solomon (or David, according to circumstances) both in word and in picture, and this was assiduously promoted, so that even the illiterate would not have been unaware of these presentations. In spite of the controversial nature of his later policies, and the gross caricature of a man which he had become by 1545, Henry won the battle for the hearts and minds of his subjects. The Royal Supremacy became the 'English way' of coping with the problems of the Church, and the King's triumphant entry into Boulogne in 1544 apparently set the seal on a lifetime of military ambition. The reality was less splendid. Henry died at the age of 55, beset by private and sexual uncertainties, leaving his Crown to a nine-year-old boy and a regime at war with the Scots and at odds with both the Emperor and the King of France. Nevertheless he was held to be a great king, and his like would not be seen again upon the throne of England.[25]

Henry would have been a hard act to follow, and fortunately his young son was not constrained to try. He was not a magnificent physical specimen, and his enthusiasm for war games was still that of a child. It might be necessary to pursue the war in Scotland, but that was the Lord Protector's policy, not the King's. A little later, the court painter, Willem Scrots, had a go at representing Edward in an imitation of his father's famous pose, but the result was unconvincing and not really relevant. How do you create a convincing power image for a King who is, for all practical purposes, a schoolboy? In his earliest public appearances, giving audience to his new council and undergoing the rite of coronation, he was presented as a solemn little figure, at once dignified, isolated and vulnerable.[26] That there may have been a mischievous side to Edward is indicated not long after in his dealings with John Fowler, a groom of the Privy Chamber, who had been recruited to assist Lord Seymour's quest for the hand of the Queen Dowager. While agreeing that Lord Seymour should wed, the King tried to divert his attention to his own sister, Mary, knowing perfectly well how averse she would be to any such approach. The royal sense of humour does not very often surface in the records, but this was surely a joke at Seymour's expense.[27] Similarly, the journal which Edward kept almost from the beginning of his reign until late in 1552 was in the nature of a school exercise, which expressed his youthful interests, but did not allow much of his boyish personality to surface. It was intended to be a record of events, not a personal diary, and does not even reveal much about the religious allegiance which we know from other sources meant a lot to him. Even before his accession, Edward had been presented as the heir to his father's virtues, as well as to his throne, but this was a hard claim to substantiate. More importantly, he must be shown to excel in those exercises appropriate to his age – in other words, he must be the model schoolboy. In the spring of 1549 Martin Bucer, who was not yet in England and had probably been fed his lines by Thomas Cranmer, wrote of him as 'leaned to a miracle'. He was, the Strasburg reformer continued:

> [...] well acquainted with Latin and has a fair knowledge of Greek. He speaks Italian and is learning French. He is now studying moral philosophy from Cicero and Aristotle, but no study delights him more than that of the Holy Scriptures.[28]

The King's own letters go some way towards substantiating this picture, even before his accession, showing the solemnity of a boy fitting himself for the highest office, or, more probably, being so fitted by his tutors. They display his command of Latin, which they were no doubt designed to do, and a moral earnestness well beyond his years. Although there is no specific evidence to that effect, he must have been brought up in the reformed faith, because he showed himself almost from the start eager to promote that cause, and in March 1551 intervened personally in the case of his sister Mary's Mass to insist that it was contrary to his conscience that his laws should not be obeyed.[29] In 1552 he was also sympathetic to the scruples of John Hooper, who did not want to be consecrated Bishop wearing vestments, and was only persuaded to withdraw his support over this same question of the obedience to law. It is not surprising that the Protestant reformers developed their own image of Edward, describing him as a 'Godly Imp'. Given his conscientious objections to the Mass and his support for the iconoclastic moves made by his council in 1550 and 1551, it is not surprising that they fastened on the Old Testament figure of Josiah to represent him. According to the book of Chronicles, Josiah was eight years old when he came to the throne of Israel and 'did what was right in the sight of the Lord', removing the hill shrines and images which his father Amon and his grandfather Manasseh had tolerated.[30] So Edward became the new Josiah, and his earnestness in pursuit of reform was taken not only as evidence of his fitness to rule, but also as confirmation of the rightness of the Royal Supremacy. During the last two years of his life particularly, Edward was being prepared for the day when he would take over power, and rule as well as reign. He attended council meetings and wrote position papers on issues of state, which show a precocious grasp of political reality. The signs are that, if he had achieved his majority, he would have been just as formidable a King as his father had been, although without that physical prowess which had given the young Henry such a flying start. He seems to have been puritanical, even priggish, in his personal morality, although it is hard to tell with one who died at the age of fifteen.[31]

Edward's image is thus a story of what might have been, rather than what actually was. In spite of Josiah, he never exercised any real authority, coming (in the words of W. K. Jordan) only to the 'threshold of power'. He was an industrious and accomplished scholar, an enthusiastic but not very competent war-gamer, and an earnest Protestant, so his councillors did their best with what they had. However, it all remained potential, and how Edward really saw himself we do not know. Too many of his writings and pronouncements were made under the eyes of his mentors – and designed to please them – for us to be sure how he saw himself.[32] The one thing that seems to be clear is that he never had any doubt about his royalty, or about the responsibilities which that would one day bring. He grew from being a biddable child into a well-disciplined youth, but whether he ever saw himself as Josiah, we do not know. The only hint comes, ironically, in the last days of his life, when we can be reasonably certain that the plan to divert the succession from Mary to Jane Grey was the King's own. The Duke of Northumberland supported it, and may even have suggested it, but the plan was Edward's. He insisted upon it and secured the allegiance (as he thought) of the council, so his one action of undisputed kingship came as he was about to give up both his office and his life. Josiah had reigned for thirty-one years.[33]

Edward may have been a child, but he was at least male, and could in due course have been fitted into one of the various alternative images of royalty historically available. But a ruling Queen presented a challenge of a quite different kind. There were no traditional power images of women, who were thought of as being weak creatures, dependent on their male kindred for everything except their dynastic significance. A Queen was a child-bearer and helpmate to a King, not a sovereign in her own right. There were exceptions to this generalization, but they were not flattering. A woman might be a whore, trading sexual favours for money or other advantages, or she might be a witch, dealing with dark diabolical forces to give her power of a most unacceptable kind. Margaret of Anjou, the consort of Henry VI, had not been a ruler, but had performed many of the functions of which her husband had been incapable, and had been reputed freakish and unnatural.[34] Isabella of Castile, who had been a sovereign, was far off, and had cloaked her steely determination under a cover of piety, so that she was known as 'the crowned nun'. Isabella offered the best role model for Mary, but there is no sign that she wished to adopt it. Her first thought seems to have been for symbolism rather than for image. She was already the symbolic head of all those who adhered to the Old Faith, and this she confirmed in her proclamation of 18 August.[35] She also set out to be the symbol of tradition and normality, a settling and calming presence after the upheavals of her brother's reign. With this in mind, she released and restored the conservative Bishops of Durham and Winchester and annulled the attainder of the old Duke of Norfolk. The 'Queen's proceedings' were generally popular, and her image (insofar as she had one at this early stage) was that of a godly virgin, doing justice and righting wrongs. She had a taste for magnificent clothing, which she indulged to the full, and her coronation was carried out with all the pomp of tradition, omitting only the anointing on the breast. However, she was the only Tudor not to hold a coronation tournament, which was equally traditional, and this indicates the uncertainty in her own mind. She could not, for obvious reasons, use the martial imagery which her father had employed, let alone take part in such exercises herself, but it never seems to have occurred to her that there was a chivalric image available to her in the tournament, and that was as president – the Queen of Faerie – the damsel for whose favour the knights contested. Not only did she miss that opportunity, but the revels of the first few months of her reign were unduly restrained, even by comparison with those of her brother's regime. It is said that the Duke of Northumberland deliberately devised 'triumphs' to distract the young King's attention from more earnest matters. That may not be true, but the Revels of Edward's last year cost £717, as opposed to just £24 for the first year of Mary. [36] That modest figure did not include the costs of either the coronation or her wedding, but is a fair reflection of a very low level of activity. The Queen, we are forced to conclude, simply did not know how to enjoy herself, and that was a sad contrast with her predecessors – even her grandfather had known how to keep up appearances! She was not reluctant to appear in public, but processing to High Mass was more in keeping with her notions of display than anything more ostentatious, which was good for her image of piety but not quite what her subjects were looking for.

There was also the question of the succession. If Mary wanted heirs of her body, that meant marriage, and quickly, since she was already 37. As we have seen, she opted for Philip of Spain, and quite apart from the political tensions which that choice generated, there were also problems with the imagery of a married couple. Quite simply, a wife and a sovereign were incompatible. As a married woman, Mary was supposed to be meek, obedient and supportive of her husband; but as a ruler she was supposed to be decisive and assertive, standing up for her own realm against all manner of foreign interference. Parliament had settled the constitutional issue and 'ungendered' the Crown, while her council had negotiated a treaty which gave Philip very little real power.[37] However, neither of these achievements solved the problem of imagery. The wedding itself revealed the nature of the issue, because it was carefully choreographed to give Mary the upper hand; even the sword of state, the symbol of power, was not borne before Philip until after the ceremony, to emphasize his dependent status. The King was accustomed to the ceremonies of power, but he had no idea how to project himself as a King of England. The best that he could do was to trade on his masculinity by staging and taking part in a number of war games. He lacked an impressive physique, but was a competent swordsman, and his efforts were well received by the military aristocracy. However his numerous enemies mocked him, and there is little sign that these tournaments made him any more popular.[38] It would have required a massive public relations exercise to have turned that situation around, which Philip had neither the mind nor the resources to mount. Meanwhile, Mary was doing her best to capitalize on her married state by claiming to be pregnant. The news was warmly welcomed by her subjects, and both the image and the fact of motherhood would have transformed her political situation. The ballad-mongers, who had been busily singing her praises ever since her accession, now struck a new note:

> Now sing, now spring
> Our care is exiled,
> Our virtuous Queen
> Is quickened with child...[39]

wrote one, with more optimism that accuracy. However, it was not to be. Her pregnancy turned out to be a phantom, and with it went her best chance of squaring the circle between married woman and Queen. As soon as he decently could, a disappointed Philip departed for The Netherlands, leaving Mary to pick up the pieces as best she could.

This was not without advantages from her point of view. The withdrawal of his council and household meant that Philip's role in the government of England was reduced from the minimal to the notional. Formal documents continued to pass in both their names, and he was kept informed of English business by a Select Council which he had briefed for that purpose, but in terms of imagery, he was now an absentee. In January 1556, he took over the Crowns of Spain from his father and concentrated thereafter on building himself into an ideal Spanish monarch, a guise in which he appears in the King's window which he gave to St Janskeerk in Gouda. Although the donation was made in the names of the King and Queen of England in 1557, Mary appears merely as a consort.[40] This imagery created problems of its own in The Netherlands, but that is another story. Philip had, in 1556, made a determined effort to secure an English coronation, more for the sake of his honour that for any tangible advantage which it would have brought him, but this bid was defeated by his spouse, who was not disposed to humour this ambition in one who refused to share her burden.[41] His brief return to England, and the involvement of Mary in his war with France, may have enhanced his credibility with the military gentry but did nothing for his popularity in the country as whole, and when Calais was lost in January 1558, thanks to the negligence of the English Council, Philip got the blame.

In the last year of her reign, Mary had a number of different images. To the Catholic clergy she was a Godly Princess; one who had restored the true Church and revived the ancient faith. That is the way in which she appears in a number of popular writings, such as John Heywood's *The Spider and the Fly*, in which she features as the handmaid of the Lord.[42] To opposition writers, on the other hand, she was merely the dupe of an unfaithful husband, trailing behind him as he brought back the Pope and generally fulfilled his European priorities. The Protestant image of her as Athalia, or 'Bloody Mary', existed mainly among the religious exiles (for obvious reasons) and the triumph of that portrayal after her death is a measure of the failure of her policies rather than of public relations. Mary's portraits are perhaps the best measure of her lack of creative imagination. They show her magnificently clad, but stony-faced, without any of the allegories of royalty which Elizabeth was to deploy so freely.[43] Perhaps it was her piety, or perhaps her puritanical upbringing, but Mary simply did not know how to deploy her sexuality to any sort of advantage. Her once-attractive face had faded, and the Venetian Ambassador, describing her in 1557, wrote:

> She is of low rather than middling stature, but although short she has no personal defect in her limbs, nor is any part of her body deformed. She is of spare and delicate frame, quite unlike her father, who was tall and stout; nor does she resemble her mother, who, if not tall, was nevertheless bulky. Her face is well formed [...] as seen by her portraits [...] At present, with the exception of some wrinkles, caused more by anxiety than by age, which makes her appear some years older, her aspect for the rest is very grave [...] [44]

which could be considered damning with faint praise. Mary was constrained by circumstances to find an imagery suitable for England's first female ruler, but lack of sexual self-confidence meant that she adopted a predominantly religious persona, which eventually backfired on her disastrously.

Elizabeth was a complete contrast. In a sense she had it easy, because her sister had already broken the ice for her. There was no longer any constitutional uncertainty about the nature of her position; she was a king who happened to be female. Mary had also posted a warning about the hazards of marriage, because she had endured a lot of personal unhappiness as well as political confusion – and all for the sake of children who had never appeared. The new Queen was not at all puritanical. She inherited her mother's feistiness and her flirtatious disposition. Whereas Mary had spent her adolescence being closely watched and guarded against undesirable male company, Elizabeth had been exposed, at the age of fourteen, to the attentions of Thomas Seymour. This encounter had taught her a lot about herself; that she was attractive to men, and that sexual adventures carried appalling risks for anyone in her position.[45] She had drawn back, and adopted a puritanical pose during her sister's reign in self-defence, declaring a complete lack of interest when Philip tried to marry her to the Duke of Savoy. She thus came to the throne without any personal commitment, and quickly decided to use her gender as a political weapon. She proclaimed herself an English maid – 'Bessy' to her people, as in the popular ballad 'Come over the borne, Bessy', the author of which proclaimed a love affair between Queen and Country which was to form the theme of much that followed.[46] Far from eschewing coronation tilts and the accompanying revels, Elizabeth threw herself into both with enthusiasm, presiding as a dominatrix who must be served by all the contestants, and coyly dropping her favours to selected knights. The revels costs for her first year came to £603, as against the £254 which had been expended in 1554–5, the year in which Philip's presence had boosted expenditure.[47] Instead of proclaiming her religious intentions as Mary had done, Elizabeth made use of studied gestures such as embracing the English Bible during her coronation entry, which did not constitute a commitment, and reserved the right to change her mind, not once but often. Although her restoration of the Royal Supremacy was sufficiently decisive, she drew back from the full implications of enforcement and baffled her newly established bishops by her equivocations. The Queen appears to have decided to use the conventional image of a woman as being indecisive to her advantage, and baffled her ministers constantly by procrastination and by deviousness in making even the most important of decisions. Sir William Cecil, her Principal Secretary and key adviser, was at first driven to distraction by this behaviour, and only later came to recognize the subtle political brain which lay behind these changes.

Under pressure from her council to marry, she paraded herself on the marriage market and entered into a number of negotiations, but no one knew (or knows now) how seriously these were intended. She was, after all, the most desirable match in Europe, and seems to have exploited potential bridegrooms in the interests of a foreign policy which was directed entirely at her own security.[48] Her image during these early years is summed up in her coronation portrait, in which her face is beautiful but totally mask-like and enigmatic, surrounded by the trappings of royalty which proclaim the uniqueness of her status. Only once in these early years did her sexuality betray her, and that was in her relationship with Lord Robert Dudley. Elizabeth fell in love with Dudley, and might well have married him if the circumstances of his wife's death which made him available to her had not also made such an outcome politically impossible. Her behaviour during the summer of 1560 certainly damaged her reputation around the court, but whether it made any difference to her image overall may be doubted. She had already declared that she was married to the realm of England, but her subjects had heard similar language from her sister, and they probably did not take it very seriously. Most people regarded her marriage as inevitable and preferred the prospect of an English spouse to some foreign prince who might well try to take over the kingdom. Her flirtation with Lord Robert merely demonstrated that she was a woman, like any other, and subject to the predictable impulses of lust. However, she did not marry him, and her image as the bride of England remained intact. Her reputation abroad may have been more damaged than it was at home; 'the Queen of England is to marry her horsemaster', Catherine de Medici is alleged to have scoffed.[49]

Most of the imagery we associate with Elizabeth belongs to the latter part of her reign, from the 1570s onwards. She had already been hailed by John Foxe as the New Constantine, and the papal Bull *Regnans in Excelsis* made her (against her own will) the Champion of Protestant Europe, the symbol of the reformed Church and the damsel crowned with the sun. The Protestants had already cast her as Deborah, the Judge of Israel, but that imagery had faded somewhat with her reluctance to promote further godly reform beyond that which had been instituted by her settlement of 1559.[50] Now it was revived and, as foreign Catholic plots (real and imagined) challenged her life and the integrity of her realm, took off in spectacular fashion. By 1580, as the prospect of her marriage receded, she had become the Virgin Queen, the damsel whom all her subjects were honoured to adore. As the Accession Day tilts grew in their visual appeal, the language of devotion became stereotyped, and was used by ministers in their routine correspondence as well as in their communications with Her Majesty. As John Stubbs's *Gaping Gulf*, aimed against the last flickers of the Anjou marriage proposal, demonstrated, she now had more to lose than to gain by entering into any such engagement.[51] By the early 1580s the integrity of her virgin body had become a symbol for the inviolability of England, an association famously exploited in her great Tilbury speech of 1588:

> I know I have the body of a weak and feeble woman, but I have the heart and stomach of a king, and of a king of England too – and take foul scorn that Parma or any prince of Europe, should dare to invade the borders of my realm...'[52]

In a sense, the war against Spain – and particularly, victory over the Armada – made that image convincing, as is demonstrated by the Armada portrait and others painted at about the same time, which show her surrounded by allegorical representations of virginity and victory. By that time, her real appearance mattered little. In 1563, worried that the smallpox had marred her beauty, Elizabeth had endeavoured to control the publication of images of her self by confining reproduction to a single authorized original. This proclamation survives only in draft, and may never have been issued, but if it was, it had little effect.[53] Twenty years later, it did not matter. By that time the Queen's love affair with her realm was a trope, and the courtiers who supported it by writing fulsome poetry praising her loveliness hardly noticed that their tongues were firmly in their cheeks. She was the symbol of England, protestant and defiant. How far Elizabeth herself was responsible for this imagery, and how far it was the work of those about her, it is difficult to say. Virginity, for example, was hardly appropriate to a woman actively seeking matrimony, and may well have emerged as a subtle way of telling her that her time had passed. Marriage to England was, however, undoubtedly the Queen's own idea, as was the use of various classical models to represent her virtues. Astrea and Belphoebe may well have been dredged out of Elizabeth's classical education and suggested to poets like Sidney and Spenser as appropriate metaphors. In 1599, John Dekker summed up this vein of flattery when he wrote in *Old Fortunatus*:

> Are you then travelling to the temple of Eliza?
>
> Even to her temple are my feeble limbs travelling. Some call her Pandora, some Gloriana, some Cynthia, some Belphoebe, some Astrea; all by several names to express several loves: yet all those names make but one celestial body, as all those loves meet to create but one soul.
>
> I am of her country. And we adore her by the name of Eliza ...[54]

By 1603 the sober reality was that she was a very tiresome old lady, but somehow or other the magic persisted. In spite of setbacks in Ireland and grumblings over monopolies, she was Gloriana, the victorious virgin, at once unattainable and mysterious. The price which she paid for this triumphant imagery was that when she died, her throne passed to her 'good brother' of Scotland, who found her an impossible act to follow, and wisely did not try.

The Tudors gave England identity and self-respect, largely by exploiting the opportunities presented by personal monarchy. Henry VIII and Elizabeth, both of whom presided over a realm divided by their own actions, succeeded by sheer force of personality in making themselves the symbols of their kingdom.

By remorseless propaganda, both literary and visual, and by the liberal use of patronage and courtly magnificence, each succeeded in building up an image of a prince specially favoured by God. Being a ruler under God was an essential concept to all the Tudors, to Edward and Mary no less than to Henry VII, Henry VIII and Elizabeth, and each had their own way of expressing that relationship[55]: Henry VII by doing good works of a conventional kind and by exploiting the support of the papacy; Henry VIII by proving to his own satisfaction that he was a better Catholic than the Pope, and that it was the will of God that he should rule the English Church; Edward VI was the Godly Imp, and Mary the restorer of the True Faith. Elizabeth's approach was more subtle, because she set out to demonstrate the validity of female rule as well as of her chosen faith, but all of them claimed a special relationship with the Almighty. Henry VIII represented England as she would wish to be seen, victorious in battle and governed by law, whereas Elizabeth presented a country supreme upon the seas, and, in John Foxe's words, an 'elect nation'. Abroad, Henry VII was the most successful, being recognized as a prudent and formidable prince. Henry VIII was a lecherous tyrant, while both Edward and Mary were led by their mentors, although in different ways. Elizabeth was lauded by her friends and gained the grudging respect of her enemies through sheer skill and tenacity. None of them had the resources, either financial or military, to hold down a rebellious country, so each depended upon their personal powers of persuasion. And to each, the presentation of an acceptable image was an essential step to success. Even today we recognize Henry VIII and Elizabeth as types of monarchy – male and female respectively – which is more a measure of their public relations achievement than of the actual success of their policies.

Conclusion

What Did the Tudors Do For Us?

The Tudor monarchy was personal. That is, the King or Queen was both Head of State and Chief Executive – a bit like a hereditary president. This is so far detached from our present democratic mindset as to be hard to envisage. In theory, they were not answerable to their subjects, but only to God, and in these days when faith is considered to be a personal matter the corporate nature of sixteenth-century religion can also be hard to understand.[1] All law was divine in origin and the King, like everyone else, was expected to obey the law. Nevertheless, the Tudors moved the goalposts in a number of significant ways. In the first place, they expanded and institutionalized the concept of consent. Medieval kings had been expected, in a rather vague way, to govern, with the consent of their nobility, those great men who had once been their companions in arms and upon whose support they chiefly relied. The King's council had originally been a vehicle for the expression of that consent. However, the effective exercise of consent had already begun to move towards the Parliament by the early fifteenth century, because it was the Commons, not the Lords, who needed to consent to grants of direct taxation, and the only convenient way of obtaining that was through the Parliament. '*Quod omnes tetigit, ab omnibus approbetur*' ('that which touches all must be approved by all') was a legal precept which long antedated the sixteenth century.[2] Consequently, altera-tions or expansions to the King's laws also needed the consent of the Lords and Commons, and this was an established principle before the Tudors obtained the Crown. However, by using the Parliament to establish and approve the Royal Supremacy over the Church, Henry VIII moved the boundaries of its jurisdiction exponentially. He was not intending to do this, because the wording of the statutes make it clear that what the Parliament was being called upon to do was to recognize an ancient authority which was deemed to reside in the King – an authority which was personal to himself and his successors. It was the succession of a minor and two women which transferred that authority to the Crown-in-Parliament and turned the Church into a department of State.[3]

Having subdued the greatest liberty of them all, Henry proceeded to use Parliament to reduce the secular franchises, to dissolve the monasteries and to determine the succession to the Crown; all matters which would have been considered *ultra vires* before 1530. He thus established it as the prime institution for the conduct of legal business and raised the concept of consent to a new level of importance. During the reign of Elizabeth, there were those in the House of Commons who believed that they had a right, as a royal council, to be consulted over all important issues of state. This was a position which neither the Queen nor the majority of the House accepted, but it pointed to an attitude which became increasingly prevalent as the seventeenth century advanced, and led to a fundamental clash with the King at the time of the Civil War.[4] It was therefore the Tudors who turned the medieval estates, with their limited function, into that sovereign legislative assembly which remained in place until the advent of the European Union. What they did not concede was their own responsibility to select advisers who had the confidence of Parliament. In other words, the executive remained independent of the legislature because the monarch, as a personal ruler, remained responsible for all political decisions, and this was another dichotomy which was to be resolved in the following century. Tudor government was not remotely democratic, but it did shift the definition of law from God to the community by determining, in effect, that the law of God was what the Lords and Commons said it was.[5] The disadvantage of that was that it brought appreciably nearer the time when the monarch would become responsible, not to God, but to the Parliament. Henry's idea that that institution formed a biddable constituency to carry out his business for him thus had long-term consequences which he could not possibly have foreseen.

Another change of long-term significance, although not of much importance in the twenty-first century, was the delegation of local government to Commissions of Peace. These commissions were established before 1485, but principally as judicial tribunals. It was the Tudors who began to use them in an administrative capacity until by the reign of Elizabeth, in the words of William Lambarde, they had 'stacks of statutes' to enforce, many of them of a social or economic nature which had little to do with their primary function of law enforcement.[6] These commissions were symbolic of what was effectively a new partnership in government between the Crown and the county gentry, a partnership which endured until the development of elected county and rural district councils in the nineteenth century. Today the partnership between local politicians and their Westminster counterparts may not be very obvious, but throughout the seventeenth and eighteenth centuries those same gentlemen who served as Justices of the Peace also sat in the House of Commons and were directly in touch with the government of the day. In the sixteenth century this partnership was important because it replaced an older partnership with the nobility. A medieval King expected to rule his realm through his nobles. Sometimes they held offices of state, sometimes not, but they were expected to use their local power, and their affinities, to enforce the King's laws and to support his judges on their assize circuits. Unfortunately, when the Crown was weak, they might take these laws into their own hands and enforce them to suit themselves, which was what happened in the 1450s. Edward IV began to break this down by using 'curial' sheriffs – that is to say, gentlemen of his household – to take over these key local offices.[7] Henry VII used Commissions of the Peace instead, placing gentlemen of his own affinity as Justices in order to guarantee conciliar control. His son and grandchildren continued this process, gradually detaching the nobility from local control and turning them instead into courtiers. As late as 1536, the attitudes of noblemen such as the Earl of Derby and Shrewsbury was crucial to the outcome of the Pilgrimage of Grace. But they decided to support the King, and when old-fashioned Earls like those of Northumberland and Westmorland endeavoured to mobilize their affinities against the Crown in 1569, they miscalculated their influence. Nor were the nobility used in war in the way they had been. Nobles might still command armies, as the Dukes of Norfolk and Suffolk did under Henry VIII and the Earl of Essex as late as 1596, but they were no longer expected to raise them on the basis of their own retinues. The King raised his soldiers directly by commissions of array, so there was no question of mediate or alternative loyalties intruding into their operations. They were the King's men, and his alone.[8] As a result of these policies, the *ancien régime* was phased out in England, beginning in the late fifteenth century and eventually becoming the political and party networks of the eighteenth century. It was probably this gradual emasculation which meant that England had no revolution in the nineteenth century and that we still have the remains of an hereditary aristocracy today.

At a more mundane level, Henry VIII created the Admiralty. He did this in stages between 1514, when he established a standing navy, and 1546, when he created the Council for Marine Causes. That council, which was in its day a very sophisticated institution, was the direct ancestor of the Admiralty Board which Samuel Pepys served, and hence of the Ministry of Defence as it exists now.[9] Henry built up the navy which Elizabeth was to use to such good effect, and initiated through the office of Cartographer Royal that development in English navigational technology which was to result in Francis Drake's circumnavigation and in the widespread commercial and colonial enterprises of the seventeenth century. It would be an exaggeration to describe either Henry VIII or Elizabeth as the founder of the British Empire, but the diversification of trade certainly dates from the latter reign, and was partly at least the result of royal initiative. The first English colony in the New World was an abortive operation at Roanoake in 1586,[10] and Elizabeth bequeathed to her successors a navy which was one of the most efficient fighting machines of the period. Other exercises in administrative reorganization were more controversial and lasted less well. The prerogative courts of Star Chamber, Requests and High Commission went down in a storm of indignation in 1641, and the financial courts established in the 1530s did not survive the reign of Mary. In Ireland, the Tudor legacy was almost entirely malign, because in spite of establishing counties on the English model, rebellion, dispossession and the Protestant ascendancy left a bitter heritage which was not finally eliminated until 1922.[11] Another Tudor failure – of great significance for a while – was over taxation. The medieval subsidy was collectively assessed by town, village or lordship, which was then left to collect its own contribution. This was replaced, by Wolsey, with individual assessment, a laborious but superficially more efficient system. Unfortunately, as a result of special pleading and official slackness, these assessments dwindled over the years, which, combined with the effects of inflation, drastically reduced the return from subsidies voted during Elizabeth's reign, so in spite of receiving double and even triple subsidies, the royal revenues could not keep pace with the costs of government – especially in wartime.[12] The Crown urgently needed a more efficient system to tap into the increasing wealth of English society, but that was an issue which the Queen (ever concerned for her popular image) did not choose to face. It was to explode in the face of Charles I with devastating effect.

The Church of England was, of course, another Tudor creation. As a Protestant establishment it dates from 1559, but without Henry VIII's precedent of the Royal Supremacy it would probably never have happened. Elizabeth, brought up as a Protestant, got the Church that she wanted when she came to the throne; a unique combination of reformed doctrine and conservative ecclesiology, which became enshrined in the national mythology of subsequent generations as being a peculiarly English (and successful) way of managing God. The days when everyone was required by law to attend their parish church have long since gone, and only a minority of English people now do so, but the establishment remains, and is still called upon from time to time when a voice of Christian conscience is required.[13] For the best part of three hundred years it was synonymous with English (and latterly British) identity, foreign policy and Imperialism. The coincidence that Scotland also had a Protestant establishment – albeit a different one – meant that 'popery' became another term for foreign interference in the domestic affairs of the British Isles. The ecclesiastical establishment thus remained a bulwark of the monarchy as that moved from a personal to a constitutional basis. God no longer plays much part in the government of Britain, but it should be remembered that our present democratic institutions are based on the assumption that the voice of the people is the voice of God – *vox populi vox dei* – and that far from encouraging secularism, the identity of a Christian Church with a Christian State was of fundamental constitutional importance. It was only the progressive exclusion of the clergy from public office, which began in Elizabeth's reign, that created the illusion of a secular society – an illusion which one glance at Victorian Britain should be sufficient to dispel.[14] Anyone attending traditional Anglican worship in the present day is using a prayer book which goes back to 1549 and even the Church's more progressive liturgies still contain echoes of Thomas Cranmer's matchless prose.

The sixteenth century saw the development of English as a literary language. That process had begun when the royal court switched from French in the fourteenth century, and had come of age in the era of Chaucer, Lydgate and Fortescue in the fifteenth century, but it was still the Tudor period which saw it achieve a status of full equality with French or Spanish or German. We associate that with Shakespeare, Sidney, Spenser and the other Elizabethan masters, but in truth it goes back to the controversial literature which was produced by and for Henry VIII at the time of his 'Great Matter' – to the *Glass of the Truth* and to the writings of Morison, St Germain and Crowley. English was not yet an international language and diplomacy was conducted in French, Italian or Latin, but by 1603 it was a fully developed medium of vernacular expression and was used as such by English merchants doing business abroad. It would have been heard on the quays of Hamburg, Amsterdam and San Lucar as well as on the streets of London or Bristol, and of course it was the normal language of the court and of Parliament, but not at school or in the universities, where Latin still reigned supreme.[15] We tend to think of the Tudors as being great patrons of education because of the number of surviving schools which trace their foundations to the sixteenth century, but in fact they were nothing out of the ordinary. Henry VIII established Regius Chairs in the universities, and founded two large colleges, but these absorbed only a small fraction of the income which he derived from the dissolution of the abbeys.[16] Schools were founded in the name of Edward VI, but not by him, being mostly municipal efforts based on chantry property which the towns had acquired by purchase. Mary endowed scholarships for poor students and made modest gifts to both universities, but Elizabeth did virtually nothing. The large number of schools which were undoubtedly founded were created by private benefactors, inspired no doubt by the intellectual culture of the court, but not directly financed by it. What the Tudors did do was to create a climate which was favourable to humanist education, and that was immensely influential. St John's College, Oxford and Emmanuel College, Cambridge, founded by Sir Thomas White and Sir Walter Mildmay, were typical of the constructive response to that critical initiative, as were Gresham's school at Holt in Norfolk and Simon Wisdom's foundation at Burford in Oxfordshire.[17] The Tudors deserve the credit for creating the cultural climate in which educational patronage could flourish, rather than for being great patrons in their own right. Both music and drama also flourished at Elizabeth's court, which set an example for the aristocracy to imitate, and created that entertainment industry which caused the London theatres to be developed and provided them with their clientele.

Other things happened in the sixteenth century which had nothing directly to do with the Tudors. Tobacco and potatoes were introduced from the New World, as were different kinds of spices from the Far East. Lighter cloths were developed for markets in the Levant and Africa, thanks to the initiative of various immigrant groups which took refuge in this country, and the manufacture of glass and clocks and other instruments was stimulated. Book production (which the monarchy was mainly interested in controlling) flourished thanks to the initiatives inspired by religious controversy, but becoming also a branch of the entertainment industry.[18] By the end of the sixteenth century, every gentleman worthy of the name had served his time at a university and had a library in his house – and that was a cultural revolution of immense significance for the future government of the country. Although we no longer follow renaissance curricula in our schools, and Latin has become a dead language, the value attached to 'book learning' has not diminished, and skills which in the Middle Ages would have been thought appropriate only to clergy have, since the Tudor period, become the possession of all. Who could now imagine a professional career without literacy and numeracy? And we still watch Shakespeare's plays and listen to the music of Tallis and Byrd. Ironically, the Tudors themselves are best known to us now through our own entertainment industry, in fictitious reconstructions of their sex lives. Henry VIII and Elizabeth 'in love' have been the subject of many films and television programmes over the last few years, usually portraying them quite unhistorically as modern people with twentieth- or twenty-first-century preoccupations. Such portrayals serve to keep them in the public eye but do nothing for their historical significance. 'Bluff King Hall', 'Bloody Mary' and 'Good Queen Bess' are testimonies to their lasting mythology rather than their real importance. A great deal of water has flowed under the political and constitutional bridges since the sixteenth century, and we are not well advised to look for too much direct influence upon our own preoccupations, but it is worth reflecting that the evolutionary nature of the political changes which have taken place in this country since Tudor times owes a great deal to the initiatives which they took. The gradual expansion of the notion of consent; the progressive domestication of the nobility and the growth of the 'gentry commonwealth'; above all, perhaps, the moderate nature of the Elizabethan religious settlement, have all served to take the edge off revolutionary enthusiasms. Britain only began to become a democracy in 1832 – in which it lagged behind the United States of America – but by that time it had a constitution sufficiently robust to stand the strain. That toughness it owes largely to the Tudors.

Notes

Chapter 1: Getting To Know the Family

1 R. R. Davies, *The Revolt of Owain Glyn Dwr* (1997), p. 130.
2 A. D. Carr, 'Welshmen and the Hundred Years War', *Welsh Historical Review*, 4, 1960, pp. 1, 37.
3 S. B. Chrimes, *Henry VII*, (1972), pp. 6–7.
4 Polydore Vergil, *Three Books of English History*, ed. H. Ellis (Camden Society, 29, 1844), p. 62.
5 *Calendar of the Close Rolls, Henry VI*, III, 1435–41, (1937), pp. 155, 225.
6 Chrimes, *Henry VII*, pp. 10–11.
7 Ibid, p. 13.
8 *Rotuli Parliamentorum*, VI, c.3, pp. 244–9.
9 This was Maud, who subsequently married (c.1476) Henry Percy, 8th Earl of Northumberland.
10 Bernard Andree, *De Vita atque Gestis Henrici septimi*, ed. James Gairdner (1858), p. 17.
11 Polydore Vergil, *Three Books of English History*, pp. 158–9, 164–7.
12 A. J. Pollard, *Richard III* (1991), p. 94.
13 Ibid, p. 96.
14 M. K. Jones and Malcolm Underwood, *The King's Mother* (1992), pp. 62–3.
15 Carole Rawcliffe, *The Staffords, Earls of Stafford and Dukes of Buckingham* (1978), pp. 30–2.
16 Chrimes, *Henry VII*, p. 26. Polydore Vergil says that this attempt was made on 10 October. The Act of Attainder says 19th.
17 Rawcliffe, *The Staffords*, p. 35.
18 James Gairdner, *History of the Life and Reign of Richard III* (1898), pp. 165–6.
19 Chrimes, *Henry VII*, pp. 29–30.
20 John de Vere had been a Lancastrian commander at Barnet, but had escaped. He had fled to France, and taken part in a failed raid on St Michael's Mount in 1473. He had been imprisoned at Hammes since 1475.
21 Ann died on 16 March 1485, when Richard was 33. Hostile rumour attributed her death to poison, and to Richard's designs on his niece, but there is no evidence to substantiate either of these surmises.

22 By the treaty of Bourges. The fall and death of Pierre Landois on 19 July probably facili-
    tated this agreement. A. Dupuy, *Histoire de la Réunion de la Bretagne à la France* (1880).
23 Chrimes, *Henry VII*, p. 39. Morgan, who was a priest, became Dean of Windsor shortly
    after Henry's accession, and was appointed Bishop of St Davids in 1496.
24 D. Rees, *The Son of Prophecy* (1985), p. 41. G. Williams, 'Prophecy, Politics and Poetry in
    Medieval and Tudor Wales', in H. Hearder and H. L. Loyn, eds, *British Government and
    Administration* (1974).
25 R. A. Griffiths, Sir Rhys ap *Thomas and his Family* (1993).
26 Chrimes, *Henry VII*, pp. 44–5. Pollard, *Richard III*, p. 168.
27 Ibid, p. 169.
28 *Three Books of English History*, pp. 223–4.
29 Ibid, p. 226. The story of the crown being found in a hawthorn bush is almost certainly
    apocryphal. S. Anglo, 'The foundation of the Tudor dynasty', *Guildhall Miscellany*, II,
    1960.
30 C. H. Williams, 'The rebellion of Humphrey Stafford in 1486', *English Historical Review*,
    43, 1928, pp. 181–9.
31 S. G. Ellis, *Tudor Ireland* (1985), pp. 68, 327.
32 Polydore Vergil, *Anglica Historia*, ed. D. Hay (Camden Society ns.74, 1950), pp. 12–26.
33 Sir Francis Bacon, *History of the Reign of King Henry the Seventh*, ed. R. Lockyer (1971),
    p. 130.
34 Ian Arthurson, *The Perkin Warbeck Conspiracy, 1491–1499* (1994). T. Rymer Foedera
    (1704–1735), XII, pp. 710–12.
35 Chrimes, *Henry VII*, p. 83.
36 W. A. J. Archbold, 'Sir William Stanley and Perkin Warbeck', *English Historical Review*, 14,
    1899.
37 Fourteen persons were subsequently attainted for this endeavour. *Rotuli Parliamentorum*,
    VI, pp. 503–7.
38 Agnes Conway, *Henry VII's Relations with Scotland and Ireland* (1932), p. 31.
39 *Rotuli scaccarii regnum Scotorum* (1878–1908), II, p. 520. Conway, *Henry VII's Relations*,
    p. 103.
40 Chrimes, *Henry VII*, p. 90. For the resulting attainders, see *Rotuli Parliamentorum*, VI,
    p. 544.
41 Arthurson, *The Perkin Warbeck Conspiracy*, pp. 182–3.
42 Ibid, pp. 199–201.
43 J. Scarisbrick, *Henry VIII* (1968), pp. 135–6.
44 For a full account of these events, see Hazel Pierce, *Margaret Pole, Countess of Salisbury,
    1473–1541* (2003), pp. 115–41.
45 The daughter of James V, and granddaughter of James IV. Born December 1542.
46 David Loades, *The Cecils; Privilege and Power behind the Throne* (2007), pp. 10–11.
47 *Calendar of the Patent Rolls, Henry VII*, I, p. 47. Penry Williams, *The Council in the
    Marches of Wales* (1958).
48 *Materials for a History of the Reign of Henry VII*, ed. W. Campbell (Rolls Series, 1873–7),
    II, pp. 541–2.

49 *Calendar of the Patent Rolls, Henry VII*, II, p. 471.

50 For a discussion of this issue, see Rees, *The Revolt of Owain Glyn Dwr*, pp. 65–97.

51 Chrimes, *Henry VII*, pp. 256–7.

52 C. A. J. Skeel, 'Wales under Henry VII' in *Tudor Studies*, ed. R. W. Seton Watson (1924), p. 13.

Chapter 2: The Kings and Their Marriages: Henry VIII's 'Great Matter'

1 *Rotuli Parliamentorum*, VI, p. 278

2 This repeal of attainders was tricky because it involved the attainder passed against Henry VI, by which he had forfeited the Duchy of Lancaster. By a majority decision the judges ruled that Henry's readeption in 1470 had voided his attainder, but it was still felt necessary to repeal it. *RP*, VI, pp. 273–5, 278–86, 288, 290–1, 298, 305. *Year Books*, 1 Henry VII, Mich., pl.5.

3 Chrimes, *Henry VII*, p. 66.

4 David Loades, *The Tudor Queens of England* (2009), pp. 78–9.

5 N. H. Nicolas, ed., *The Privy Purse Expenses of Elizabeth of York* (1830).

6 Catherine consistently denied consummation and was insistent that she had come to Henry VIII as a virgin. For a full description of the ceremonies surrounding their wedding, see Sydney Anglo, *Spectacle, Pageantry and Early Tudor Policy* (1969), pp. 56–98.

7 He got as far as sending envoys to Valencia to appraise the recently widowed Joanna of Naples, and their report leaves little to the imagination. *Memorials of King Henry VII*, ed. J. Gairdner (Rolls Series, 1858), pp. 223–39. That he had his eyes on Catherine is pure contemporary gossip.

8 According to the Spanish envoy Fuensalida, he was kept in virtual seclusion and treated as a young girl might have been. Like most of his reports, this was a gross exaggeration, based upon ignorance of the court. *Correpondencia de Gutierre Gomez de Fuensalida*, ed. El Duque de Berwick y de Alba (1907), p. 449.

9 Henry VII changed his mind about the desirability of this marriage, having fallen out with Ferdinand, and caused his son to repudiate the agreement a few days before his fourteenth birthday, on which day he would have come of age for matrimonial purposes.

10 Loades, *The Six Wives of Henry VIII*, p. 25.

11 *Letters of Richard Fox*, ed. P. S. and H. M. Allen (1929), p. 93. Scarisbrick, *Henry VIII*, p. 25.

12 Hall, *Chronicle*, p. 519.

13 Scarisbrick, *Henry VIII*, pp. 55–6.

14 Beverly Murphy, *Bastard Prince* (2001), pp. 25–7.

15 Patricia Crawford, *Blood, Bodies and Families in Early Modern England* (2004), pp. 96–7.

16 There was no good reason why Henry should have failed to acknowledge a bastard son, if it had indeed been his. This story was told by one John Hale, vicar of Isleworth, and dates from 1535. *Letters and Papers of the Reign of Henry VIII* (1862–1910), VIII, no.567.

17 Murphy, *Bastard Prince*, pp. 69–107.

18 Guy Bedouelle and Patrick Le Gal, *Le 'Divorce' du Roi Henry VIII* (1987), pp. 35–41.

19 Nicholas Pocock, *Records of the Reformation, the Divorce 1527–1533* (1870), I, p. 11.

20 *Letters and Papers*, IV, no.4002. *Calendar of State Papers, Spanish*, III. ii, pp. 367, 386. A decretal commission was one from which no appeal was allowed, and which had been carefully withheld in this case.

21 For a full account of the circumstances surrounding the fall of Cardinal Wolsey, see Peter Gwyn, *The King's Cardinal* (1990).

22 Eric Ives, T*he Life and Death of Anne Boleyn* (2004), pp. 81–93.

23 Ibid, p. 147. *L & P*, V, no.337.

24 Scarisbrick, *Henry VIII*, pp. 273–4.

25 Diarmaid MacCulloch, *Thomas Cranmer* (1996), pp. 84–9.

26 Statute 24 Henry VIII, c.12. *Statutes of the Realm*, III, pp. 427–9.

27 A view of Catherine's expenses from 19 December 1533 to 30 September 1534, after the second reduction of her household, shows an income of £3,000 and an expenditure of £2,950. *L & P*, VII, no.208.

28 Ives, *Life and Death*, pp. 189–204.

29 Ibid, pp. 316–18.

30 Retha Warnicke, *The Rise and Fall of Anne Boleyn* (1989), Chapter 8. Ives, *Life and Death*, pp. 296–7.

31 Ibid, pp. 324–5.

32 Scarisbrick, *Henry VIII*, p. 349.

33 For a consideration of Jane's role in this, see Ives, *Life and Death*, pp. 303–5.

34 The Queen's attainder and death were sufficient to remove her from the scene. The annulment of their marriage and bastardization of Elizabeth can only have been the result of Henry's conviction that he had been tricked into the marriage in the first place. MacCulloch, *Thomas Cranmer*, pp. 157–9. *Cal.Span.*, 1536–8, p. 121; *L & P*, X, no.909.

35 Loades, *Six Wives*, pp. 92–3

36 Statute 35 Henry VIII, c.1.*Statutes of the Realm*, III, p. 955.

37 Hall, *Chronicle*, p. 825.

38 Loades, *Six Wives*, p. 100.

39 Hall, *Chronicle*, p. 825.

40 *L & P*, XIII, I, no.1198.

41 Hans Holbein's well-known portrait of Anne was one of the products of these investigations. *L & P*, XIV, ii, nos.33, 117.

42 Retha Warnicke, *The Marrying of Anne of Cleves* (2000), pp. 127–54.

43 Ibid, p. 231.

44 According to Ralph Morice, Cranmer's secretary. *Narratives of the Days of the Reformation*, p. 260.

45 L. B. Smith, *A Tudor Tragedy* (1961), pp. 45–9. Her first lover had been the music teacher, Henry Manox.

46 Ibid, pp. 155–6. Scarisbrick, *Henry VIII*, p. 427.

47 Smith, *A Tudor Tragedy*, pp. 167–70.

48 MacCulloch, *Thomas Cranmer*, pp. 287–8.
49 *Proceedings and Ordinances of the Privy Council of England*, ed. H. Nicolas (1834–7), VII, pp. 354–5.
50 TNA SP1/167, f.167 et seq., *L & P*, XVI, no.1325.
51 Statute 35 Henry VIII, c.1. *Statutes of the Realm*, III, p. 955.
52 Ibid.
53 J. R. Tanner, *Tudor Constitutional Documents* (1951), p. 397.
54 *L & P*, XVIII, no.804.
55 Loades, *Tudor Queens of England*, p. 165.
56 David Loades, *John Dudley, Duke of Northumberland* (1996), pp. 238–41.
57 Inner Temple, Petyt MS 47, f.316. J.G. Nicholas, *Literary Remains of King Edward VI*, (1857), II, pp. 571–2.
    David Loades, *Mary Tudor; a Life* (1989), pp. 175–80.
58 G. Redworth, *English Historical Review* (1997), p. 112.

Chapter 3: Two Queens in Search of an Heir

1   Statute 35 Henry VIII, c.1. *Statutes of the Realm*, III, p. 955.
2   Redworth, '"Matters impertinent to Women"...'
3   Loades, *Mary Tudor*, p. 200.
4   *Cal.Span.* XI, pp. 131, 153–4.
5   Ibid, pp. 181, 183. In fact Lord Paget seems to have introduced the name of Philip, quite independently of Renard's instructions, which was a bonus for the ambassador.
6   Ibid, pp. 319, 327.
7   For a discussion of the circumstances surrounding this move, see M.-J. Rodriguez Salgado, *The Changing Face of Empire* (1988), pp. 35–7.
8   He deposited a writing ad cautelem in every section of his archive dealing with English affairs, declaring that he was swearing to observe the articles 'in order that his marriage with the said Queen of England might take place, but by no means in order to bind himself or his heirs to observe the articles...' *Cal. Span.*, XII, pp. 4–6.
9   For a full discussion of this rebellion, and of the circumstances surrounding the Duke of Suffolk's execution, see David Loades, *Two Tudor Conspiracies* (1965).
10 Rodriguez-Salgado, *The Changing Face of Empire*, pp. 83–5. Eventually he settled on his sister Juana as Regent.
11 *Cal.Span.* XII, p. 309.
12 'The Copie of a Letter sent into Scotland' (by John Elder). *The Chronicle of Queen Jane*, Appendix, x, p. 140.
13 *Cal.Span.* XIII, p. 11.
14 Ruy Gomez to Francisco de Eraso (the Emperor's Secretary), 27 July 1554. *Cal.Span.*, XIII, p. 2.
15 Loades, *Mary Tudor*, p. 229.
16 David Loades, 'Philip II and the Government of England'. *Law and Government under the Tudors*, ed. Cross, Loades and Scarisbrick (1988), pp. 177–95.

17 Statute 1 & 2 Philip and Mary, c.10. *Statutes of the Realm*, IV, pp. 255–7.

18 *The Diary of Henry Machyn*, p. 86. Loades, *Mary Tudor*, pp. 248–50.

19 It was provided in the treaty that any child of the marriage would inherit the Low Countries in addition to England, but would have no claim to the Crowns of Spain, which were already settled on Philip's existing son, Don Carlos. Hughes and Larkin, *Tudor Royal Proclamations*, II, pp. 21–6.

20 *Calendar of State Papers, Venetian*, VI, p. 212.

21 *Cal.Span.*, XIII, pp. 378–80. BL Cotton MS Titus B II, f.109. Strype, *Ecclesiastical Memorials*, III, ii, p. 418.

22 Michel Surian to the Doge and Senate, 15 January 1558. Cal.Ven., VI, p. 1427. Philip to Pole, 21 January 1558. *Cal.Span.*, XIII, p. 340.

23 'The Count of Feria's Dispatch to Philip II of 14th November 1558', ed. M.-J. Rodriguez-Salgado and Simon Adams (*Camden Miscellany*, 28, 1984), pp. 302–45.

24 He was about 60 per cent right in his predictions. Ibid.

25 Feria reported that Elizabeth was on the worst possible terms with Pole, but that he had visited him and endeavoured to comfort him. Ibid, p. 341.

26 Archivo de la casa de Medinaceli, caja 7. legajo 249, ff. 11–12. Cited and translated in G. Parker and C. Martin, *The Spanish Armada* (1988), p. 281.

27 Deposition by Catherine Ashley, 4 February 1549. TNA SP10/6, no.23.

28 *Elizabeth I: Collected Works*, ed. L. S. Marcus, J. Mueller and M. B. Rose (2000), pp. 58–60.

29 Susan Doran, *Monarchy and Matrimony* (1996), pp. 40–72.

30 Feria to Philip II, 18 and 29 April 1559. *Cal.Span.*, 1558–67, pp. 57–8, 63.

31 Kervyn de Lettenhove, *Relations Politiques des Pay Bas et de l'Angleterre sous la regne de Philippe II* (1888–1900), II, pp. 123–4.

32 Doran, *Monarchy and Matrimony*, pp. 42–3.

33 David Loades, *Elizabeth I* (2003), p. 144.

34 *Cal.Span., 1558–67*, pp. 422, 513.

35 The doctrine of the real presence postulated a spiritual presence of Christ in the Eucharistic elements, as distinct from the Catholic position of transubstantiation (physical presence), or the Zwinglian position, which treated the Eucharist as a mere memorial.

36 Victor Von Klarwill, *Queen Elizabeth and Some Foreigners* (1928), pp. 208–9.

37 Doran, *Monarchy and Matrimony*, p. 81.

38 Sir Henry Norris to Cecil, 23 June 1568. TNA SP70/98 f.277. *Cal.S.P. For.*, 1566–8, p. 494.

39 W. MacCaffrey, *The Shaping of the Elizabethan Regime, 1558–1572* (1968), p. 188.

40 Conference between Walsingham and Paul de Foix, 28 April 1571. Sir Dudley Digges, *The Complete Ambassador* (1655), pp. 90–2.

41 W. MacCaffrey, *Queen Elizabeth and the Making of Policy, 1572–1588* (1981), pp. 164–90.

42 Doran, *Monarchy and Matrimony*, p. 130.

43 Smith to Burghley, 10 January 1572. TNA SP70/122, f.50.

44 Mark Holt, *The Duke of Anjou and the Politique Struggle during the Wars of Religion* (1986), pp. 93–101.

45 William Camden, *The History of the Most Renowned and Victorious Princess Elizabeth, Queen of England* (1688), p. 227.

46 Doran, *Monarchy and Matrimony*, pp. 162–4.

47 TNA PRO31/3/27 f.397. Ibid, pp. 164–5.

48 *Cal.Span., 1580–86*, p. 227.

49 Mortimer Levine, *The Early Elizabethan Succession Question* (1966), pp. 13–30.

50 Particularly in the Parliament of 1563. Ibid, pp. 45–61.

51 J. Wormald, *Mary Queen of Scots: a Study in Failure* (1988).

52 Levine, *Succession Question*, pp. 201.

53 See above, p. 44. Mary created him Duke of Albany before they were married.

54 Throgmorton to Elizabeth, 26 July 1567. *Calendar of State Papers Relating to Scotland, 1563–1569*, pp. 362–4.

55 Hastings was descended from Thomas of Woodstock through his daughter Anne, who had married Edmund, Earl of Stafford. From him descended Henry Stafford, Duke of Buckingham, whose daughter (another Anne) married Henry's grandfather, George, Earl of Huntingdon.

56 Loades, *Elizabeth I*, p. 181.

57 Camden, *The History of the Most Renowned Princess Elizabeth*, p. 202.

58 R. Parsons [R. Doleman], *A Conference about the next succession to the Crown of England* (1594).

59 David Loades, *The Cecils*, pp. 259–60.

60 Ibid.

Chapter 4: The Monarch and the Realm: The Uses of Parliament

1 A nobleman's jurisdiction was determined by his status as a Tenant-in-Chief of the King. By that right he held Honour Courts, to which the manor courts of the Honour were answerable. K. B. MacFarlane, *The Nobility of Later Medieval England* (1973), pp. 213–28. The Church as a landholder was subject to the normal feudal jurisdiction of the Crown, but legislated its own canons without the King's consent.

2 G. L. Harriss, 'Aids, Loans and Benevolences', *Historical Journal* 6, 1963, pp. 1–19. Harriss, *King, Parliament and Public Finance to 1369* (1975), pp. 509–10.

3 R. Somerville, *History of the Duchy of Lancaster* (1953–70).

4 Peter Coss, *The Origins of the English Gentry* (2003). P. J. Holmes, 'The Great Council in the Reign of Henry VII', *English Historical Review*, 101, 1986, pp. 840–62.

5 J. S. Roskell, *The Commons and their Speakers in English Parliaments, 1376–1523* (1965).

6 J. H. Baker, *The Oxford History of the Laws of England, 1483–1558* (2003).

7 P. R. Cavill, *The English Parliaments of Henry VII*, 1485–1504 (2009), pp. 205–12.

8 Loades, *Tudor Government* (1997), p. 39. The clergy were represented in their Provincial Convocations, which were not part of the Parliament.

9 J. F. Baldwin, *The King's Council in the Middle Ages* (1913). A. L Brown, 'The King's Councillors in Fifteenth Century England', *Transactions of the Royal Historical Society*, 5th series, 19, 1959, pp. 95–118. R. L. Storey, *The End of the House of Lancaster* (1966).

10 See, for example, Sir John Fortescue, *De Laudibus Legum Anglie*, ed S. B. Chrimes (1942).

11 G. R. Elton, *The Tudor Constitution* (1982), pp. 163–86.

12 Ibid, p. 103.

13 Loades, *Reign of Mary* (1991), pp. 18–25.

14 I. S.Leadam, *Select Cases in the Court of Requests* (Selden Society, 1898), p. xx.

15 Edward IV had occasionally presided at the Court of King's Bench, but when James I investigated the possibility of doing the same, he was told that it was not permitted.

16 Charles Ross, *Edward IV* (1974), p. 374. Both Henry VII and Henry VIII continued this practice down to the reorganisation of the 1530s, when the Treasury of the Chamber was superseded by the Court of Augmentations and other fiscal courts. These courts were reabsorbed into the Exchequer in 1554, when the Lancastrian procedures were (more or less) restored.

17 S. B. Chrimes, *Henry VII* (1972), p. 217. Loades, *The Tudor Court* (1986), pp. 20–1.

18 S. Anglo, *Spectacle, Pageantry and Early Tudor Policy* (1969), pp. 10–21, 56–97.

19 D. Starkey, 'Intimacy and Innovation; the rise of the Privy Chamber, 1485–1547' in Starkey, ed., *The English Court from the Wars of the Roses to the Civil War* (1987), pp. 71–118.

20 Pam Wright, 'A change of direction; the ramifications of a female household, 1558–1603' in Starkey, *The English Court*, pp. 147–72.

21 Cavill, *English Parliaments*, pp. 78–92.

22 J. A. Guy, *The Cardinal's Court; the Impact of Wolsey in Star Chamber* (1977).

23 Elton, *Tudor Constitution*, pp. 198–9.

24 Ibid, pp. 199–203. The fact that these courts were agencies of the central government was critical to their survival.

25 The sheriff controlled the County Court, almost the last function of which was the return of members to Parliament. He was also responsible for the empanelling of juries, and for commanding the shire militia before the advent of the Lord Lieutenant in the middle years of the century.

26 Every Commission of the Peace included at least one councillor or officer of the central government, and the commissions were overseen by the Justices of Assize.

27 K. N. Houghton, 'Theory and Practice in Borough Elections to Parliament during the later Fifteenth Century', *Bulletin of the Institute of Historical Research*, 39, 1966, pp. 130–40.

28 For full accounts of Henry's financial policies, see Chrimes, *Henry VII*, pp. 194–218, and Cavill, *English Parliaments*, pp. 46–71.

29 Ibid, pp. 245–6.

30 S. E. Lehmberg, *The Reformation Parliament, 1529–1536* (1970), p. 84.

31 Guy Bedouelle and Patrick Le Gal, *Le Divorce du Roi Henry VIII* (1987), pp. 19–26.

32 J. S. Roskell, C. Rawcliffe and L. Clark *The History of Parliament; The House of Commons 1386–1421* (1992). For the praemunire indictments in this context, see J. Scarisbrick, *Henry VIII* (1968), pp. 273–4.

33 Lehmberg, *Reformation Parliament*, pp. 174–5.

34 Elton, *Tudor Constitution*, pp. 338–77. Loades, *Tudor Government*, pp. 44–5.

35 Sir Thomas More expressed this view at his trial, denouncing his indictment as being 'grounded upon an act of parliament directly repugnant to the laws of God and His Holy

Church...', to which the Lord Chief Justice responded that if the Act of Parliament was lawful, then the indictment was good enough. Nicholas Harpefield, *The Life and Death of Sir Thomas More, Knight*, ed. E. V. Hitchcock and R. W. Chambers (1932), pp. 193, 196–7.

36 An issue addressed by Christopher St Germain in 1528. St Germain, *Doctor and Student*, ed. T. F. T. Plucknett and J. L. Barton (Selden Society, 1974), pp. 27–9, 31–3, 39–41, 47, 73.

37 Mary's letter to the council of 22 June 1549. Loades, *Mary Tudor*, p. 146.

38 Pole's letter to Mary, 13 August 1553. *Cal. Ven.*, V, p. 766.

39 Statute 1 & 2 Philip and Mary, c.6. Jennifer Loach, *Parliament and the Crown in the Reign of Mary Tudor* (1986), pp. 74–90, 105–27.

40 N. L. Jones, *Faith by Statute* (1982).

41 Smith, *De Republica Anglorum*, ed. Mary Dewar (1982), p. 78.

42 Loades, *Tudor Government*, pp. 45–6.

43 Loades, *Reign of Mary*, p. 219.

44 S. T. Bindoff, ed., *The House of Commons, 1509–1558* (1982). Loach, *Parliament and the Crown*, pp. 128–58.

45 John Foxe, *Acts and Monuments* (1583). Wallace MacCaffrey, *The Shaping of the Elizabethan Regime* (1969), pp. 55–70.

46 Sir Simonds D'Ewes, *The Journals of all the Parliaments during the Reign of Queen Elizabeth* (1682), p. 410.

47 Ibid.

48 For the full story of Grindal's falling-out with Elizabeth on the subject of prophecyings, see Patrick Collinson, *Edmund Grindal, 1519–1583; the Struggle for a Reformed Church* (1979).

49 Loades, *Tudor Government*, p. 51.

50 Elton, *Tudor Constitution*, pp. 316–25.

51 J. Wormald, *Mary Queen of Scots: a Study in Failure* (1988).

52 Loades, *Elizabeth I*, p. 224. Wallace MacCaffrey, *Queen Elizabeth and the Making of Policy, 1572–1588* (1981), p. 479.

53 Statute 27 Elizabeth I, c.1. *Statutes of the Realm*, IV, pp. 704–5.

54 William Camden, *The History of the Most Renowned Princess Elizabeth, Late Queen of England* (1688), iii, p. 202.

55 Elton, *Tudor Constitution*, pp. 267–8.

56 Loades, *Elizabeth I*, p. 293. 'The Commons Journal of Hayward Townshend, 1601', Bodleian MS Rawlinson A 100. J. E. Neale, *Elizabeth and her Parliaments* (1957), ii, pp. 352–6.

57 D'Ewes, *Journals*, p. 654.

58 W. Notestein, 'The winning of the initiative by the House of Commons', *Proceedings of the British Academy*, 11, 1926, pp. 125–76.

Chapter 5: Noble Ambitions

1 J. Green, *The Aristocracy of Norman England* (1997). P. R. Coss, *The Origins of the English Gentry* (2003).

2   M. C. Prestwich, *Armies and Warfare in the Middle Ages; the English Experience* (1996).

3   Coss, *The Origins of the English Gentry*, p. 156.

4   M. H. Keen, *Chivalry* (1984), pp. 1–17.

5   E. F. Jacob, *The Fifteenth Century; 1399–1485* (1961), pp. 317–18.

6   R. A. Griffith, *The Reign of Henry VI* (1981).

7   There are numerous discussions of these circumstances and events, which were known as 'the wars of York and Lancaster'. The term 'Wars of the Roses' was not coined until the nineteenth century. K. B. McFarlane, *The Nobility of Later Medieval England* (1973); J. Gillingham, *The Wars of the Roses* (1981); A. J. Pollard, *The Wars of the Roses* (1988).

8   Charles Ross, *Edward IV*, (1974), pp. 202–3.

9   S. B. Chrimes, *Henry VII*, pp. 53–8. P. J. Holmes, 'The Great Council in the Reign of Henry VII', *English Historical Review*, 101, 1986, pp. 840–62.

10 Chrimes, *Henry VII*, p. 102.

11 Statute 4 Henry VII, c.12, 'An act for Justices of the Peace, for the due execution of their commissions'. *Statutes of the Realm*, IV, p. 157

12 *Rotuli Parliamentorum*, V, p. 618. Elton, *Tudor Constitution*, p. 34.

13 Statute 19 Henry VII, c.14. *Statutes of the Realm*, II, pp. 658–60.

14 J. T. Rosenthal, 'The estates and finances of Richard, Duke of York', *Studies in Medieval and Renaissance History*, ii, 1965. Ross, *Edward IV*, pp. 11–21.

15 Chrimes, *Henry VII*, pp. 277–89.

16 W. H. Dunham, *Lord Hastings Indentured Retainers, 1401–1483* (1955), pp. 100–5.

17 Edward Hall, *Chronicle* (ed.1806), p. 503.

18 G. E. Cockayne, *The Complete Peerage* (1913).

19 David Loades, *Politics and the Nation, 1450–1660* (1999), p. 92.

20 Carole Rawcliffe, *The Staffords, Earls of Stafford and Dukes of Buckingham, 1394–1521* (1978), pp. 36–44.

21 D. Loades, *The Life and Career of William Paulet* (2008), p. 47.

22 For a full account of the demise of the Howards, see L. B. Smith, *Henry VIII, the Mask of Royalty* (1971), pp. 254–9.

23 Laurence Stone, *The Crisis of the Aristocracy, 1558–1640* (1965), p. 758.

24 Elton, *The Tudor Constitution*, pp. 338–77.

25 The evidence for this 'schoolroom' is inconclusive, but Edward certainly – and Elizabeth probably – shared their lessons with other children. That is how Edward first became acquainted with his friend Barnaby Fitzpatrick, and possibly how Elizabeth first met Robert Dudley.

26 Helen Miller, *Henry VIII and the English Nobility*, pp. 220–2.

27 W. K. Jordan, *Edward VI; the Young King* (1968), pp. 63–5.

28 Loades, *John Dudley, Duke of Northumberland* (1996), Appendix I.

29 Jordan, *Edward VI*, pp. 494–523. Loades, *John Dudley*, pp. 130–41.

30 Ibid.

31 Jordan, *Edward VI: the Threshold of Power* (1970), pp. 70–97.

32 D. Loades, *The Cecils: Privilege and Power behind the Throne* (2007), pp. 35–9.

33 For a loyalist account of this assembly, see 'The Vita Mariae Angliae Reginae of Robert Wingfield of Brantham', ed. D. MacCulloch (*Camden Miscellany*, 28, 1984).

34 Loades, *John Dudley*, pp. 254–66.

35 For a full account of Pole's position, see T. F. Meyer, *Reginald Pole, Prince and Prophet* (2000).

36 Cockayne, *The Complete Peerage, sub* Norfolk.

37 J. G. Nichols, ed., *The Chronicle of Queen Jane* (Camden Society, 48, 1849), p. 14.

38 P. G. Boscher, 'The Anglo-Scottish Border, 1550–1560' (Durham University PhD, 1985).

39 D. Loades, *The Reign of Mary Tudor* (1991), pp. 194–231.

40 Loades, *The Life and Career of William Paulet*, pp. 122–3.

41 M. C. Fissell, *English Warfare, 1511–1642*, (2001), pp. 8–13.

42 Wallace MacCaffrey, *The Shaping of the Elizabethan Regime* (1969), pp. 27–40.

43 Loades, *Elizabeth I* (2003), pp. 129–30, 257–8.

44 Ibid, pp. 143–5.

45 Loades, *The Cecils*, p. 81.

46 *Calendar of State Papers, Domestic, Addenda, 1566–1579*, p. 89.

47 Richard Norton was a veteran of the Pilgrimage of Grace. The Duke of Alba was Philip II's Governor in The Netherlands, having been sent there to suppress dissent in 1566. He was not interested in supporting a movement which had so little 'substance'. Pope Pius V belatedly backed the rebels by issuing the Bull *Regnans in Excelsis*, excommunicating and deposing Elizabeth, in February 1570. MacCaffrey, *The Shaping of the Elizabethan Regime*, pp. 232–3.

48 Ibid, pp. 227–9.

49 For the correspondence relating to these moves, see Sir Cuthbert Sharp, ed., *The 1569 Rebellion* (1840, repr. 1975), pp. 49–127.

50 Cockayne, *The Complete Peerage, sub* Northumberland. He succeeded by the terms of the original patent of creation.

51 R. T. Spence, *The Privateering Earl (George, 3rd Earl of Cumberland)* (1995). MacCaffrey, *The Shaping of the Elizabethan Regime*, pp. 228–9.

52 Ibid, p. 232.

53 Raphael Holinshed, *Chronicles*, ed. John Hooker et al. (1587), III, p. 252.

54 Loades, *The Fighting Tudors* (2009), pp. 197–204.

55 L. O. Boynton, *The Elizabethan Militia* (1967).

56 Loades, *The Fighting Tudors*, pp. 189–92.

57 L. B. Smith, *Treason in Tudor England: Politics and Paranoia* (1986), pp. 218–38.

58 Camden, *Elizabeth*, p. 606. Francis Bacon, 'A declaration of the practices and treasons attempted and committed by Robert, late Earl of Essex' in Bacon, *Works*, ed. J. Spedding (1857–74), III, pp. 136–65.

59 Harry Kelsey, *Sir Francis Drake: the Queen's Pirate* (1998).

60 Stone, *The Crisis of the Aristocracy*, p. 237.

61 Ibid.

62 Ibid, p. 238.

63 Smith, *Treason in Tudor England*, pp. 261–6.

64 M. E. James, 'English Politics and concept of Honour', *Past and Present*, Supplement 3, 1978.

Chapter 6: The Tudors and Their Neighbours

1 Notably in the use of massed pikes, which was a Swiss innovation, and in the development of hand-held firearms, in which the leaders were the French. Mark Fissell, *English Warfare, 1511–1642*, pp. 4–8.

2 Agnes Conway, *Henry VII's relations with Scotland and Ireland, 1485–1498* (1932).

3 Rymer, *Foedera*, XII, p. 680. Chrimes, *Henry VII*, p. 91.

4 S. G. Ellis, *Tudor Ireland* (1985), pp. 19–32.

5 Ibid, p. 75.

6 H. G. Richardson and G. O. Sayles, *The Irish Parliament in the Later Middle Ages* (1952), p. 274.

7 For an account of these feuds, and their effect on the politics of Ireland, see Ellis, *Tudor Ireland*, pp. 85–105. The most energetically pursued quarrel was between the FitzGeralds and the Butler Earls of Ormond.

8 Chrimes, *Henry VII*, p. 280. For the treaty of Redon, see Rymer, *Foedera*, XII, pp. 362–72.

9 Ibid, pp. 497 et seq. The treaty of Etaples was confirmed by Act of Parliament; statute 11 Henry VII, c.65. *Statutes of the Realm*, II, p. 635.

10 Ian Arthurson, *The Perkin Warbeck Conspiracy, 1491–1499* (1994), pp. 116–17.

11 *Cal.Span.* I, nos.13, 14.

12 For a full account of these ceremonies, see Anglo, *Spectacle, Pageantry and Early Tudor Policy*, pp. 56–97.

13 J. Gairdner, *Memorials of King Henry VII* (1858), pp. 223–39. *Cal.Span*, I, pp. 429 et seq.

14 Chrimes, *Henry VII*, p. 288.

15 Although chilly, relations with Ferdinand remained correct, and in 1507 the latter even accredited his daughter as an additional ambassador. *Cal.Span*. I, no.551.

16 Mark Fissell, *English Warfare*, p. 3, citing an unpublished paper by Clifford Davies.

17 In the summer of 1514 Henry had taken the unusual step of mothballing his fleet instead of disposing of it. He had by this time over thirty ships, and appointed two additional officers to look after them. D. Loades, *The Tudor Navy* (1992), pp. 67–9.

18 Rymer, *Foedera*, XIII, p. 413. *Letters and Papers*, I, nos.3101, 3171.

19 Scarisbrick, *Henry VIII*, pp. 59–62.

20 Rymer, *Foedera*, XIII, p. 624. Scarisbrick, *Henry VIII*, pp. 72–3.

21 J. G. Russell, *The Field of Cloth of Gold* (1969), pp. 105–39.

22 S. J. Gunn, 'The Duke of Suffolk's March on Paris, 1523', *English Historical Review*, 101, 1986, pp. 596–634.

23 Scarisbrick, *Henry VIII*, pp. 141–2.

24 There is good reason to suppose that Henry had anticipated this outcome, perhaps as early as 1523, but it offered an additional reason to break with Charles at this point.

25 Peter Gwynn, *The King's Cardinal* (1990). David Loades, *Cardinal Wolsey, c.1472–1530; Tudor Statesman and Chancellor* (2008), p. 31.

26 Ellis, *Tudor Ireland*, pp. 122–4.

27 Ellis, 'Henry VIII, rebellion and the rule of law', *Historical Journal*, 24, 1981, pp. 527–9.

28 This was the policy of 'surrender and regrant', whereby the Irish chieftains surrendered their

tribal lands to the King, and in return he regranted the same lands on a feudal tenure, along with an appropriate title. The new peer then had a right to sit in the Irish House of Lords.

29 *Letters and Papers*, XVIII, nos.7, 22, 44.

30 D. Loades and C. Knighton, *Letters from the Mary Rose* (2002), pp. 106–20.

31 Jordan, *Edward VI: the Young King*, pp. 237–9.

32 M. L. Bush, *The Government Policy of Protector Somerset* (1975), p. 27.

33 Rymer, *Foedera*, XV, pp. 212–15. 400,000 crowns was approximately £160,000, roughly equivalent to a year's ordinary income.

34 The effective agent of this enterprise was Sebastian Cabot, who had returned to England from Spain in 1548. D. Loades, *England's Maritime Empire, 1490–1690* (2000), pp. 66–7.

35 W. K. Jordan, *Edward VI: the Threshold of Power*, pp. 131–3. For Edward's enthusiasm, see Jordan, *The Chronicle and Political Papers of King Edward VI* (1966), pp. 70–3.

36 Loades, *Mary Tudor*, pp. 199–204.

37 Loades, 'Philip II and the Government of England', *Law and Government under the Tudors*, ed. Cross, Loades and Scarisbrick (1987), pp. 177–94.

38 Bishop of Arras to Feria, 26 May 1558. *Cal.Span.*, XIII, p. 388.

39 Loades, 'Philip II and the Government of England'.

40 R. Dunlop, 'The Plantation of Leix and Offaly', *English Historical Review*, 6, 1891, pp. 67–70.

41 Harry Kelsey, *John Hawkins; Queen Elizabeth's Slave Trader* (2003), pp. 1–33.

42 *Calendar of State Papers Relating to Scotland, 1560–61*, pp. 413–15.

43 Mary was kept in indefinite confinement in England, because Elizabeth refused to hand her over to the Scots and was unwilling to allow her to proceed to France, where her kindred, the Guises, were locked in war with the Huguenots. This arrangement suited the Regency government of Scotland.

44 Holinshed, *Chronicle*, p. 205. Conyers Read, *Mr Secretary Cecil and Queen Elizabeth* (1955), pp. 259–60.

45 Mark Greengrass, *The French Reformation* (1987). N. M. Sutherland, *The Huguenot Struggle for Recognition* (1980).

46 Charles had been born in Ghent and brought up in the Low Countries. He was also multilingual, unlike Philip who was fluent only in Spanish and Latin.

47 Jonathan Israel, *The Dutch Republic, 1477–1806* (1995), pp. 137–54.

48 W. S. Maltby, *Alba; a Biography of Fernando Alvarez de Toledo, Third Duke of Alba, 1507–82* (1983), pp. 143–7.

49 Israel, *The Dutch Republic*, pp. 169–78.

50 Geoffrey Parker, *The Dutch Revolt* (1979).

51 Harry Kelsey, *Sir Francis Drake: the Queen's Pirate* (1998), pp. 280–304.

52 Geoffrey Parker and Colin Martin, *The Spanish Armada* (1988), p. 147.

53 Ibid, pp. 179–94. On Medina Sidonia's failure to communicate with Parma, see pp. 180–1.

54 Loades, *The Making of the Elizabethan Navy, 1540–1590* (2009), pp. 199–201.

55 S. and E. Usherwood, *The Counter Armada, 1596* (1983). Taken from the journal of the *Mary Rose*.

56 Mark Fissell, *English Warfare*, pp. 154–8.

57 Ellis, *Tudor Ireland*, pp. 305–6.

58 N. P. Canny, 'Why the Reformation failed in Ireland; une question mal posée', *Journal of Ecclesiastical History*, 30, 1979. J. J. Silke, *Ireland and Europe, 1559–1607* (1966).

59 J. Wormald, *Court, Kirk and Community; Scotland 1470–1625* (1981).

60 The story that she did so on her deathbed is derived from Camden's *Annales*, without contemporary confirmation.

61 Chapuys was committed to involving Charles V in England on the side of Queen Catherine, and all his despatches have to be read with that priority in mind. Charles was reluctant, and rejected his advice.

62 On these 'special operations' see Alan Haynes, *Invisible Power; the Elizabethan Secret Services* (1992).

Chapter 7: The Trouble With God

1 E. Duffy, *The Stripping of the Altars* (1992), pp. 170, 313–27.

2 Durham University Library, Cosin MS v.v.19, cited in Dickens, *The English Reformation*, p. 3.

3 M. C. Knowles, *The Religious Orders in England, III, The Tudor Age* (1959).

4 Ben Lowe, *Commonwealth and the English Reformation; Protestantism and the Politics of Religious Change in the Gloucester Vale, 1483–1560* (2010), pp. 31–62.

5 D. Loades, 'Anticlericalism in the Church of England before 1558. An "eating canker"?' in Nigel Aston and Matthew Cragoe, *Anticlericalism* (2000), pp. 1–17.

6 Christopher Harper Bill, *The Pre-Reformation Church in England, 1400–1530* (1989).

7 J. H. Lupton, *The Life of John Colet* (1887), Appendix C, p. 293.

8 Peter Marshall, *Reformation England* (2003), pp. 19–25.

9 S. B. Chrimes, *Henry VII* (1972), Appendix D, pp. 330–2.

10 Statute 4 Henry VII, c.14. *Statutes of the Realm*, II, pp. 533–4.

11 J. A. F. Thompson, *The Later Lollards, 1414–1529* (1965), pp. 237–8. Chrimes, *Henry VII*, p. 240.

12 Anthony Goodman, 'Henry VII and Christian Renewal'; *Studies in Church History*, 17, 1981, pp. 115–25. Robert Swanson, *Church and Society in Late Medieval England* (1989), p. 190.

13 P. Gwynn, *The King's Cardinal* (1990).

14 Book of King's payments for the first five years of his reign. *Letters and Papers*, II, p. 1446 et seq.

15 J. D. M. Derrett, 'The Affair of Richard Hunne and Friar Standish', in Thomas More, *The Apology*, ed. J. B. Trapp (1979). Marshall, *Reformation England*, p. 22.

16 For Henry's first moves in this direction, see Eric Ives, *The Life and Death of Anne Boleyn* (2004), pp. 63–80.

17 Guy Bedouelle, 'Le déroulement historique', Bedouelle and Le Gal, *Le Divorce du Roi Henry VIII* (1987), pp. 19–28.

18 J. Scarisbrick, *Henry VIII* (1968), pp. 241–305.

19 Statute 26 Henry VIII, c.1. *Statutes of the Realm*, III, p. 492.

20 David Daniell, *The Bible in English; Its History and Influence* (2003).

21 Statute 31 Henry VIII, c.14, *Statutes of the Realm*, III, pp. 739–43. T. A. Lacey, ed., *The King's Book* (1932).

22 G. W. Bernard, *The King's Reformation* (2005).

23 Joyce Youings, *The Dissolution of the Monasteries* (1971).

24 Statute 27 Henry VIII, c.28. *Statutes of the Realm*, III, p. 575.

25 The last to fall was Waltham Abbey in Essex. Knowles, *The Religious Orders in England, III, The Tudor Age.*

26 Ben Lowe, *Commonwealth and the English Reformation*, pp. 115–40.

27 John Foxe, *Acts and Monuments* (1583), pp. 1120–1.

28 G. R. Elton, *Policy and Police* (1972), p. 258.

29 Alan Kreider, *English Chantries; The Road to Dissolution* (1979), pp. 186–210. Statute 1 Edward VI, c.14. *Statutes of the Realm*, IV, pp. 24–33.

30 Joyce Youings, 'The South Western Rebellion of 1549', *Southern History*, I, 1979, pp. 99–122.

31 A. G. Dickens, *The English Reformation*, pp. 244–6.

32 W. K. Jordan, *Edward VI: The Young King* (1968), pp. 206–9. Jordan, *Edward VI: The Threshold of Power* (1970), pp. 256–64.

33 Ibid. Diarmaid MacCulloch, *Tudor Church Militant* (1999), pp. 36–9.

34 J. Ketley, ed., *The Two Liturgies...Set Forth by Authority in the Reign of King Edward VI* (1844).

35 There had been only muted opposition to the reforming legislation of Edward's parliaments, but it is only fair to add that substantially the same men voted for the repeal of those same acts in the autumn of 1553. S. T. Bindoff, ed., *The House of Commons, 1509–1558* (1982).

36 D. Loades, *Mary Tudor: A Life* (1989), pp. 145–6.

37 Statute 1 Mary, st.2, c.2. *Statutes of the Realm*, IV, p. 202.

38 D. Loades, *The Reign of Mary Tudor* (1991), pp. 108–9.

39 For a discussion of the implications of this, see Jennifer Loach, *Parliament and the Crown in the Reign of Mary Tudor* (1986), pp. 105–27.

40 W. Wizeman, *The Theology and Spirituality of Mary Tudor's Church* (2006).

41 Ibid. E. Duffy, *Fires of Faith: Catholic England under Mary Tudor* (2009).

42 C. H. Garrett, *The Marian Exiles* (1938). D. Loades, 'The Essex Inqusitions of 1556', *Politics, Censorship and the English Reformation* (1991), pp. 16–27.

43 Duffy, *Fires of Faith*. D. Loades, 'The Personal Religion of Mary I', in Loades and Duffy, eds, *The Church of Mary Tudor* (2006), pp. 1–29.

44 D. Loades, *The Religious Culture of Marian England* (2010), pp. 129–44.

45 W. P. Haugaard, 'Elizabeth Tudor's Book of Devotions; a Neglected Clue to the Queen's Life and Character', *Sixteenth Century Journal*, 12, 1981, pp. 79–105.

46 'The Count of Feria's despatch to Philip II of 14 November 1558', ed. M.-J. Rodriguez Salgado and Simon Adams, *Camden Miscellany*, 28, 1984, p. 332.

47 N. L. Jones, *Faith by Statute* (1982).

48 Wallace MacCaffrey, *The Shaping of the Elizabethan Regime* (1969), pp. 55–70.

49 Open Catholics were excluded from the House of Commons in 1563, and from the Council in 1567, but many continued to dissemble their religious allegiance, and the Bishops were unhappy about the composition of many Commissions of the Peace.

50 D. Loades, *Elizabeth I* (2003), p. 170.

51 John Larocca, 'Popery and pounds; the effect of the Jesuit mission on penal legislation', in *The Reckoned Expense; Edmund Campion and the Early English Jesuits*, ed. Thomas McCoog (1996), pp. 249–64.

52 Peter Holmes, *Resistance and Compromise: the Political Thought of the Elizabethan Catholics* (1982).

53 Statutes 13 Elizabeth I, c.2, 23 Elizabeth I, c.1, 27 Elizabeth I, c.2. *Statutes of the Realm*, IV, pp. 528–31, 657–8, 706–8.

54 Patrick Collinson, *The Elizabethan Puritan Movement* (1967), pp. 391–6.

55 Statute 35 Elizabeth I, c.1. *Statutes of the Realm*, IV, p. 841.

56 Tom Betteridge, 'From Prophetic to Apocalyptic; John Foxe and the Writing of History' in *John Foxe and the English Reformation*, ed. D. Loades (1997), pp. 210–32.

57 Ibid.

58 See Thomas Deloney, 'Three Ballads of the Armada Fight' in A. F. Pollard, *Tudor Tracts*, pp. 485–502: 'O Noble England, fall down upon thy knee!

    And praise thy GOD with thankful heart,

      which still maintaineth thee!

59 Jennifer Loach, *Edward VI* (1999).

60 Wallace MacCaffrey, *Elizabeth I: War and Politics, 1588–1603* (1992), p. 3.

Chapter 8: Merchant Matters

1 D. Loades, *England's Maritime Empire, 1490–1690* (2000), p. 15. T. H. Lloyd, *The English Wool Trade in the Middle Ages* (1977).

2 Ibid.

3 Rymer, *Foedera* (1704–35), IV, p. 107.

4 C. Ross, *Edward IV* (1974), pp. 353–4.

5 'Historiae Croylandensis Continuatio', in *Rerum Anglicarum Scriptores Veterum*, ed. W. Fulman (1684), p. 569.

6 D. Loades, 'The King's Ships and the Keeping of the Seas, 1413–1480', *Medieval History*, 1, 1991, pp. 93–104.

7 By 1498 it had risen to 69,000. E. M. Carus Wilson and E. Coleman, *England's Export Trade, 1275–1547* (1963).

8 Loades, *England's Maritime Empire*, p. 29.

9 Statute 12 Henry VII, c.6. *Statutes of the Realm*, II, p. 639.

10 G. Schantz, *Englische Handelspolitik gegen Ende des Mittelalters* (1881), I, p. 549.

11 E. M. Carus Wilson, 'The origin and early development of the Merchant Adventurers', *Economic History Review*, 2nd series, 4, 1932, pp. 147–76.

12 *Cal.Span.*, I, p. 21. Rymer, *Foedera*, XII, pp. 420–8.

13 Henry's relations with Ferdinand cooled markedly after Isabella's death, and he decided to support Juana and Philip in their bid for the Castilian succession. *Foedera*, XII, pp. 578–88.

14 S. B. Chrimes, *Henry VII* (1972), p. 238.

15 The rates seem to have varied, perhaps with the size of the ship. In 1488 a vessel of 140 tons attracted a bounty of 3s 10d a ton, while in 1490 one of 400 tons was paid at the rate of 5s a ton. B. Dietz, 'The royal bounty and English shipping in the sixteenth and seventeenth centuries', *Mariners Mirror*, 77, 1991, pp. 5–21.

16 Rymer, *Foedera*, XII, p. 595.

17 J. A. Williamson, *The Cabot Voyages and Bristol Discovery under Henry VII* (1962), pp. 116–44.

18 Ibid, pp. 145–72.

19 Ralph Davis. *English Overseas Trade, 1500–1700* (1973), p. 52. Having delivered a declaration of war against the Emperor in January 1528, Henry promptly concluded a truce with Margaret to protect English trade. *Letters and Papers*, IV, nos.3879, 4147, 4426.

20 J. A. Williamson, *The Voyages of the Cabots...under Henry VII and Henry VIII* (1929), pp. 85 et seq., 244 et seq.

21 Ibid, pp. 94 et seq., 248 et seq.

22 Richard Hakluyt, *The principall navigations, voiages and discoveries of the English nation* (1589), p. 520.

23 Ibid, p. 517. E. G. R. Taylor, 'Master Hore's voyage of 1536', *Geographical Journal*, 77, 1931, pp. 460–70.

24 E. G. R. Taylor, *Tudor Geography, 1485–1583* (1930), pp. 48–52.

25 C. E. Challis, *The Tudor Coinage* (1978), pp. 81–112, 248.

26 P. L. Hughes and J. F. Larkin, *Tudor Royal Proclamations*, I (1964), pp. 518–19.

27 *Cal.Pat. Edward VI*, I, p. 320.

28 Loades, *England's Maritime Empire*, p. 56.

29 John Stow, *The Annals of England Faithfully collected* (1592), p. 609.

30 Loades, *England's Maritime Empire*, pp. 59–60. *Acts of the Privy Council*, III, p. 489.

31 F. C. Dietz, *English Government Finance* (1964), p. 196.

32 'Great was the triumph here in London. For my time I never saw the like...', *The Chronicle of Queen Jane*, ed. J. G. Nichols (Camden Society, 48, 1851), p. 11.

33 Forty-five of the Whitecoats were executed in London, twenty-two others in Kent and an uncertain number in Southwark. Probably about a hundred died overall. *The Diary of Henry Machyn*, ed. J. G. Nichols (Camden Society, 42, 1848), p. 55.

34 TNA SP11/4, no.36.

35 Loades, *Mary Tudor*, p. 297. Philip to the Privy Council, 31 January 1558, *Cal.Span.*, XIII, p. 348.

36 *Cal.Pat., Philip and Mary*, II, pp. 55–8.

37 Sir William Foster, *England's Quest for Eastern Trade* (1933), p. 17.

38 Davis, *English Overseas Trade*, p. 52.

39 *The Passage of our most Dread Sovereign Lady, Queen Elizabeth...the day before her Coronation* (1558/9). A. F. Pollard, *Tudor Tracts* (1903), pp. 365–95.

40 Dee had been employed in some capacity by John Dudley, Duke of Northumberland, and was introduced to the Queen by Lord Robert Dudley. He is alleged to have cast the horoscope for her coronation.

41 Harry Kelsey, *Sir John Hawkins; Queen Elizabeth's Slave Trader* (2003), pp. 11–15.

42 Conyers Read, 'Queen Elizabeth's seizure of Alba's pay ships', *Journal of Modern History*, 5, 1933, pp. 443–64.

43 Kelsey, *Sir John Hawkins*, pp. 19–33.

44 Ibid, pp. 99–104

45 Harry Kelsey, *Sir Francis Drake; Queen Elizabeth's Pirate* (1998), pp. 63, 81–9.

46 John Dee, *General and rare memorials pertaining to the Perfect Arte of Navigation* (1577) [RSTC 6459].

47 Kelsey, *Sir Francis Drake*, p. 93.

48 Ibid, pp. 106–9.

49 Ibid, p. 204.

50 D. R. Bisson, *The Merchant Adventurers of England* (1993), p. 68.

51 Davis, *Overseas Trade*, pp. 41–3.

52 T. K. Rabb, *Enterprise and Empire, 1575–1630* (1967), p. 104.

53 Ibid.

54 Foster, *England's Quest of Eastern Trade*, p. 69.

55 Samuel Purchas, *Hakluytus posthumus or Purchas his pilgrimes* (1625). Hakluyt Society, VIII (1905–7) pp. 449 et seq.

56 D. Loades, *The Cecils; Privilege and Power Behind the Throne* (2007). Cheryl A. Fury, *Tides in the Affairs of Men; The Social History of Elizabethan Seamen, 1580–1603* (2002).

57 D. C. Coleman, 'An Innovation and its Diffusion; the New Draperies', *Economic History Review*, 2nd Series, 21, 1968. Andrew Pettegree, *Foreign Protestant Congregations in Sixteenth Century London* (1986).

58 For the net Exchequer receipts from 1594 to 1603, see F. C. Dietz, *English Public Finance, 1558–1641* (1964), p. 328 note.

Chapter 9: The Good Lord and His Servants

1 Marc Bloch, trs. L. A. Manyon, *Feudal Society* (1961). F. L. Ganshof, trs. Philip Grierson, *Feudalism* (1964).

2 Their lands were allodial, and not part of the manor in which they were situated. A. W. B. Simpson, *A History of the Land Law* (1986).

3 Only a man who was personally unfree was bound to his tenement by law, and was subject to the jurisdiction of the manor court for all offences. Ibid.

4 Ben Lowe, *Commonwealth and the English Reformation* (2010), pp. 31–62.

5 D. Loades, *Cardinal Wolsey* (2008), pp. 11–12. J. Cornwall, *The Revolt of the Peasantry, 1549* (1977).

6   J. R. Jones, *The Tudor Commonwealth* (1970), pp. 43–64.
7   D. Loades, *Tudor Government* (1997), pp. 160–6.
8   W. Hudson and J. C. Tingey, *The Records of the City of Norwich (1906).* S. Rappaport, *Worlds within Worlds; the Structures of Life in Sixteenth Century London* (1989).
9   A. D. Dyer, *Decline and Growth in English Towns, 1400–1640* (1991).
10 Statute 27 Henry VIII, c.25. *Statutes of the Realm*, III, p. 558.
11 For example, 18 Elizabeth I, c.3; 39 Elizabeth I c.4; 43 Elizabeth I, c.2. These acts made local assessments compulsory, but did not provide any assistance.
12 E. F. Jacob, *The Fifteenth Century* (1961), pp. 520–2.
13 K. B. McFarlane, *The Nobility of Later Medieval England* (1973), p. 106.
14 Loades, *Tudor Government*, pp. 1–16.
15 Majorie Chibnall, *Anglo–Norman England, 1066–1166* (1986), pp. 161–83.
16 *Certain Homilies appointed by the King's Majesty to be declared and read* (1547), reprinted in J. Griffiths, *Homilies Appointed to be Read in Churches* (1859).
17 R. A. Houlbrooke, *Church Courts and the People during the English Reformation* (1979), pp. 30–4.
18 D. Loades, *Politics and the Nation, 1450–1660* (1999), p. 13; 'the complaint of the men of Kent'.
19 The Court of Star Chamber was properly a creation of Cardinal Wolsey, but Henry VII's council met in the Star Chamber for this kind of business, so the term is used here to distinguish a function. S. B. Chrimes, *Henry VII*, p. 99.
20 Sir Thomas Smith, *De Republica Anglorum*, ed. Mary Dewar (1982), p. 78.
21 Helen Miller, *Henry VIII and the English Nobility* (1986), pp. 73–4.
22 G. R. Elton, *Policy and Police* (1972).
23 M. C. Fissel, *English Warfare, 1511–1642* (2001), pp. 8–13.
24 Chrimes, *Henry VII*, p 69.
25 Ian Arthurson, *The Perkin Warbeck Conspiracy, 1491–1499* (1994), pp. 84–6.
26 Chrimes, *Henry VII*, p. 90.
27 J. R. Lander, *Government and Community in England, 1450–1509* (1980), p. 340. Miller, *Henry VIII and the English Nobility*, pp. 133–4.
28 J. Scarisbrick, *Henry VIII* (1968), pp. 3–20.
29 E. Hall, *Chronicle* (ed.1806), pp. 588 et seq. *Calendar of State Papers*, Venetian, II, pp. 876, 881–2, 887.
30 Ibid.
31 F. C. Dietz, *English Government Finance, 1485–1558* (1964), p. 94.
32 G. W. Bernard, *War, Taxation and Rebellion in Early Tudor England; Henry VIII, Wolsey and the Amicable Grant of 1525* (1986).
33 For the nature of Henry's understanding of his relationship with God, see G. W. Bernard, *The King's Reformation* (2005).
34 A viewpoint set out in the preambles to various reformation statutes. 24 Henry VIII, c.12 (An Act in Restraint of Appeals); 25 Henry VIII, c.20 (An Act Restraining the Payment of Annates); 26 Henry VIII, c.1 (The Act of Supremacy); and 28 Henry VIII, c.10 (An Act Extinguishing the Authority of the Bishop of Rome).

35 J. S. Block, *Factional Politics and the English Reformation, 1520–1540* (1993). Ellen A. Macek, *The Loyal Opposition, Tudor Traditionalist Polemic, 1535–1558* (1996).

36 Bernard, *The King's Reformation.*

37 For a full discussion of Cromwell's sources of information, see Elton, *Policy and Police.*

38 R. W. Hoyle, *The Pilgrimage of Grace and the Politics of the 1530s* (2001), pp. 459–63.

39 Ibid, pp. 339–64.

40 Ibid, pp. 362–3.

41 Elton, *Policy and Police*, p. 387.

42 Diarmaid MacCulloch, *Tudor Church Militant: Edward VI and the Protestant Reformation* (1999), pp. 57–104.

43 Frances Rose-Troup, *The Western Rebellion of 1549* (1913), pp. 492–4.

44 W. K. Jordan, *Edward VI: the Young King* (1968), pp. 477–93.

45 S. T. Bindoff, *Kett's Rebellion*, 1549 (1949). M. L. Bush, *The Government Policy of Protector Somerset* (1975), pp. 84–9.

46 F. W. Russell, *Kett's Rebellion in Norfolk* (1859), pp. 87–98.

47 D. Loades, *John Dudley, Duke of Northumberland* (1996), pp. 125–79. B. L. Beer, *Rebellion and Riot: Popular Disorders in England in the Reign of Edward VI* (1982).

48 Jennifer Loach, *Edward VI* (1999).

49 The only man with any claim was Reginald Pole, the grandson of George, Duke of Clarence, who was ruled out for a number of reasons – not least that he was an attainted traitor.

50 D. Loades, *Mary Tudor: a Life* (1989), pp. 201–4.

51 D. Loades, *Two Tudor Conspiracies* (1965), pp. 113–27.

52 Glyn Redworth, '"Matters impertinent to women": Male and Female Monarchy under Philip and Mary', *English Historical Review*, 112, 1997, pp. 597–613.

53 D. Loades, *Mary Tudor: the Tragical history of the first Queen of England* (2006), pp. 145–61.

54 Wallace MacCaffrey, *The Shaping of the Elizabethan Regime* (1969).

55 Susan Doran, *Monarchy and Matrimony: the Courtships of Elizabeth I* (1996). Simon Adams, *Leicester and the Court* (2002), pp. 133–50.

56 Mortimer Levine, *The Early Elizabethan Succession Question* (1966), pp. 30–59.

57 Conyers Read, *Mr. Secretary Cecil and Queen Elizabeth* (1955), pp. 440–3.

58 *Calendar of State Papers, Domestic, Addenda 1566–79*, p. 89.

59 Sir Cuthbert Sharp, *The 1569 Rebellion* (1840), ed. and with a foreword by Robert Wood (1975), pp. xxv–vi.

60 Ibid.

61 The Duke of Norfolk had secured the Dacre inheritance through a lawsuit with Leonard Dacre. It became forfeit to the Crown on his attainder in 1572.

62 Conyers Read, *Mr. Secretary Walsingham and the Policy of Queen Elizabeth* (1925), II, pp. 364 et seq. J.H. Pollen, *Mary Queen of Scots and the Babington Plot* (1922), pp. 63–6.

63 Statute 43 Elizabeth I, c.13. *Statutes of the Realm*, IV, p. 979.

64 W. Lambarde, *Eirenarcha, or the Office of the Justice of the Peace* (1602), pp. 34–7.

65 D. MacCulloch, 'Bondmen under the Tudors' in Cross, Loades and Scarisbrick, eds, *Law and Government under the Tudors* (1988), pp. 91–110.

Chapter 10: *The Selling of the Monarchy*

1   *Bacon's History of Henry VII*, ed. J. R. Lumby (1902), p. 5.
2   Kevin Sharpe, *Selling the Tudor Monarchy: Authority and Image in Sixteenth Century England* (2009), p. 64.
3   S. Anglo, *Images of Tudor Kingship* (1992), p. 20
4   Edward Hall, *Chronicle*, ed. H. Ellis (1809), pp. 426–8. J. C. Meacher, 'The First Progress of Henry VII', *Renaissance Drama*, 1, 1968, pp. 45–74.
5   Sharpe, *Selling the Tudor Monarchy*, p. 64.
6   E. Cavell, 'Henry VII, the North of England and the First Provincial Progress of 1486', *Northern History*, 29, 2002, pp. 187–208.
7   S. B. Chrimes, *Henry VII*, (1972), pp. 64–7. Cavell, op. cit., p. 201.
8   BL Add. MSS 7099, 59899.
9   Lumby, *Bacon's History of Henry VII*, p. 219.
10   S. Anglo, *Spectacle, Pageantry and Early Tudor Policy* (1969), pp. 108–23.
11   William Roper, *The Lyfe of Sir Thomas More, knight*, ed. E. V. Hitchcock (Early English Text Society, 1935), p. 11.
12   Hall, *Chronicle*, p. 507.
13   *Letters and Papers*, 1, no.162.
14   On the strong Francophobia prevalent in the council, see *Letters and Papers*, II, no.539. For Wolsey's hijacking of Leo's plan, see Peter Gwyn, *The King's Cardinal* (1990), p. 15.
15   J. Scarisbrick, *Henry VIII*, pp. 73–4.
16   *Cal.Span.*, II, pp. 285, 288. *Cal.Ven.*, III, p. 98.
17   RSTC 13078. F. Macnamara, *Miscellaneous Writings of Henry VIII* (1924), pp. 25–154.
18   P. L.Hughes and J. F. Larkin, *Tudor Royal Proclamations*, I (1964), p. 6. Scarisbrick, *Henry VIII*, p. 113.
19   Sharpe, *Selling the Tudor Monarchy*, pp. 81–90.
20   RSTC 11918. S. Haas, 'Henry VIII's Glasse of the Truthe', *History*, 64, 1979, pp. 65–72. See also R. Rex, 'Redating Henry VIII's Glass of the Truth', *The Library*, 7th series, 4, 2003, pp. 16–27.
21   G. R. Elton, *The Tudor Constitution* (1982).
22   J. P. Carley, *The Books of Henry VIII and his Wives* (2004), p. 114.
23   N. Sanders, *De Origine ac Progressu Schismatis Anglicani Liber* (1585). R. Parsons, *De Persecutione Anglicana Epistola* (1581).
24   'O stranger, if you desire to see pictures with all the appearance of life, look on these which Holbein's hand has created' (Nicholas Bourbon, 1503–1550). *Holbein and the Court of Henry VIII* (1978), p. 6.
25   Lacey Baldwin Smith, *Henry VIII; the Mask of Royalty* (1971).
26   W. K. Jordan, *Edward VI: the Young King* (1968), p. 51.
27   Deposition of John Fowler, January 1549. TNA SP10/6, no.10.
28   Martin Bucer to Johannes Brentius, 15 May 1550. J. G. Nichols, *Literary Remains of Edward VI*, I (1857), p. cxliv.
29   W. K. Jordan, *The Chronicle and Political Papers of King Edward VI* (1966), p. 55.

30 2 Chronicles 34.

31 Jennifer Loach, *Edward VI* (1999).

32 For a discussion of Edward's political education, see D. Loades, *John Dudley, Duke of Northumberland* (1996), pp. 191–5.

33 Ibid, pp. 238–41.

34 Agnes Strickland, *Lives of the Queens of England*, III (1902), p. 109.

35 Hughes and Larkin, *Tudor Royal Proclamations*, II (1969), pp. 5–8.

36 A. Feuillerat, *Documents Relating to the Office of the Revels in the Reigns of Edward VI and Mary* (1914), p. 161.

37 Statute 1 Mary, st.3, c.1. Hughes and Larkin, *Tudor Royal Proclamations*, II, pp. 21–6.

38 D. Loades, *Intrigue and Treason; the Tudor Court 1547–1558* (2004), pp. 191–2.

39 D. Loades, *Mary Tudor: A Life* (1989), p. 232.

40 Wim de Groot, *The Seventh Window* (2005), pp. 217–20.

41 The reasons for Mary's refusal to accede to this demand were never made clear. She claimed that Parliament would not allow it, but as Philip pointed out, it was none of Parliament's business. Loades, *Mary Tudor*, pp. 257–9.

42 Sharpe, *Selling the Tudor Monarchy*, pp. 273–4.

43 Particularly that by Anthonis Mor, commissioned by Philip. The original is now in the Prado. For a discussion of this portrait, see Roy Strong, *Tudor and Jacobean Portraiture* (1969).

44 Giovanni Michieli, 'Narration of England'; *Cal.Ven.*, VI, pp. 1043–85.

45 Jordan, *Edward VI: the Young King*, pp. 372–4. L. Weissener, trs. C. Yonge, *The Youth of Queen Elizabeth* (1879).

46 Sharpe, *Selling the Tudor Monarchy*, pp. 348–57.

47 A Fueillerat, *Documents Relating to the Office of the Revels in the Reign of Queen Elizabeth* (1908), pp. 79–108.

48 Susan Doran, *Monarchy and Matrimony; the Courtships of Elizabeth I* (1996).

49 Throgmorton to Chamberlain, 29 October 1560. TNA SP70/19, no.132.

50 *The Passage of Our Most Dread Sovereign Lady Queen Elizabeth through the City of London* (1559), in Pollard, *Tudor Tracts*, pp. 387–8.

51 D. Loades, *Elizabeth I* (2003), pp. 210–11.

52 L. S. Marcus, Janel Muller and M. B. Rose, eds, *Elizabeth I: Collected Works* (2000), pp. 325–6. 'Gathered by one that heard it and was commanded to utter it.'

53 Hughes and Larkin, *Tudor Royal Proclamations*, II, p. 240, December 1563.

54 *Thomas Dekker, Works* (1873), I, p. 83. Roy Strong, *The Cult of Elizabeth* (1977), p. 15.

55 Sharpe, *Selling the Tudor Monarchy*, pp. 61–3.

Conclusion: What Did the Tudors Do For Us?

1 In medieval England it was inconceivable that any member of the community would not be a member of the Church. So a monarch had to relate to his (or her) subjects in two different ways, and society was at once temporal and religious. Because of their

sacramental authority, the clergy had a claim to allegiance which was independent of the King, and it was that problem which Henry VIII set out to address.

2   David Little, *Religion, Order and Law; a study in pre-revolutionary England* (1968).

3   Whatever might have been claimed for Henry VIII, there was no precedent for the exercise of ecclesiastical jurisdiction by a minor, and the Royal Supremacy had to be borne, along with the rest of the Crown's executive power, by Edward's council. The use of Parliament was a natural fail-safe. Following the Act of 1554, Elizabeth was entitled to call herself Supreme Head, but chose Supreme Governor as a gesture of conciliation to conservative opinion.

4   This was the point of Peter Wentworth's questions, posed in 1587. G. R. Elton, *The Tudor Constitution* (1982), pp. 273–4.

5   Once Henry's religious legislation had been extended, repealed and then reinstated, there was no realistic alternative to regarding the will of God and the will of Parliament as being identical, although that was never accepted in principle.

6   William Lambarde on Justices of the Peace. *Eirenarcha* (1602), Bk 4, pp. 366–9.

7   This was true in troublesome counties such as Norfolk. Elsewhere he still tended to rely on baronial supporters. Charles Ross, *Edward IV* (1974), pp. 332–9.

8   M. C. Fissell, *English Warfare, 1511–1642* (2001), pp. 8–13.

9   C. S. Knighton, *Pepys and the Navy* (2003). There was no major discontinuity in the evolution of naval administration until the late twentieth century.

10 The Roanoake colony was undertaken by Sir Walter Raleigh, although with the Queen's encouragement. Carole Shammas, 'English Commercial Development and American Colonisation, 1560–1620', in K. R. Andrews, N. P. Canny and P. E. H Hair, *The Westward Enterprise* (1978), pp. 131–74.

11 When the independence of the Irish Republic was recognized. The Protestant/Catholic division persists in Northern Ireland.

12 F. C. Dietz, *English Public Finance, 1558–1642* (1964), pp. 53–66.

13 The role of the Church of England is now most noticeable when the government is seeking endorsement for an 'ethical' choice of policy. It played a significant part in the deconstruction of apartheid in South Africa.

14 For the part played by his Christian faith in the career of one great Victorian statesman, see Richard Shannon, *Gladstone; Heroic Minister, 1865–1898* (1999).

15 Joan Simon, *Education and Society in Tudor England* (1966).

16 The average net receipts from monastic sources were about £130,000 a year from 1536 to the end of the reign. Of this about 7 per cent was bestowed on the universities.

17 J. K. McConica, ed., *The Collegiate University of Oxford* (1986). Sarah Bendall, Christopher Brooke and Patrick Collison, *A History of Emmanuel College, Cambridge* (1999). Antonia Catchpole, David Clark, Robert Peberdy, eds, *Burford...a Cotswold Town* (2008).

18 David Cressy, *Literacy and the Social Order; Reading and Writing in Tudor and Stuart England* (1980), p. 47.

Bibliography

RSTC = *Revised Short Title Catalogue of books printed in England, Scotland and Ireland, and of English Books printed Abroad, 1475–1640,* by A. W. Pollard and G. R. Redgrave, revised by W. A. Jackson and F. S. Ferguson (1976)

Wing = *A Short Title Catalogue of books printed in England, Scotland, Ireland, Wales, and British North America, and of English Books printed in other countries, 1640–1700,* by D. G. Wing (1945–51)

A. MANUSCRIPTS

The National Archive

SP1, SP10, SP11, SP12, SP46, SP69, SP70
E101, E351
PRO31

The British Library

Add.MSS 7099, 59899
Cotton MS Titus B II

Magdalene College, Cambridge, Pepys Library

MSS 2875, 2876

Inner Temple Library

Petyt MS 47

Bodleian Library, Oxford

Rawlinson MS A.100, 200, 201.

B. CONTEMPORARY PRINTED WORKS AND MODERN EDITIONS

Assertio Septem Saramentorum (1521) [RSTC 13078]

Bacon, Sir Francis, *History of the Reign of King Henry the Seventh*, (1622) [RSTC 1159], ed. R. Lockyer (1971)

Dee, John, *General and rare monuments pertaining to the perfect Arte of Navigation* (1577) [RSTC 6459]

Digges, Sir Dudley, *The Compleat Ambassador* (1655) [Wing 1453]

Deloney, T., *Three Ballads of the Armada Fight* [RSTC 6557, 6558, 6565], in A. F. Pollard, *Tudor Tracts* (1903)

Fortescue, Sir John, *De Laudibus Legum Anglie* [RSTC 11197], ed. S. B. Chrimes (1942)

Foxe, John, *Acts and Monuments of the English Martyrs* (1583) [RSTC 11225]

A Glasse of the Truthe (1532) [RSTC 11918]

Hakluyt, Richard, *The principall navigations, voiages, and discoveries of the English nation* (1589) [RSTC 12625]

Hall, Edward, *The Union of the two noble and illustre famelies of York and Lancaster* [RSTC 12721] (*Chronicle*), ed. H. Ellis (1809)

Holinshed, Raphael, *Chronicles*, ed. J. Hooker et al. (1587) [RSTC 13569.5]

Homilies Appointed to be read in Churches [RSTC 13638.5], ed. J. Griffiths (1859)

The King's Book, (*A Necessary Doctrine and Erudition for any Christen Man*) [RSTC 13087], ed. T. A. Lacey (1932)

Lambarde, William, *Eirenarcha, or the Office of Justice of the Peace* (1602) [RSTC 15170]

More, Sir Thomas, *The Apology* [RSTC 18078], ed. J. B. Trapp (1979)

Parsons, R., *De Persecutione Anglicanae Epistolae* (1581) [trs. G. T., RSTC 19406]

Parsons, R. [R. Doleman], *A conference about the next succession to the Crown of England* (1594) [RSTC 19398]

The passage of our most Dread Sovereign Lady, Queen Elizabeth…the day before her coronation (1559) [by Richard Mulcaster] [RSTC 2589.5], in Pollard, *Tudor Tracts*, pp.365–95.

Purchas, Samuel, *Hakluytus Posthumus or Purchas his Pilgrimes* (1625) [RSTC 20509] (Hakluyt Society, VIII, 1905–7)

Roper, W., *The life of Sir Thomas More, Knight* (1557) [RSTC 21316], ed. E. V. Hitchcock (Early English Text Society, 1935)

St. Germain, Christopher, *Doctor and Student* [RSTC 21505], ed. T. F. T. Plucknett and J. L. Barton (Selden Society, 1974)

Sanders, Nicholas, *De Origine ac Progressu Schismatis Anglicana Liber* (1585) [Adams S284]

Smith, Sir Thomas, *De Republica Anglorum* [RSTC 22857], ed. M. Dewar (1982)

Stow, John, *The Annals of England faithfully collected* (1592) [RSTC 23334]

Two Liturgies set Forth by Authority in the reign of King Edward VI [RSTC 16267, 16279] ed. J. Kelley (1844)

Vergil, Polydore, *Three Books of English History* [RSTC 24645], ed. H. Ellis (Camden Society, 29, 1844)

Vergil, Polydore, *Anglica Historia* [RSTC 24645], ed. D. Hay (Camden Society, n.s.74, 1950)

C. CALENDARS AND DOCUMENTS

Acts of the Privy Council, ed. J. R. Dasent et al. (1890–1907)

Adams, S., and Rodriguez-Salgado, M.-J., 'The Count of Feria's despatch to Philip II of 14 November 1558' (*Camden Miscellany*, 28, 1984)

Allen, P. S., and H. M., *The Letters of Richard Fox* (1929)

Andree, Bernard, *De Vita atque Gestis Henrici Septimi*, ed. James Gairdner (1858)

Bacon, F., *History of Henry VII*, ed. J. Lumby (1902)

Calendar of the Close Rolls – Henry VI (6 vols, 1933–9)

Calendar of the Patent Rolls, 1485–1494 (1914)

Calendar of the Patent Rolls, 1494–1509 (1916)

Calendar of the Patent Rolls, 1547–1553 (1924–9)

Calendar of the Patent Rolls, 1553–1558 (1936–9)

Calendar of State Papers, Domestic, 1547–1704, ed. R. Lemon et al. (1856–1947)

Calendar of State Papers, Domestic, 1547–1553, ed. C. S. Knighton (1992)

Calendar of State Papers, Domestic, 1553–1558, ed. C. S. Knighton (1998)

Calendar of State Papers, Foreign, 1547–1592, ed. W. Turnbull et al. (1861–1980)

Calendar of the State Papers, Spanish, ed. G. A. Bergenroth et al. (1862–1954)

Calendar of State Papers Relating to Scotland, ed. Jos. Bain (Edinburgh, 1898)

Calendar of State Papers, Venetian, ed. Rawdon Brown et al. (1864–98)

Campbell, W., ed., *Materials for a History of the Reign of Henry VII* (Rolls Series, 1873–7)

Cockayne, G. E., *The Complete Peerage*, ed. V. Gibbs et al. (1910–59)

Correspondencia de Gutierre Gomez de Fuensalida, ed. El Duque de Berwick y de Alba (Madrid, 1907)

D'Ewes, Sir Symonds, *The Journals of all the Parliaments during the Reign of Queen Elizabeth* (1682)

Elizabeth I: Collected Works, ed. L. S. Markus, J. Mueller, and M. B. Rose (Yale, 2000)

Elton, G. R., *The Tudor Constitution* (1982)

Feuillerat, A., *Documents Relating to the Office of the Revels in the Reign of Queen Elizabeth* (1908)

Feuillerat, A., *Documents Relating to the Office of the Revels in the Reigns of Edward VI and Mary* (1914)

Foedera, Conventiones, Literae, etc., ed. T. Rymer (1739–45/1967)

Gairdner, James, *Memorials of King Henry VII* (1858)

Harpesfield, Nicholas, *The Life and Death of Sir Thomas More, Knight*, ed. E. V. Hitchcock and R. W. Chambers (Early English Text Society, 1932)

'Historia Croylandensis Continuatio', in *Rerum Anglicarum Scriptores Veterum*, ed. W. Fulman (1684)

Hudson, W., and J. C. Tingay, *The Records of the City of Norwich* (1906)

Jordan, W. K., *The Chronicle and Political Papers of King Edward VI* (1966)

Leadam, I. S., *Select Cases in the Court of Requests* (Selden Society, 1898)

Letters and Papers, Foreign and Domestic, of the Reign of Henry VIII, ed. J.S. Brewer et al. (1862–1910)

Loades, D., and C. S. Knighton, eds, *Letters from the Mary Rose* (2002)

MacCulloch, D., 'The Vita Mariae Angliae Reginae of Robert Wingfield of Brantham'
   (*Camden Miscellany,* 28, 1984)
Macnamarra, C. F., ed., *Miscellaneous Writings of King Henry VIII* (1924)
Nichols, J. G., *The Diary of Henry Machyn* (Camden Society, 42, 1848)
Nichols, J. G., *The Chronicle of Queen Jane* (Camden Society, 48, 1850)
Nichols, J. G., *Literary Remains of King Edward VI* (Roxburgh Club, 1857)
Nichols, J. G., ed., *Narratives of the Days of the Reformation* (Camden Society, 77, 1860)
Nicolas, N. H., *The Privy Purse Expenses of Elizabeth of York* (1830)
Pocock, Nicholas, *Records of the Reformation: the Divorce, 1527–1533* (1870)
Proceedings and Ordinances of the Privy Council of England, ed. N. H. Nicolas (1834–7)
Rotuli Parliamentorum, ed. J. Strachey et al. (1767–77)
State Papers of Henry VIII (1830–52)
Statutes of the Realm, ed. A. Luders et al. (1810–28)
Tanner, J. R., *Tudor Constitutional Documents* (1951)
Tudor Royal Proclamations, ed. P. L. Hughes and J. F. Larkin (Princeton, 1964–9)

D. SECONDARY WORKS: BOOKS

Adams, S., *Leicester and the Court* (2002)
Andrew, K. R., N. P. Canny and P. E. H. Hair, *The Westward Enterprise* (1978)
Anglo, S., *Spectacle, Pageantry and Early Tudor Policy* (1969)
Anglo, S., *Images of Tudor Kingship* (1992)
Arthurson, Ian, *The Perkin Warbeck Conspiracy* (1994)
Baker, J. H., *The Oxford History of the Laws of England, 1483–1558* (2003)
Baldwin, J. F., *The King's Council in the Middle Ages* (1913)
Bedouelle, G., and Patrick le Gal, *Le 'Divorce' du Roi Henry VIII* (1987)
Beer, B. L., *Rebellion and Riot: Popular Disorders in England in the Reign of Edward VI* (1982)
Bendall, Sarah, Christopher Brook and Patrick Collinson, *A History of Emmanuel College,*
   Cambridge (1999)
Bernard, G. W., *War, Taxation and Rebellion in Early Tudor England* (1986)
Bernard, G. W., *The King's Reformation* (2005)
Bindoff, S. T., *Kett's Rebellion, 1549* (1949)
Bindoff, S. T., ed., *The House of Commons, 1509–1558* (1982)
Bisson, D. R., *The Merchant Adventurers of England* (1993)
Bloch, M., trs. L. A. Manyon, *Feudal Society* (1961)
Block, J. S., *Factional Politics and the English Reformation* (1993)
Boynton, L. O., *The Elizabethan Militia* (1967)
Bush, M. L., *The Government Policy of Protector Somerset* (1975)
Camden, William, *The History of the Most Renowned and Victorious Princess, Elizabeth Queen*
   of England (1688)
Carley, J. P., *The Books of Henry VIII and his Wives* (2004)
Carus-Wilson, E. M., and E. Coleman, *England's Export Trade, 1275–1547* (1963)
Cavill, P., *The English Parliaments of Henry VII, 1485–1504* (2009)

Challis, C. E., *The Tudor Coinage* (1978)

Chibnall, M., *Anglo-Norman England 1066-1166* (1986)

Chrimes, S. B, *Henry VII* (1972)

Collinson, P., *The Elizabethan Puritan Movement* (1967)

Collinson, P., *Edmund Grindal, 1519-1583: the Struggle for a Reformed Church* (1979)

Conway, Agnes, *Henry VII's Relations with Scotland and Ireland* (1932)

Coss, Peter, *The Origins of the English Gentry* (2003)

Crawford, P., *Blood, Bodies and Families in Early Modern England* (2004)

Cressy, David, *Literacy and the Social Order: Reading and Writing in Tudor and Stuart England* (1980)

Daniell, David, *The Bible in English: Its History and Influence* (2003)

Davies, R. R., *The Revolt of Owain Glyndwr* (1997)

Davis, Ralph, *English Overseas Trade, 1500-1700* (1973)

Dickens, A. G., *The English Reformation* (1964 rep. 1989)

Dietz, F. C., *English Government Finance, 1485-1558* (1921 rep. 1964)

Dietz, F. C., *English Public Finance, 1558-1641* (1932 rep.1964)

Doran, Susan, *Monarchy and Matrimony: the Courtships of Elizabeth I* (1996)

Duffy, E., *The Stripping of the Altars* (1992)

Duffy, E., *Fires of Faith; Catholic England under Mary Tudor* (2009)

Duffy, E., and David Loades, *The Church of Mary Tudor* (2006)

Dunham, W. II., *Lord Hastings Indentured Retainers, 1401-1483* (1933)

Dupuy, A., *Histoire de la Réunion de la Bretagne à la France* (1880)

Dyer, A. D., *Decline and Growth in English Towns, 1400-1640* (1991)

Ellis, S. G., *Tudor Ireland* (1985)

Elton, G. R., *The Tudor Revolution in Government* (1953)

Elton, G. R., *Policy and Police* (1972)

Fissell, M. C., *English Warfare, 1511-1642* (2001)

Foster, Sir William, *England's Quest for Eastern Trade* (1933)

Fury, C. A., *Tides in the Affairs of Men: the Social History of Elizabethan Seamen, 1580-1603* (2002)

Gairdner, James. *A History of the Life and Reign of Richard III* (1898)

Ganshof, F. L., trs. Philip Grierson, *Feudalism* (1964)

Garrett, C. H., *The Marian Exiles* (1938)

Gillingham, J., *The Wars of the Roses* (1981)

Green, J., *The Aristocracy of Norman England* (1997)

Greengrass, Mark, *The French Reformation* (1987)

Griffiths R. A., *The Reign of Henry VI* (1981)

Griffiths, R. A., *Sir Rhys ap Thomas and his Family* (1993)

Groot, Wim de, *The Seventh Window* (2005)

Guy, J. A., *The Cardinal's Court; the Impact of Wolsey on Star Chamber* (1977)

Gwyn, P., *The King's Cardinal* (1990)

Hall, Mark, *The Duke of Anjou and the Politique Struggle during the Wars of Religion* (1986)

Harper-Bill, C., *The Pre-Reformation Church in England, 1400-1530* (1989)

Harriss, G. L., *King, Parliament and Public Finance to 1369* (1975)

Haynes, Alan, *Invisible Powers: The Elizabethan Secret Services* (1992)

Holmes, Peter, *Resistance and Compromise: the Political Thought of the Elizabethan Catholics* (1982)

Houlbrooke, R. A., *Church Courts and the People during the English Reformation* (1979)

Hoyle, R. W., *The Pilgrimage of Grace and the Politics of the 1530s* (2001)

Israel, J., *The Dutch Republic, 1477–1806* (1995)

Ives, E. W., *The Life and Death of Anne Boleyn* (2004)

Jacob, E. F., *The Fifteenth Century, 1399–1485* (1961)

Jones, J. R., *The Tudor Commonwealth* (1970)

Jones, M. K., and M. Underwood, *The King's Mother* (1992)

Jones, N. L., *Faith by Statute* (1982)

Jordan, W.K., *Edward VI: the Young King* (1968)

Jordan, W. K., *Edward VI: the Threshold of Power* (1970)

Keen, M., *Chivalry* (1984)

Kelsey, Harry, *Sir Francis Drake: the Queen's Pirate* (1998)

Kelsey, Harry, *John Hawkins: Queen Elizabeth's Slave Trader* (2003)

Knighton, C. S., *Pepys and the Navy* (2003)

Knowles, M. C., *The Religious Orders in England, Vol.III, The Tudor Age* (1959)

Kreider, Alan, *English Chantries: the Road to Dissolution* (1979)

Lander, J. R., *Government and Community in England 1450–1509* (1980)

Lehmberg, S. E., *The Reformation Parliament, 1529–1536* (1970)

Lettenhove, Kervyn de, *Relations Politiques des Pays Bas et de l'Angleterre sous la Regne de Philip II* (1888–1900)

Levine, M., *The Early Elizabethan Succession Question* (1966)

Little, David, *Religion, Order and Law: A Study in Pre-Revolutionary England* (1968)

Lloyd, T. H., *The English Wool Trade in the Middle Ages* (1977)

Loach, J., *Parliament and the Crown in the Reign of Mary Tudor* (1986)

Loach, J., *Edward VI* (1999)

Loades, D., *Two Tudor Conspiracies* (1965)

Loades, D., *The Tudor Court* (1986)

Loades, D., *Mary Tudor: A Life* (1989)

Loades, D., *The Reign of Mary Tudor* (1991)

Loades, D., *The Tudor Navy* (1992)

Loades, D., *John Dudley, Duke of Northumberland* (1996)

Loades, D., *Tudor Government* (1997)

Loades, D., ed., *John Foxe and the English Reformation* (1997)

Loades, D., *England's Maritime Empire, 1490–1690* (2000)

Loades, D., *Elizabeth I* (2003)

Loades, D., *Intrigue and Treason: the Tudor Court 1547–1558* (2004)

Loades, D., *The Cecils; Privilege and Power behind the Throne* (2007)

Loades, D., *The Life and Career of William Paulet* (2008)

Loades, D., *The Tudor Queens of England* (2009)

Loades, D., *The Six Wives of Henry VIII* (2009)

Loades, D., *The Fighting Tudors* (2009)

Loades, D., *The Making of the Elizabethan Navy 1545–1590* (2009)

Loades, D., *The Religious Culture of Marian England* (2010)

Lowe, Ben., *Commonwealth and the English Reformation: Protestantism and the Politics of Religious Change in the Gloucester Vale* (2010)

Lupton, J. H., *The Life of John Colet* (1887)

MacCaffrey, W., *The Shaping of the Elizabethan Regime, 1558–1572* (1968)

MacCaffrey, W., *Queen Elizabeth and the Making of Policy, 1572–1588* (1981)

MacCaffrey, W., *Elizabeth I: War and Politics, 1588–1603* (1992)

MacCulloch, D., *Thomas Cranmer* (1996)

MacCulloch, D., *Tudor Church Militant* (1999)

Macek, Ellen A., *The Loyal Opposition: Tudor Traditionalist Polemic, 1535–1558* (1996)

MacFarlane, K. B., *The Nobility of Late Medieval England* (1973)

Maltby, W. S., *Alba: a Biography of Fernando Alvarez de Toledo, Third Duke of Alba, 1507–1582* (1983)

Marshall, P., *Reformation England* (2003)

Mayer, T. F., *Reginald Pole: Prince and Prophet* (2000)

McConica, J. K., ed., *The Collegiate University of Oxford* (1986)

McCoog, T., *The Reckoned Expense: Edmund Campion and the Early English Jesuits* (1996)

Miller, Helen, *Henry VIII and the English Nobility* (1986)

Murphy, B., *Bastard Prince: Henry VIII's Lost Son* (2001)

Neale, J. E., *Elizabeth I and her Parliaments* (1957)

Parker, G., *The Dutch Revolt* (1979)

Parker, G., and C. Martin, *The Spanish Armada* (1988)

Pettegree, A., *Foreign Protestant Congregations in Sixteenth Century London* (1986)

Pierce, Hazel, *Margaret Pole, Countess of Salisbury, 1473–1541* (2003)

Pollard, A. J., *The Wars of the Roses* (1988)

Pollard, A. J., *Richard III* (1991)

Pollen, J. H., *Mary Queen of Scots and the Babington Plot* (1922)

Prestwich, M. C., *Armies and Warfare in the Middle Ages: the English Experience* (1996)

Rabb, T. K., *Enterprise and Empire, 1575–1630* (1967)

Rappaport, S., *Worlds within Worlds; the Structures of Life in Sixteenth Century London* (1989)

Rawcliffe, Carole, *The Staffords, Earls of Stafford and Dukes of Buckingham* (1978)

Read, Conyers, *Mr. Secretary Walsingham and the Policy of Queen Elizabeth* (1925)

Read, Conyers, *Mr. Secretary Cecil and Queen Elizabeth* (1955)

Rees, D., *The Son of Prophecy* (1985)

Richardson. H. G., and G. O. Sayles, *The Irish Parliament in the Late Middle Ages* (1952)

Rodriguez-Salgado, M.-J., *The Changing Face of Empire* (1988)

Rose Troup, Frances, *The Western Rebellion of 1549* (1913)

Roskell, J. S., *The Commons and their Speakers in English Parliaments, 1376–1523* (1965)

Roskell, J. S., C. Rawcliffe and L. Clark, *The House of Commons, 1386–1421* (1992)

Ross, Charles, *Edward IV* (1974)

Russell, F. W., *Kett's Rebellion in Norfolk* (1859)
Russell, J. G., *The Field of Cloth of Gold* (1969)
Scarisbrick, J. J., *Henry VIII* (1968)
Sharp, Sir Cuthbert, *The 1569 Rebellion* (1840, rep. 1975)
Sharpe, Kevin, *Selling the Tudor Monarchy: Authority and Image in Sixteenth Century England* (2009)
Silke, J. J., *Ireland and Europe* (1966)
Simon, Joan, *Education and Society in Tudor England* (1966)
Simpson, A. W. B., *A History of the Land Law* (1986)
Smith, L. B., *A Tudor Tragedy* (1961)
Smith, L. B., *Henry VIII: the Mask of Royalty* (1971)
Smith, L. B., *Treason in Tudor England: Politics and Paranoia* (1986)
Somerville, R., *History of the Duchy of Lancaster* (1955–70)
Spence, R. T., *The Privateering Earl* (1995)
Starkey, D., *The English Court from the War of the Roses to the Civil War* (1987)
Stone, L., *The Crisis of the Aristocracy, 1558–1640* (1965)
Storey, A. L., *The End of the House of Lancaster* (1966)
Strickland, Agnes, *The Lives of the Queens of England* (1902)
Strong, Roy, *Tudor and Jacobean Portraiture* (1969)
Strong, Roy, *The Cult of Elizabeth* (1977)
Strype, J., *Ecclesiastical Memorials* (1721)
Sutherland, N. M., *The Huguenot Struggle for Recognition* (1980)
Swanson, Robert, *Church and Society in Late Medieval England* (1989)
Taylor, E. G. R., *Tudor Geography, 1485–1583* (1930)
Thompson, J. A. F., *The Later Lollards, 1414–1529* (1965)
Usherwood, S., and E., *The Counter Armada, 1596* (1983)
Von Klarwill, V., *Queen Elizabeth and Some Foreigners* (1928)
Warnicke, Retha, *The Rise and Fall of Anne Boleyn* (1989)
Warnicke, Retha, *The Marrying of Anne of Cleves* (2000)
Weissener, L., trs. C.Yonge, *The Youth of Queen Elizabeth* (1879)
Williams, Penry, *The Council in the Marches of Wales under Elizabeth* (1958)
Williams, Penry, *The Tudor Regime* (1979)
Williamson, J. A., *The Voyages of the Cabots under Henry VII and Henry VIII* (1929)
Williamson, J. A., *The Cabot Voyages and Bristol Discovery under Henry VII* (1962)
Wizeman, W., *The Theology and Spirituality of Mary Tudor's Church* (2006)
Wormald, J., *Court, Kirk, and Community: Scotland 1470–1625* (1981)
Wormald, J., *Mary Queen of Scots: a Study in Failure* (1988)
Youings, J., *The Dissolution of the Monasteries* (1971)

ARTICLES, PAPERS AND THESES

Anglo, S., 'The Foundation of the Tudor Dynasty', *Guildhall Miscellany*, 2, 1960
Boscher, P. G., 'The Anglo-Scottish Borders, 1550–1560' (Durham Univ., Ph.D, 1985)

Brown, A. L., 'The King's Councillors in fifteenth century England', *Transactions of the Royal Historical Society*, 5th ser., 19, 1959

Carr, A. D., 'Welshmen in the Hundred Years War', *Welsh Historical Review*, 4, 1960

Carus Wilson, E. M., 'The origin and early development of the Merchant Adventurers', *Economic History Review*, 2nd series, 4, 1932

Cavell, E., 'Henry VII, the north of England, and the first provincial progress of 1486', *Northern History*, 29, 2002

Dietz, B., 'The royal bounty and English shipping in the sixteenth and seventeenth centuries', *Mariners Mirror*, 77, 1991

Gunn, S. J. 'The Duke of Suffolk's march on Paris, 1523', *English Historical Review*, 101, 1986

Harriss, G. L., 'Aids, Loans and Benevolences', *Historical Journal*, 6, 1963

Haugaard, W. P., 'Elizabeth Tudor's Book of Devotions; a neglected clue to the Queen's life and character', *Sixteenth Century Journal*, 12, 1981

Holmes, P. J., 'The Great Council in the Reign of Henry VII', *English Historical Review*, 101, 1986

Houghton, K. H., 'Theory and Practice in Borough Elections to Parliament during the Fifteenth Century', *Bulletin of the Institute of Historical Research*, 39, 1966

James, M. E., 'English Politics and the Concept of Honour', *Past and Present*, Supplement 3, 1978

Loades, D., 'Philip II and the Government of England' in Loades, C. Cross and J. Scarisbrick, *Law and Government under the Tudors* (1988)

Loades, D., 'The King's Ships and the Keeping of the Seas, 1413–1489', *Medieval History*, 1, 1991

MacCulloch, D., 'Bondmen under the Tudors', in *Law and Government under the Tudors*

Meacher, J. C., 'The First Progress of Henry VII', *Renaissance Drama*, 1, 1968

Notestein, W., 'The winning of the initiative by the House of Commons', *Proceedings of the British Academy*, 11, 1926.

Read, Conyers, 'Queen Elizabeth's seizure of Alba's pay ships', *Journal of Modern History*, 5, 1933

Redworth, Glyn, '"Matters impertinent to women", male and female monarchy under Philip and Mary', *English Historical Review*, 112, 1997

Rex, Richard, 'Redating Henry VIII's Glasse of the Truthe', *The Library*, 7th series, 4, 2003

Rosenthal, J. T., 'The Estates and Finances of Richard, Duke of York', *Studies in Medieval and Renaissance History*, 2, 1965

Skeel, C. A. J., 'Wales under Henry VII', in R. W. Seton Watson, ed., *Tudor Studies* (1974)

Taylor, E. G. R., 'Master Hore's voyage of 1536', *Geographical Journal*, 77, 1931

Williams, C. H., 'The Rebellion of Humphrey Stafford in 1486', *English Historical Review*, 43, 1928

Youings, Joyce, 'The South Western Rebellion of 1549', *Southern History*, 1, 1979

Index